STILL CRAZY

about

Aunt Carrie's !

Love Judy Prescott Marshall

ALSO BY JUDY PRESCOTT MARSHALL

BE STRONG ENOUGH

STILL CRAZY

INSPIRED BY A TRUE LOVE STORY

BY
JUDY PRESCOTT MARSHALL

STILL CRAZY. Copyright © 2021 by Judy Prescott Marshall. All rights reserved. Printed in the United States of America.
For information, address Writing Studio 12 May Knoll Dover Plains, New York 12522

www.judyprescottmarshall.com

ISBN 978-0-9910273-3-0 (hardcover)
ISBN 978-0-9910273-4-7 (softcover)
ISBN 978-0-9910273-2-3 (e-book)
ISBN 978-0-9910273-5-4 (audible)

Books may be purchased by going to the author's website or at any one of the following locations:

AMAZON
APPLE
AUDIBLE BAKER and TAYLOR BAM!
BARNES and NOBLE
GOOGLE PLAY
INDIE BOUND
KOBO
OVERDRIVE

Please support your local library and indie bookstore.
Formatting Performed by Ardent Artist Books
Audio read by Susan McGurl

For David — my every dream, desire and prayer.

Contents

Early Praise

James A. Cox, Editor-in-Chief, Midwest Book Review: I'm very pleased to announce that the November 2020 issue of our online book review magazine "Small Press Bookwatch" features a review of Still Crazy. Deftly scripted by an author with a genuine flair for the kind of entertaining and narrative driven storytelling that will swiftly engage the reader's total attention.

Kyle Page, Owner – Lake City Books and Writers Nook: This was a perfect antidote to the crazy we call life right now. I thoroughly enjoyed reading this book.

Ellen Levine, former Editorial Consultant to Hearst Magazines: I started reading in the afternoon and didn't stop until one-thirty a.m. in the morning. I laughed, cried and loved it! Love is a golden gift! **Sally Jessy Raphael, former Talk Show Host:**

The reader can make an emotional connection to so many aspects of the story…the end brought tears to my eyes.

BookLife reviews Still Crazy:

This cozy tribute to faith and unconditional love will please hopeless romantics. Great for fans of: Debbie Macomber and Nicholas Sparks. Carol L. Caton, Ph. D, Prof. of Social Medical Sciences (Psychiatry), College of Physicians and Surgeons, Columbia University (Author of THE OPEN DOOR):

Judy Prescott Marshall is one of those rare writers who can engage the reader from the very first sentence. Millennials, this one's for you!

Rodney Plimpton, Ph. D, in Organizational Behavior: The better parts of you will be touched by reading Still Crazy. Inspiring for men and women of all ages.

Rathna Pattabhi, (former classmate Michigan State University: The style of writing is simply engaging!

Readers' Favorite Five Star review by Lesley Jones:

Still Crazy by Judy Prescott Marshall will sweep you instantly into the tormented world of Julie Holliday. The next novel, The Inn in Rhode Island is highly anticipated.

Janet Pole Cousineau, Librarian:

The book has some great characters and a gripping plot and I will highly recommend it to book clubs as we ladies love to talk about issues like this. FABULOUS BOOK – READ IT! [Capitalization in original]

Joan Wright, NetGalley reviewer:

It is a book that will keep you reading to the end!

OnlineBookClub.org:

With her compelling style of writing, Prescott Marshall draws readers in with such an honest and uplifting plot. Still Crazy is a work of art that has such originality to it. The heartfelt ending was so unexpected and beautiful that it brought tears to my eyes.

PART ONE

*She stood in the storm
and when the wind did not blow her way,
she adjusted her sails*

Elizabeth Edwards

Chapter 1

At 3 a.m., I finally slid out of our bed. The moon was bright enough to light up the room. I stood in the living room for a minute. Something was wrong. I could feel it. The light of the moon had nothing to do with my lying awake for hours. I wandered into my husband's office as if that piece of paper had been calling to me the entire night. My hands shook as I picked it up.

"Nooo…" I whispered as I held the flowery paper in my hand. It was a woman's handwriting. Instantly, my eyes began to well up. I read her name and phone number over and over again, then closed my eyes.

My heart started beating faster and faster, my breathing became erratic. I felt my chest tighten. I refused to have another panic attack. I fought it off. I have been through his chicanery too many times.

Imagining my husband wrapped up in yet another woman's arms was not where I'd saw myself at forty-nine.

My lower lip quivered as I set the paper down. When I reached for a handful of tissues, I knocked over the photo of us taken during our 25th year together. The heavy ornate silver frame was a gift from Lynnae. She had it engraved, *Dan and Julie Holliday: When forever means forever after.*

I held the frame in my hand for a moment before setting it down. I knew it would have broken Lynnae's heart if I told her. She had been only eighteen when she came into our lives. Ten years later and she's like a daughter to both of us. There was no way I could let her know about my suspicions. When I stepped back, I banged into the gun cabinet. The stainless-steel barrel on my Smith & Wesson handgun shone in the light.

Shaking to the core, I stumbled out of Dan's office and went out the front door. I sat down onto the frozen Welcome Home doormat, my legs on the even colder bluestone patio. I took a deep, shuddering breath, filled my lungs with the cold night air and gasped. Above my shivering body, stars shone as bright as the moon.

I groaned audibly as I looked up at them. *How dare they?* In the distance, a lone coyote yelped.

Another icy shudder racked my body.

The man I built my life with. "Oh, God," I whispered. "Why? I don't deserve this."

Memories flashed before me. Kayaking, hiking, Dan sitting in the canoe waiting for a fish to jump, me reading. Us cooking together every night. Dan holding my hand on movie night. So many memories. All good, until…

"Why?" I cried out into the night.

Realizing my legs were so cold they were numb, I had to crawl back into the house. As I was struggling to pull myself up, I caught sight of my reflection in the entryway mirror – shock. My face was pale, practically blue, and my hair was stuck to my robe. *What am I turning into?* I moaned, "Who is this?"

Tears trailed down my cheeks and I couldn't stomach looking at myself any longer. I stepped away from my reflection, went into the guest bedroom and took off my frozen robe. Another mirror stood before me, four times the size of the previous. I dropped the robe and my panties on the floor and snatched two blankets from the closet. For a moment, I held the blankets in my arms. Since the day we met, Dan had always told me I personify sexy.

I took one more glance at myself, shook my head and blew out a breath. I was a good-looking woman. A willing lover. Two nights ago, I was on top of Dan, and I thought my head was going to explode from the orgasms. "What is *wrong* with him?"

My eyes began to well up again. I wrapped the blankets around myself, curled up in a corner of the window seat and stared out at the river, trying to gather my thoughts. I rested my forehead against the icy windowpane. Outside, the water was glowing from the moon's reflection, but I could not stop seeing her name in my mind. *I cannot go through that again.* My suspicions were tearing me apart. I refused to give him the opportunity to call me crazy.

I had to find a way to be strong. Strong enough to what... leave him?

An hour later, my body finally stopped shaking, but my head refused to stop. I thought he was done. How *could* he keep putting me through this? My God, why? I blew out a long breath as every painful detail came swimming to the surface. In 1977, we had been dating a year when I saw a woman on the back of his motorcycle. Dan swore to me that he was only giving her a ride home. With words and kisses, he *promised.* I believed him, and I thought I would never have to go through that again.

In spite of suspecting him of cheating a few *more* times, in 1989 I finally said yes and married Dan. And for a while we were both happy. But in 1997, I suspected he was having an affair with a woman he had done work for. When I confronted him, he said I was being paranoid. That's when I had my first panic attack. My panic attacks were uncontrollable, devastating, and strong enough to make me pass out. Back then, he was convincing, and I had no proof. But honestly, how many times could I play the fool?

For thirty years, I have racked my mind and heart to know if my suspicions were true or not. I hugged my legs to my chest. Buried my face to my knees. I was sitting in the comfort of our home – the home I designed, yet it felt like I was sitting in the electric chair waiting for him to flip on the current.

In the end, I knew there would be no peace for me. I had no good answer as to why I stayed with a man I suspected had no self-control. Over the years, my separation anxiety would not allow me to walk away. As many times as I tried to be strong and independent, I'd failed. I couldn't even go to my niece's wedding by myself. I spent the entire weekend vomiting. While my family enjoyed the Florida sun, I stayed in a bathroom.

Seeing yet another name on his desk, I no longer cared if I vomited every day for the rest of my life. I was done with sitting still, worrying about every damn woman who had round heels, who winked at him or gave him her phone number. My heart hurt just thinking about it.

Truth was I was scared to death.

I had no idea how I was supposed to live without him. Dan was my first and only love. He told everyone... I was his best friend.

I made myself get up, went back into his office, turned on the reading lamp and read the note one more time. I made a mental note: *investigate the matter before I say a word to him.* I needed *proof.*

Chapter 2

A t 5 a.m., after mulling the situation over for two hours, I wanted to wake Dan up. Shake the life out of him. Scream at him. But I didn't. Because I never let that woman out from inside me. I hated confrontation. Besides, even I knew Dan wanted me to find that note.

I tiptoed back to our bedroom and managed to snap up my clothes without waking Dan. Thankfully, our dog Lady slept on my side of the room. I was able to get in and out without disturbing them. I took a quick shower in the guest bathroom and got dressed. "Great. Brown hair, brown eyes, shirt, pants and boots." My wardrobe matched my crappy mood.

Next to the coffee pot, I left a note saying I had forgotten about an early pick-up. I went to the bakery, because I had nowhere else to go. Other than Dan, my bakery was my life. It was also where my best friend, Lynnae, worked.

I drove in a daze. When I reached the bakery, I parked my car, opened the front door and turned off the alarm. "Alarm…" I looked up at the camera. I should install a security system at the house. The clock caught my eye and I remembered a friend of mine telling me

about a hidden camera in the clock at the local card shop. "Huh."

With no actual early pick-ups, I knew Lynnae would be wondering why I was there before her, but I didn't care. My heart calmed down as I stepped into the kitchen. I loved my bakery. I especially loved the three women I worked with. I stood there taking in every detail: the mixers, ovens, the cooling racks. The big spice cabinet. My cookbooks: *Once Upon a Tart, The Sweet Spot,* and the must have book in every bakery, *The Professional Pastry Chef* by Bo Friberg.

I blew a breath into my cold hands. I looked at the worktable in the center of the room. The one Dan custom-built for me. The bakery was a lifelong dream of mine. When I finally got it up and running; Dan made sure I had every piece of equipment necessary; he even bought me a cinnamon-bun scented candle as a joke. "A little motivation to get ya started," he said.

Just as I was ready to flip the table over, I heard the bell on the front door, and I knew Lynnae had arrived. When she found me in the office a few moments later, she was holding two take-out cups.

"Morning, Julie," she said as she handed me a cup of coffee. Black. "Morning," I replied, yawning.

"I turned the ovens on," Lynnae said as she picked up the clipboard containing the day's orders. When she stopped in the doorway, she added, "You look like crap."

"I'm fine," I replied.

"Yeah, well, I'm gonna get started," she said, a little unsure, as she left the office.

"I'll be out in a minute," I replied, but still sat there, lifeless, when I should have been working.

Maybe it was from the lack of sleep from the night before or perhaps it was the multiple flashbacks. *Affairs?* The word still made me sick. Suspected or real? I didn't know. What I did know was no woman should have to suspect her husband of having an affair numerous times in her life. Could I have been wrong about the ones before we were married? Certainly not about all of them. Ten years ago, was the last time I suspected Dan. "I'm exhausted," I said under my breath.

"Hey, if you're not doing anything important in there, can you frost the cupcakes?" I heard Lynnae say, after about an hour had gone by.

"I'll be right out," I hollered back.

Twenty minutes later, I was standing next to Lynnae at the worktable. I was still thinking about that damn flowery note and not the cupcakes in front of me and hadn't realized I had managed to get icing all over my apron.

"Hey, meticulous, you're making some mess over there," Lynnae said as she put a tray of crumb cake in the oven.

Once again, I yawned.

"Julie...?" Lynnae tapped her hand on mine. "Hey, are you all right?"

"Of course," I replied. Realizing she knew something was wrong, I frosted the last cupcake, and carried the tray out to the front room. My heart hurt. I wished I were more like Lynnae. She would have confronted Dan within seconds of finding a note from another woman. No, she would have run, the very first time. Hell, any other woman would be bawling her eyes out. Pride is an awful thing to possess. Actually, I was embarrassed. I especially didn't want the rest of my staff, Brooke and Stephanie, to know my personal business. They were too young and innocent.

Somehow, I managed to place the cupcakes in the display case without dropping any of them on the floor. Even though I was exhausted, I took care of a few customers, wiped down the tables, and filled the display case with Lynnae's fresh baked goods.

Anything to keep myself busy and away from Lynnae's line of fire.

Several times, I caught her peeking through the glass in the kitchen door. It would not be long before she asked me what was going on. As much as I wanted to tell her my suspicions, I couldn't. Not that day, anyway. All I wanted to do was go to bed, yet I could not make myself leave. If only Lynnae were older. I wish she didn't love Dan like a father. I needed her. I needed my friend.

Even more than a shoulder to cry on, at that moment, all I needed was sleep.

Finally, when several customers commented on how tired I looked, I decided it was time to go home. Every time I heard the bell on the front door ring, I looked at the clock. Twenty-two minutes, Brooke and Stephanie would arrive, then I would go home.

I lined everything up in all the display cases, filled the napkin holders, and heard the bell on the door. That time, the bell gave me some relief.

"Good morning, Julie."

"Good morning, Brooke. Good morning, Stephanie," I said as they passed through the front room on their way to the kitchen.

I waited a few minutes, went back to the kitchen and said, "Hey, I'm gonna go home and take a nap. My head is killing me."

"You better." Lynnae gave me that look. The one she gives me when she knows something is up but isn't quite sure what to say. "I'll call you later," I said.

She waved her hand at me. "Don't worry. I got this. Hey, don't be bullheaded, take something for that headache."

As I left the kitchen, I heard Lynnae ask Stephanie to open the door between the kitchen and the front room.

By the time I got into my car, I was numb. Somehow, I managed to put the car in drive.

When I made it home, I was glad Dan was gone for the day, and he had taken Lady to work with him. I was too tired to take her out for a run. "Sleep," I said. "Julie, just go to bed."

I figured I had a few hours to take a little nap and wake up in plenty of time to prepare dinner. *After all, I am nothing if not a good wife, no matter what my husband does.*

For a moment, I stood in the doorway, staring at our bed – it was the one bedroom set we both fell in love with. Our entire home was filled with oak furniture, and in every room, a Hayden Lambson print, or two. When the bedroom set arrived, so did a few surprises.

A chaise lounge and a lingerie chest. "Spin it around," Dan had said. "It has a full-length mirror on the backside."

My eyes moved to the chaise and then to the print above it. Two bucks and a doe standing in a meadow. The caption read: *Over My Dead Body.*

On my nightstand sat my favorite photo of Dan. I picked it up and tossed it across the room. Bang! It landed somewhere in our closet. I had to be stronger. I could not make the same mistake. Normally, I would have confronted Dan about my suspicions. Not this time. I was done playing his game. I was not going to confront him. Not about to give him the opportunity to lie and deny everything and tell me I was crazy. I had to think about myself. My future. As much as I loved Dan, I had to find a way to let go of him.

"Damn you!" I hollered. "You were the only man I ever wanted." He was the handsome bad boy. The kind of man my mother warned me about, the kind of man who would break my heart. The type that never stayed long. "Why didn't I listen…?" I asked, as if my mother, or God Himself, could tell me the answer.

"Huh!" It was my mother who also told me not to date too many guys. She said, "Those girls get a bad reputation."

Ring! Ring! I jumped at the sound. "Good heavens!" I shouted before answering. "Hello."

"Mrs. Holliday, this is Jane Bushnell. I'm a reporter from the *Herald.* We're doing a story about your husband and…"

I sat on the edge of the bed and cracked my neck, first to the right and then to the left. The damn article was Lynnae's idea. Of course, I agreed to it. She had said, "Dan always does the right thing.

He deserves to be recognized."

My eyes caught sight of the back of the oak picture frame, it was lying on the closet floor.

"The newspaper article? I'm sorry, now is not a good time," I told her.

"The story is set to run in Sunday's paper. This will only take a minute or two of your time. I just need a quote or two."

I held the phone to my leg. "You have got to be kidding me," I said under my breath before returning the phone to my ear.

"Your husband made a generous donation to the town. Because of him, Main Street now has flowering trees. His success is inspiring. I understand you were there from the beginning..."

From the beginning? Dan was twenty-three, tall and thin when we met. His hair was longer than my own. Back then, Dan had not one penny in the bank. I covered my mouth with my hand, hoping she didn't hear me yawn.

"And now, without any college, he's a self-made millionaire," she continued. "With a lot of iron."

A self-made *millionaire*? I had to answer that. "I don't know that I would go as far to say he's a millionaire. And by iron, you mean equipment? Yes, he does have the tools necessary to work and yes Dan and I have been together long enough to start both of our businesses."

I looked at the picture hanging above our bed. That one was Dan's favorite. A buck and a doe lying together. I read the caption, *Secret Place*. Then snapped my neck again, to relieve the mounting tension.

"Thank you, Mrs. Holliday, you've been very helpful. The article will appear in the Sunday edition of the paper."

"I'm glad I could help. We look forward to reading the article."

I went out to the kitchen, made myself a piece of cinnamon toast and a cup of tea. I drank the tea, took two bites of the toast and went back to our bedroom. A half-hour later, I heard Dan calling for Lady to come inside. Of all days for him to come home early.

When he came into the bedroom, I pretended to be asleep. I heard him exhale. For an hour or so more, I could hear Dan roaming from one room to the next. At quarter to three, I heard the phone ring. "Hello." Dan picked up on the first ring. He must have been in the kitchen because I could hear every word he was saying. "I'm whispering because Julie's asleep. No, she's out cold. Snoring like a baby. Nah, she got up early. No, she didn't see her flowers, she's sleeping. I'll give 'em to her later. I want her to sleep.

I'm making Bolognese sauce for tonight, want some? You sure? I wanna start early tomorrow. Yeah, yeah, just get here by eight."

Dan is one of those rare men who picks up after himself, loves to cook, and even shares his Häagen-Dazs. When the Bolognese sauce was near ready, I knew he would drop the pasta into the boiling water, set the table, cut the French bread and pour two glasses of his signature homemade iced tea.

With dinner on the table, he came back to the bedroom and softly called my name. I tried not move. My insides were trembling. "Julie," he said again. Then came over and gently touched my shoulder. He called out my name several times, sounding like he was having a moment of panic. When he leaned in closer to me and heard me "snoring", he closed the door and I finally fell asleep.

Chapter 3

I slept for twelve hours straight.

When I woke up, I saw where Dan had slept between the sheets and where he had pulled the bedspread over me. I kicked the bedspread to the bottom of the bed. Grabbed the photo from the closet and set it back on my nightstand. Thankfully, the glass hadn't broken.

Out in the kitchen, Dan was waiting for me with a breakfast of eggs and shitake mushrooms on the table.

"I heard you flush, so I poured the coffee," he said as he handed me a cup.

During breakfast, he asked me several times if I was okay. I nodded my head yes, staring at the flowers. "The sunflowers are beautiful."

He was brushing his fingers across the top of my hand. "Are we hiking this morning?"

I glanced over at the clock. We still had plenty of time to get our morning hike in before either of us had to be at work. I inhaled, exhaled, and answered him, "Yes, of course." Then I took my last bite and cleared the table. I was standing at the sink, rinsing the last plate when Dan approached me from behind. When he kissed the back of my neck, I flinched.

"You okay?" he asked me. "What's going on?"

"I'm fine. I'm almost done." When the lump in my throat formed, I took a deep breath and told myself to breathe.

I hiked about ten feet behind Dan, following him through the woods, over the railroad tracks, down the hill, over streambeds. I never once raised my eyes to look at him. My hands were freezing.

Of course, I'd snapped up the wrong gloves.

The wind must have been blowing from the east, because I could smell Dan's shave cream – I inhaled the scent and my heart nearly exploded.

Usually, Lady runs up ahead of us. That morning, my beautiful chocolate Labrador retriever walked between Dan and me. Several times, she sat and waited for me to catch up. Each time, I would motion to her to get going. I tried to focus on the sound of happy birds coming from the trees, but the wind was picking up, starting to howl. All I wanted to do was go home and take a hot shower.

Suddenly, Dan stopped in his tracks, and he gestured to me to be silent with a movement of his finger to his lips. I stood still, wondering what he was looking at. When he motioned for me to come closer, up ahead, in the open field, I saw two small deer nibbling on a berry bush.

Dan reached for my hand, our eyes met and held. His deep blue eyes intense. He whispered against my temple, "I love you," then shot me a questioning look, but all I could do was nod. I caught my breath and mouthed, "Olive juice." In that instant, that second, something passed between us.

"They're last year's fawns. I don't see their mother, do you?" he asked and then pulled me in closer to where he was standing. "Be very quiet, she's not far away," he whispered, and then moved me so I was standing in front of him. "Uh-oh, look to your right. She's coming out from the cedar trees. Don't move."

We watched as she gathered her two youngsters, and waited for them to move to the lower field before continuing our trek. "Are you cold?" Dan asked.

"Freezing," was the only word I could muster.

He took his vest off and put it on me. "I figured you were cold. Put your hands in your pockets."

My heart was bleeding. Dan could be so gentle and tender at times that he took my breath away.

Immediately upon our return, we both headed for the bathroom. Dan grabbed our towels and hung them over the shower before turning both showerheads on. I did not want to be near him. I tried to think of a reason not to enter the same space, but Dan opened the shower door for me and I stepped inside. I had to turn away from him. I couldn't resist him, or his heart piercing smile. As the warm water poured down my face, so did my tears.

We both finished at the same time. I watched as Dan dried himself off. Usually, I cannot keep my eyes off him. Naked, he went by me. Same as every other morning, Dan pinched my butt. He went into the closet; half work clothes, half camo. He owns one suit, which hangs in the downstairs cedar closet. I could see him getting dressed and he could see me, rubbing lotion on my body.

"I'll see you tonight." He kissed me. "Mmmm, you smell good," he said as he winked my way. He stopped in the doorway. "How much do I love you?" he asked with a seductive smile on his face, then he stretched out his arms as my breath left my lungs in small bursts.

I could not go to work. I just couldn't. At six-thirty-nine, I called Lynnae at the bakery and told her that I would not be coming in. If she needed me, she could call my cell phone.

"Are you okay? What's wrong?" Lynnae said.

"I'm fine."

"No, you're not." Lynnae said with an iciness in her tone. "Call me later so I know what's going on."

As soon as I hung up, I got in my car, turned on the radio, and drove. I didn't care where I went. It was at least two hours before I stopped for gas, then I parked the car in front of The Metro Café, a small café at the end of a plaza. To the right was an ice cream shop, Fudgy's, and next to that, a dance studio. Thankfully, there were only a few cars in the parking lot. I could only hope they were all dancing.

I didn't go in. I just sat there, letting the car idle. Making rash decisions would only make things worse. I hit the dashboard with my fists and grunted. Ran my hands through my hair as if I were pulling it out. I needed to be alone. Yet I was feeling terrified because I knew I could not do it on my own. I needed another cup of coffee. Strong. As I reached for the key to turn it to the off position, "Jesus Take the Wheel" began to play on the radio. I sang every word, crying. When the song ended, I wiped my eyes, shook my head and smiled. *I love you, Lord.*

In the café, I took a seat in the back, away from everyone, and ordered a cup of black coffee. I moved the red-checkered curtain, looked out the window and watched as the wind blew a woman's tan and brown scarf across the parking lot.

After my second cup of coffee, I decided I could not take it anymore. Between the lump in my throat and my pounding headache, it was time to leave.

I paid for my coffee, went out to my car and wondered what my life without Dan would be. *How can this be? Why does it feel like I am in mourning, when he is still alive?* I cried, knowing that I would have to give up my business. I was so mad. Damn it, I was happy.

I rested my head on the steering wheel, feeling like Forrest Gump. Dan's love for me was not as deep as my love for him. At least that's how it felt. Where would I find the strength to tell him that I could not live like that anymore?

It was so cold outside I had to leave the car running. I sat there, knowing that if I were to keep my sanity, I would have to leave Dan. A surge went through my body and I quivered at the thought. Because I knew, leaving could be the very thing that destroyed me completely.

"Why, God? Why would you put Dan in my path? Knowingly. Lord, I accepted You into my heart when I was twelve years old. I have tried my best to be a good Christian, daughter, and wife.

Please...make me understand. Tell me why, Lord. What have I done wrong?"

Tears were running down my face. My head ached from straining to think. Of course, there were no tissues in my car. I wiped my nose on the back of my hand. Banged my head on the window, then I looked up at the sky and realized it was ice blue. In front of me, ice crystals were everywhere. Even Dione, the water goddess, was crying for me.

"Lord, I know you're up there." I closed my eyes, hoping He was. "I stayed with Dan because I believed in my wedding vows. You know that. You know my heart better than I do. Lord, I have tried my best. Obviously, my best wasn't good enough." I opened my eyes, adding, "I'm sorry, Lord, I'm asking for your forgiveness."

At three-thirty, I drove home on the icy roads, wondering how I was supposed to make it through another night, pretending the note did not exist. That my husband loved me as I loved him. That all my suspicions were nothing but a nightmare. How was I supposed to do something so simple as cook dinner, when I didn't even know if I could carry on with my marriage?

Cooking alongside Dan...how was I supposed to get through that?

I opened the refrigerator, thinking I would start dinner. Instead, I stood there, drifting into space. When the refrigerator door alarm went off, I closed the door. Sat on the floor. With my back against the kitchen cabinets, I stretched out my legs; pulled them up to my chest and buried my face.

A few minutes later, I went into our bedroom. I thought about lying down, until I saw Dan's picture. This time, I picked it up, held it to my chest and closed my eyes.

When men shook Dan's hand, they knew he was someone they could trust. He's a man's man, not so tall, barely six feet, but solid; hair once golden blond has turned gray, making his seductive glances even more tempting. I should have married a Bill Gates. No, I had to go for the good-looking guy. Make him my world and share everything with him. Including my kitchen.

Because Dan was a homebody at heart, cooking became our passion. If we went out to eat, it was usually for dinner. Always celebratory. Whenever anyone asked Dan why he stayed home so much, he'd always say, "Why go out? I get exactly what I want every night in the comfort of my own home."

Being in the kitchen with him was one of my favorite times. I loved to watch him create his own concoctions. When Dan cooked, I was his sous-chef. Often, I would scribble down the recipe as fast as I could, so he could recreate the dish for our dinner guests.

I set the photo down. With my heart beating, I sat down on the chaise lounge.

Dan was the kind of husband every woman dreamed of marrying: a hardworking man with an excellent work ethic, handy around the house, smart, seductive, and damn if he was not good looking. Even after all those years, I still thought he was the sexiest man I had ever known. Forget all that, the man could *cook*. In fact, I rarely cooked on the weekends. Breakfast was his specialty. From omelets to serving up my eggs exactly the way I like them – over hard.

I loved being with him. Near him.

I could deal with his inability to share his emotions. Even the fact that he was a little reserved, because I believed in him. His goal in life was to keep what he had. To know that no one would take away his home, his hunting rights, his lifestyle. I admired how he never went over his means. Unlike me, he was a true saver. Unlike me, I was afraid he didn't know how to remain faithful. "Thirty years!" I hollered.

It was 1976. October 2nd. I was an innocent girl. He was the handsome best man. If I had known I was about to meet the man who would shatter my heart like Baccarat, I would have skipped my friend's wedding.

His wink and smile were intoxicating. When the wedding was over, Dan asked me to go to a private party and I accepted. Later that night, he wanted to go back to his apartment for some pot, but only if I went with him.

Before I knew it, I had a helmet on my head, and I was on the back of a motorcycle for the first time in my life. It was a

Kawasaki 900, and he knew how to handle it – and me. Five-minutes into the ride, Dan reached back and pulled me into him so tight, I thought I was driving the bike. When he took a corner, we moved as if our bodies were one. When we arrived at his apartment, all I saw was a twin bed and a stereo – nothing else. No television, no table and chairs, not even a dish to eat from. He did, however, have charisma. When we got back on that bike, I lost my heart for the first time in my life. I could not let go of him. When he called me the next day, I knew my life would never be the same again.

"Oh, Lord. What am I to do?"

I got up, went into the bathroom and took two aspirins.

When Dan got home from work, dinner was on the table. I had planned to cook chicken, but knowing chicken *piccata* was one of Dan's favorites, I opted for meatloaf. I did not want to be near him. That night, or any time soon.

I ate my dinner forkful by forkful, knowing I must learn how to live alone or lose my mind.

Chapter 4

I was driving to work when I passed a teenager driving an old Jeep Wrangler, the kind with a serious roll bar and plastic windows that zipped open and closed, that was nearly identical to Lynnae's. The car was fitting for her free spirit. She insisted on having the top down regardless of the season. The only time she put the canvas top on was when her two little sons were in the backseat. Or when it was raining or snowing. When Lynnae stopped at a traffic light, people would turn the palms of their hands up, as if to say, "What's up?" She'd smile at them and turn her music up a little louder. She didn't care if it was forty degrees outside.

She answered to no one, and everyone knew it. That was one of the things I admired about her. Lynnae was both vivacious and brilliant. She only needed to read something once, and she had a clear understanding.

She was eighteen when she started working for me. The same age I was when I met Dan. Like me, she dropped out of high school. In her first few months on the job, Lynnae was diligent, enthusiastic, and a bright-eyed employee, the sort of worker who volunteered for every project. She wanted to learn everything there was to know about the business of baking. It didn't take her long to become the best baker in the valley, and the mother of two very energetic, smart, adorable little boys. Sam was eight and Max almost five.

In spite of her having to deal with a man who refused to acknowledge his own son, and dealing with a child who had dyslexia, she was the most positive person I knew. Lynnae had a deep affection for people. My customers loved her. Her greatest asset was her gift of gab. Women loved to tell her their troubles. Men loved looking at her. I could not imagine running that bakery without her. For the past ten years, Lynnae had been the best assistant, friend and confidant a person could ask for. Ten years and such different lives, yet we shared a bond as special as any mother and daughter.

Somehow, Lynnae knew the exact moment when my spirit needed a lift. She was always there for me. She knew exactly what to say. There wasn't anything I wouldn't do for her. Including hiring additional help for her when she announced she was pregnant with her first child. As if the angels heard my prayer, Brooke and Stephanie came into the bakery looking for jobs.

If they hadn't told me they were sisters, I never would have guessed. The only things they had in common were their body sizes and the rings in their noses. Brooke was a petite blond, with blue eyes, while Stephanie had brown hair and brown eyes. Brooke was a lot like my Lynnae: chatty, loved her music and loved baking.

Stephanie, on the other hand, hated baking, but she drew masterfully. She was the quiet sister. If she said three words all day, we were surprised. She was so good, I let her do her own thing. After all – she was an artist. First thing she did was turn on her iPod, then placed the earplugs in her ears, glanced at the order board, opened her sketchpad and began drawing. Unlike Lynnae, she didn't sing.

And unlike Brooke, she didn't move to the sound of the music. When Stephanie was done, she handed her drawings over to Brooke. Brooke was a master cake decorator. I was amazed at what she could do with fondant. But it was Lynnae's food that everyone loved. Her specialty was spices. She used black and white chia seeds in her morning glory muffins to help you feel full. And in every sugar-free cupcake, she put a dash of cinnamon, ginger or turmeric.

She said it helped to reduce one's sugar cravings.

One day, a man asked if we could put a drawing of his wife's present on top of her cake. The woman actually tried to pick the pearls up! That's how good an artist Stephanie was. In fact, her goal in life was to be recognized as a true artist. The three women worked flawlessly together, creating one masterpiece after another.

I was standing at the back of the bakery, speaking to a customer about our Davey Crocket bars. "They're so simple to make," I said.

"I would love the recipe."

"Come with me, I'll write it down for you."

"Seriously?"

I wrote the recipe down. Handed it to her.

"Butter mixed with graham cracker crumbs, followed by a layer of chocolate chips, then a layer of nuts, coconut, and topped with condensed milk? That's it?" she said.

"Pretty much."

"I'm going home right now and making these. Thank you!"

I looked at Lynnae. "What?"

"Did you just give her your recipe?"

"She'll never make them the way you do."

"Hey, wanna go to the farmer's market with me?" Lynnae asked me as I turned around. "Now?"

"No. After work. Brooke and Stephanie can close. It will be good practice for them."

"Umm, sure."

"We have to be there right at six, so do whatever you have to do now."

Forty minutes later, I opened the door to Lynnae's Jeep but had to wait for her to move two magazines and a container. I sat down and she asked me, "Want one?"

I took one of the treats. "Are these Cheerios?"

Lynnae was backing out of the parking lot. When she turned to face me, she nodded her head, "Yep. I'm addicted to them. The boys love them. Just don't tell them how healthy they are."

"What do you call it?"

"A Cheerio bar."

"We should sell them…"

"Why, so you can turn around and give out the recipe? I'm joking. We should and we're gonna."

"I promise, no more handing out recipes."

"Julie…"

"Yeah?" I took another bite.

"Do you think it's wrong of me not to tell Max about his father?"

"Lynnae, Max's father was wrong to lead you on. It was *his* decision to exclude himself from Max's life. He's the one who lied to you about having a fiancée. When the time is right, by that I mean when Max is old enough to understand, you can tell him the truth. Right now, all he needs to know is… that he has a fantastic mother.

That he is a blessing to you."

We rode in silence for the next three or four miles. Then I heard her say, "I never wanna know a day without you and Dan in my life."

"Lynnae, we both love you…"

"Seriously. When I think about Max never meeting his father, I think it's a good thing. At least he doesn't have to worry about having someone you love in your life only to…"

"Lynnae." I put my hand on her leg. I turned and looked out my window. Sadness filled my heart. I didn't want to tell her about the note.

Lynnae stopped for a red light. "I frigging love you guys so much."

"And we love you."

She turned the radio on. Pink was singing a familiar song, but Lynnae was driving in silence. I glanced over at her. Her elbow was on the door, her head resting on her hand and I wondered what else she was thinking.

A moment later, Lynnae pulled into the farmer's market. "Make sure you buy whatever you can from the Fresh Gourmet. They have the best produce."

I went to get out of the car, but Lynnae reached for my hand and stopped me. "Julie, Dan loves you."

Chapter 5

Wednesday morning, people sat around the bakery drinking their coffee, nibbling on the day's special – fresh Strawberry Pavlova – or our warm cinnamon donuts, or the buttery croissants. Satisfied customers filled every seat. The line of people seemed to never end, and then there was the phone ringing off the hook with orders for the upcoming Valentine's Day celebration. Normally, I love the frenetic bustle, but not today.

"Hey, how ya doing out there?" Lynnae hollered to me.

"I'm doing fine," I said, noticing Brooke and Stephanie had both stopped what they were doing to hear my response. I flashed them a smile. Brooke continued decorating the cake she was working on, and Stephanie nodded her head at me and then went back to drawing.

Several times throughout the morning, I noticed Lynnae was staring at me.

Finally, we caught a break. At eleven o'clock, the line of people temporarily ended. I was standing at the espresso machine, ready to wipe the surface when Lynnae gently banged her hip into mine.

"Well?"

"Well, what?"

She looked at me pointedly. "Okay, Julie, what the hell is going on? Your face is as pale as death. Those circles under your eyes?

They're getting darker by the minute. And what's with your hands?" My hands were trembling.

"Julie, you're sweating more than a whore in church." She seized the cleaning cloth from my hand.

I felt tears sting my eyes.

"Well? Do you need to go home again?" She wrinkled her nose. "You might as well tell me. I am not going to stop until you tell me everything."

"I'll be fine." I was trying my best to sound okay.

"Yeah, right. I know something is going on. You're stewing about something. Please don't tell me it's what I think it is. Look at me."

Outside, the sound of thunder made me shudder.

"Relax, it'll be over soon. It's February, for God's sake. How long can it last?" Lynnae tried to reassure me. "I still can't believe your mother made you sit in a closet during thunderstorms." "She was trying to protect us from broken glass," I explained.

"Yeah, I know, you've told me that about a zillion times. Well, news flash, there's no windows back here." She twisted me around so she could see my eyes. "Julie, you don't look good to me."

My heart was pounding. I took a deep breath. "I think Dan is having an affair."

"What!" She put her hand on her forehead. "Oh, Julie… why didn't you say this yesterday?" Lynnae wrapped her arms around me. "Tell me…" She shook her head. "With who…? Why do you think…?"

"The other night, I couldn't sleep." Instantly, I could feel the tension mounting inside my body. My hands were trembling more than ever. My heart was pounding so hard I could feel its drum in my ears.

"Julie, just tell me…"

"I found a note with a name and phone number on Dan's desk." "So, okay. A note with a customer's name on it. Julie?"

"The kind of paper a woman might write her grocery list on," I explained. "Let's face it, I noticed it because it stuck out like a sore thumb. All the other notes on his desk are in his handwriting. They contain the customer's name, phone number, work details, along with a price quote. A woman with only her name and phone number on it wrote this note."

"You need to sit down. Fuck that, I need to sit down. In the office. Now!"

It was the first time I did not yell at Lynnae for using foul language.

She sat me down in one of the chairs in the office, and then she went to the front and told Brooke and Stephanie to take care of the customers, and to keep an eye on the ovens. When she returned, she set two cups of chamomile tea on the desk, along with thick slices of her famous sugar-free Paleo carrot cake. *Slam!* Lynnae closed the door with her foot, causing me to jump.

"What am I going to do?" I whined.

Lynnae picked up one of the desserts, placing it in front of me.

"You are going to take a bite. Now." She sat down next to me. "Should you test your sugar?"

"It's not my sugar."

"Well, here's what you're going to do. You're going to take a deep breath and I will tell you what you are *not* going to do. You are not going to panic."

"Trust me; I never want to experience another panic attack in my life."

"Seriously, why do you think he's having an affair? Because of a piece of paper, for Pete's sake? Don't read stuff into this that's not there. Dan's not that kind of guy."

Lynnae loved Dan. She looked at him like a father figure. *I knew she would feel this way.*

I know it in my heart. I just know it! Dan can deny it all he wants. For women like me, it was not a matter of *if* he would have another affair, it was a matter of *when*; and once again I was reminded that some things never changed. Unless I made that change.

"Lynnae," I sighed. "I *know* my husband. I'm telling you, it's as if I live with my very own weatherman, giving me all the warning signs that a storm is coming in our marriage."

"You don't know he's having an affair. Maybe she needs her driveway plowed out. You don't know."

"Her husband has a plow truck. Thank you."

"Oh crap."

"I should have known. The minute his behavior changes toward me, I know I'm in for some stormy weather."

Lynnae shook her head. "Why in God's name would you refer to an affair as a storm... might I ask?" She was almost yelling at me.

I tilted my head to the side, twirling a strand of hair. "Because they usually roll out faster than they roll in."

"Julie, I know Dan. He hasn't done anything wrong."

I was trying to be brave, but I couldn't breathe. I wanted to cry. My throat was tight from holding back my tears. My insides were trembling, and my mind rewound back – to uglier days. I wanted to tell Lynnae everything, the whole sordid truth. But... I didn't have the courage.

"Lynnae, I've suspected Dan of fooling around before."

"You *suspect?* Are you kidding me? Tell me you're joking!" she hollered. "Sorry, I didn't mean to yell."

I shook my head, "I think Dan has a terrible sickness. I... ten years ago..."

"I can't believe this. Why the hell didn't you tell me ten years ago?"

"You were so young. And I didn't want you thinking about Dan... you know... like..."

"Like what? Like family," she protested. "Did you *ask* him? What did he say?"

"He always swears to God he's not cheating. He's never admitted to any of them. Every time I've confronted him, he denied it."

"Every time? Well, maybe he didn't do anything. Did you ever think that maybe you're wrong?" Lynnae stood up. "Thanks, by the

way…"

"For what?"

"Because tonight, I'll probably eat two containers of salted caramel ice cream."

"Oh, Lynnae."

Lynnae kissed me on the cheek. "Get out of here. Go for a drive. Go home. I need to think. And Julie? I *know* Dan. He's not cheating on you."

I didn't drive far. I went straight home. As soon as I got home, I logged onto a website that offered hidden cameras. I ordered two photo frames. One for Dan's office and one for his garage. Then I logged onto her Facebook page again. Creeping like a crazy person. I was looking for clues, anything that said she was Dan's mistress.

The next morning, I couldn't wait to get outdoors. "Are you ready yet?" I hollered, and then I rang the doorbell.

"Stop it!" Dan yelled back to me, then I heard him say, "Come on, Lady. Momma is in a hurry this morning."

Through the glass in the front door, I watched him turn off the TV, set the remote control down and pick up his hiking stick. He came out wearing his heavy coat and muck boots. As he closed the door behind him with one hand, he was reaching out to touch my arm with his other. For a moment, our eyes met, holding as if lost, and again he gently touched my arm before stepping down off the front porch.

The morning sky was a brilliant blue. I wanted to go hiking. Hell, I *needed* to be in the woods. My morning hike was the best part of my day. I loved the sound the birds made. They sounded more like R2-D2 than songbirds. I was happiest when I was outdoors. We lived out in the country where the air was pure and the nights were quiet. We had been hiking on our property behind our house for thirty years.

As confused as I was... as painful as my heart felt, one minute I had the desire to hike alongside Dan, and the next minute, I wanted to run away from him. As far as I could get. If it were up to me, I would live deep in the woods. Alone.

If I didn't love Dan as much as I did, I would take Lady. She was our dog, but she and Dan always had a special bond, since the day we found her... rescued her. I remembered the day we went to see her at the pound. She was sleeping alone in a cage. When the man opened the door, Lady ran past him and right into Dan's arms. When she nuzzled her tiny face into his neck, I knew she was coming home with us. Dan even took her to work with him.

Ahead of me, Lady led the way to Dan. As I hiked behind him, I thought the saddest thing about betrayal was that it never came from your enemies. It came from friends, your loved ones. In life, I realized everyone played a role. Some tested me, some taught me. Some loved me, and some hurt me.

Ever since I'd found that note, everything he said, everything he did, triggered emotions in me. I could hear it in his tone; he knew something was bothering me. For the past few days, he either tiptoed around me, or avoided me like the plague. Nevertheless, if I asked him about the note, he would have just denied everything. Or given me another lame excuse.

Wednesday morning, we were hiking when Dan came to an abrupt stop. He looked back at me and motioned for me to catch up. "Momma deer has survived the winter," he said.

"I am so happy to see her," I replied. She was the only deer that allowed all three of us to get close to her when she fed. I smiled at her as she nonchalantly continued eating her breakfast. Momma was a large doe. We knew it was her because of her markings. A large brown spot behind her right ear.

By the time we got to the railroad tracks, the sky had taken on the color of darkness.

"What happened to my blue sky?" I asked.

"Channel Seven called for rain. Didn't you see it?"

In the distance, I could hear thunder. Followed by a flash of lightning. No surprise, we all picked up our pace.

"You knew? And you didn't mention it before we left? You know I *hate* thunder and lightning."

"You're fine. We'll be home in plenty of time," he tried to assure me, but the storm was already upon us. We ran, stumbling and sliding down the snowy slope. I felt bad for Lady. She no longer ran between us, she was running as close to Dan as she could get.

She didn't like thunder, either.

Dan took hold of my hand and we bolted for the only safety in sight – the lower run-in shed. The late winter storm was fierce. The shed only had a roof and a back wall. I was terrified the lightning would come in through the front or side at any moment. My knees shook, my heart felt like a drumbeat in my ears.

The storm roared over us, wild and ferocious. Dan reached down and patted Lady on the head, pulling her closer.

"Breathe, you're okay," he shouted in my ear, over the storm. "We're not hurt; we're all safe in here." Standing behind me, he wrapped his arms around me, holding me tight to his chest. I closed my eyes. The storm had nothing to do with my falling hard, without any attempt to catch myself. I still could not look into his eyes without wanting him. That old part of me, the undamaged part, longed for him to kiss me. But he didn't.

After a few minutes, he cocked his head, listening. "It's over.

Rain stopped. We can go home now." He stepped to my side and gave me a nod.

When I looked up, the sky appeared purple.

Not wanting our hike to end, not wanting to get back to the house and face reality – the note with the flowery border – I slowed my pace to a saunter. Hiking down the path toward the third trestle, old memories of our making love under the stars came rushing back to me. His kisses were tasty, ripe, with a hint of shock followed by sweet nectar. I could still feel his fingers pressing hard into my hipbones. When my insides began to tremble with sheer pleasure, I wanted him even more. Why? Why did he do this to me? I never said no to him. I always let him know how satisfied I was. I hated hiking this way. Every time I hiked past that damn trestle, I thought about how passionate our lovemaking was.

As we climbed up the hill toward the railroad tracks, Dan reached back to me, helping me up the hill, then he let go of me, stepped back, looked into my eyes and he knew I was remembering…

I think that was also the moment, he knew – *this time* would be different. I could see that, now, his heart was racing. He knew something was different about me. I would rather give him the freedom to be with whomever he wanted. Hell, I would rather live in a bear's den than live with a man who could not be faithful. When Dan's eyes widened, I knew he wanted to say something, but I ran to the top of the hill as fast as I could.

I heard Dan shout, "Train!"

The train went by me so fast I had to lock onto a tree.

"I hollered train," Dan shouted. "What is wrong with you?" I didn't say anything, I was too scared.

"Slow the hell down. If you want to run, run in the damn field where I can see you," he yelled even louder and began hiking ahead of me so fast I could not keep up with him. He didn't take a shower or eat breakfast. He climbed into his truck and went straight to the construction site.

Later on, I went to work and tried to be productive. An impossible endeavor.

"You need to stop thinking about him." Lynnae said this from across the counter. "Seriously. Either that or just go somewhere else, because holding your hand to your mouth is not getting that mix in the bowl, or any of this bread into the ovens."

"I'm sorry. I know I've been a wreck all week."

"Don't be sorry. I should be the one apologizing. Oh, I almost forgot, one of your tenants, Paul, dropped off his rent check yesterday. I put it on your desk."

"He's so good at paying his rent on time. Actually, both Dan and I have really good tenants." I thought for a moment. "I'm so glad we kept our money and real estate transactions separate."

"Ummm... anyway, I've been meaning to as you how do you know her husband has a plow truck?"

I did not mean to roll my eyes. But I did. "Facebook." "Oh. No shit. I'm going to prove something to you..." She started to say something more, but then suddenly she dashed across the room, picked up the phone and pressed buttons. "Hi, it's Lynnae at Bella Napoli Bakery." She snapped her fingers and mouthed the words, *"What's her name?"* I said the name.

"Hey, I have a special delivery – for..." She gave the postmaster the woman's real name. Lynnae wrote down the woman's address, went out into the front room and told Brooke and Stephanie that we would be back in twenty minutes.

We jumped into her Jeep and drove to where the woman lived. It was three o'clock in the afternoon, and a minivan was in the driveway, which was perfect. I wrote down the license plate number.

On the drive back to the bakery, I thought about how close her house was to the east-side our hundred acres.

"Lynnae, Dan can ride his Polaris Ranger right to her backdoor."

"I see that. I wasn't going to mention it but now that you did..."

"I just want the truth." I looked away. I was tired of feeling this way.

"So do I!" Lynnae pulled up to the bakery and we both went inside.

Living in a small town could be a beautiful thing. Owning a bakery and knowing every cop in the valley...well that had its benefits, too. Knowing a sheriff who would do anything for me, including running a license plate was even better. Lynnae and I went straight to the office.

"Hi, Mark. It's your favorite baker."

"Hey, beautiful. What can I do for you?" he asked, knowing I had something up my sleeve.

"Mark, can you run a plate for me?"

"Sure."

I read the plate letters and the numbers to him.

"Give me a few minutes. I'll call you back," he said.

"Well?" Lynnae said.

"He's gonna run the plate and call me right back."

"I need a cup of tea," Lynnae said. "I'll get you one." She flashed a quick smile at me. "Who's a genius?"

When Lynnae came back to the office, she had our tea and two cranberry scones. "I have a frigging headache," she said, then took a bite.

When the phone rang, Lynnae jumped and scared the crap out of me.

I listened as Mark told me about the woman. "Married, with twins, a boy and a girl."

I didn't want to answer his next question, but I did. "I think Dan's having an affair with her."

"Julie, trust me," Mark said in a stern voice. "Dan is not having an affair with this woman. Dan would not have anything to do with her." Mark let out a breath before adding, "Julie, she's having an affair with one of my co-workers. So you can get that idea out of

your head right now. You need anything else, call me." Lynnae was motioning to me. "So?" she whispered.

"Thank you." I hung up the phone.

"What'd he say?"

"Mark was able to confirm that the car *is* registered to – the same woman. He knows her. He said Dan is not having an affair with her. He told me to get that idea out of my head."

"Julie, come on. I *told* you so. I just know you can trust him." Lynnae put her hand on my back, "Julie, seriously, come on. You're getting all worked up over nothing. I'm telling you, Dan is not having an affair with this woman. Or any other woman. You have to trust him."

"Lynnae, I have to know the truth."

"What truth, Julie? Seriously, how many times are you going to accuse him, before you piss him off? How many people have to tell you he's not cheating on you?"

I left the bakery, feeling sick to my stomach.

Chapter 6

L ater that evening, I stood in the doorway to our living room. To my left, I could see Dan, he was seated before a roaring fire, he looked happy, content in the moment. I caught my breath remembering how many nights he held me in front of that fireplace. Holding me tight in his arms. The two of us talking, laughing and sharing our dreams and the desire to retire closer to a bigger body of water. The ocean…

"Join me," he said, stopping me from wondering about our future. "You look beautiful," he added, smiling. His smile, his eyes, and the way he looked at me, always got to me.

"We'll be late," I said, hoping he'd get up.

"What time's our reservations?"

"Seven," I replied and moved toward the coat closet. "Give me two seconds," Dan said as he secured the fire.

Before we reached the garage, the wind blew and I could smell his shave cream. I loved that smell – sexy and alluring. I wished for it to be October 2nd and we could start over again.

We reached the restaurant holding hands, as if it were our first date. At the table, I glanced over at him, wondering his innocence or guilt and our eyes met. Suddenly a rush came over me. I wasn't sure if it was anger or passion. I fiddled nervously with my napkin.

Dan looked up from his plate and flashed me a smile before setting his fork down. "You haven't touched your food."

He reached over and caressed my right shoulder. When he took his hand back and rubbed his hands on his thighs, my emotions rose.

Dan reached out again. This time holding my wrist and once again, I was electrified by his touch.

When we got home, he asked me if I wanted him to light a fire. I told him I was tired and had a lot work to do the next day.

Friday morning, Lynnae, Stephanie and I were all in the kitchen, watching Brooke sway to the sound of Christina Aguilera singing "Ain't No Other Man."

"I don't know how she does it. Decorating a cake while moving her hips like that?" I said as I lined a tray for oatmeal raisin cookies.

Stephanie raised her head from her sketchpad long enough to see Brooke give us a little hip action.

"Hey, what'd Dan get you for Valentine's Day?" Lynnae asked me as she seized a cookie sheet out of the oven.

"He bought me my favorite roses, a card and took me out for dinner."

"Aww, that was nice of him. See…?"

"When he handed the card to me, he told me I was a romantic." Lynnae smiled. "Oh, yeah, and like he's not? Did ya tell him, he grew up reading the same fairy tales as you and me? Dan knows he's your prince and you're his queen." She cocked her head. "Get to work. Customers just walked through the door."

I waited on the couple, hoping Lynnae was right. In fairy tales, there *is* a happily ever after. Why couldn't that be true for me? We had so much to be thankful for, and yet it felt like an abyss had opened up between us.

"Umm, hello. Did you forget something?" Lynnae asked, pointing a wooden spoon at the front room.

"What?"

"They gave you an order for next Saturday, hang it up on the board."

"Geez…" I went back to the front room, snatched the form and hung it up on the clipboard.

An hour later, Brooke and Stephanie were washing the mixing bowls. Lynnae had just cleared the worktable, and I had just put the last pie in the display case.

"That's it for the next few minutes. Julie, you need to take a little break."

I followed Lynnae out to the front room.

"Julie, let me ask you something. Why do you think Dan plows our parking lot ten times every damn snowstorm?"

"What is your point, Lynnae?"

"Because he doesn't want you stranded here after we close the shop. He wants you home. With him. If you're not here with us, who are you with?"

"Dan."

"Exactly."

"I can't believe you're sticking up for him, Lynnae." "Because I'm right! I see the way Dan is with you. Listen..." She put her hands on her hips. "Dan is your life. And you... are his whole world. He would be lost without you. My life isn't perfect. I frigging... I struggle every day as a single parent. It's not easy. Sure, I wish things turned out differently, but I deal with it the best I know how. You taught me that. Don't throw away what you have. Family is everything. Tell me something – what do the two of you do when you're both not working?"

"We love being outdoors," I admitted. "Taking long walks deep into the woods. You know that."

"And...?"

"Kayaking down the majestic river in the back of... I know what you are trying to do," I said and started cleaning one of the tables.

"No, you don't. You have no clue. Your mind is so damn tainted, you can't see straight. I'm giving you a reality check, damn it." Lynnae tossed the coffee grinds into the garbage, collected another liner and filled it with fresh coffee.

"I'm sorry you're upset. Lynnae, please..."

"Remind me – what is it the two of you do every evening?"

"You know what we do, now stop. I don't want the girls to hear…"

"They don't hear anything but the damn radio." She pulled me toward the back of the bakery.

I sat down on the floor, my back against the wall. She was standing in front of me, her hands on her hips, head tilted to the right.

"What… do… you… love the most at the end of your day? Tell me again, because I forgot." She stuck her hands out, palms up, in front of me. "Watching old black and white movies? That sound familiar? You know the last time I curled up in a man's arms to watch a movie?"

"I know what you're saying. I know how blessed I am." There were many nights when the passion, laughter, and love were so strong my feet never hit the hardwood floor.

Lynnae sat down on the floor next to me, and took my hands in hers. "Remember when you built the model of your house? Remember what Dan said when he saw it?"

That time, I gave her a wry grin. I remembered exactly what he'd said: "Let's build it." And a month after that, we were sitting down with an architect. Eighteen months later, I was dancing in my new living room all by myself. My heart began to beat faster remembering it – how when I had turned around, there was Dan.

He'd had an enormous grin on his face, and he was just as happy as I was. His eyes had sparkled; he had come and put his arms around me and his touch had melted my heart.

"Whatever you want, he gives you. He built that house for you because he loves you. Julie, your home is your castle; it's where you feel safe. I would love to have a place where I felt safe like that." "Oh, Lynnae, honey, I know. I'm sorry for complaining, but it's not all roses. I fell in love, not knowing the risk. The moment I saw him, I knew I wanted to be with him. He was molting adolescence when I caught sight of him. I fell crazy in love with him. But…"

"No buts. You still love him like crazy."

I didn't answer.

Lynnae looked at me, eyebrows raised. "Right?"

"Yes, I do. No. Oh, hell, I don't know. I don't know anything anymore."

All afternoon, I kept thinking about what I was secretly planning to do. I *had* to know.

"Hey, did you order something from Amazon?" Lynnae asked, handing me a package.

I took the package. "I ordered something for Dan."

"Nice. If you wanna go, I'll lock-up."

"Thanks," I said, taking the package in my arms; then headed for the office to get my purse. "I'll see you in the morning."

I parked my car in the garage, purposely to make sure Dan was not home yet. I went into the house, hung up my coat, made myself a cup of tea and sat down in the living room. I was grateful for the moment to be alone. I opened the package and set the additional photo frames in every room in the house, and one more in the garage.

Every day, I logged onto the site and checked for any activity. Nothing.

A week later, Mother Nature had one more blizzard up her sleeve. It snowed so much that day Dan had to call his friend Jesse to come help him plow. Jesse was a bigger version of Dan. The men had known each other since they were teenagers.

During warmer months, Jesse ran a tree service business. But in the colder months, Jesse liked to hang out with Dan. Especially in Dan's new garage. They both rode Harleys, and they were both car buffs.

Dan and Jesse plowed snow for four straight days. When the storm was over, it was truly a winter wonderland. I was sitting in the living room looking out toward the river; it had snowed so much that I could no longer see the water. A blanket of white stretched from one embankment to the other.

When I heard the trucks pull in, I gripped my cell phone and immediately logged onto the site. I needed to know if Dan had a second cell phone, because if he did, he would definitely leave it in the garage.

"I've had enough. I don't want to see snow again, until next year," I heard Dan say.

"Me either," Jesse said, agreeing with Dan. "I gotta clean this truck out."

They were standing in the middle of the garage and I could see them both.

"What the hell is that?" Dan hollered. "Throw the garbage in a bag, not on the floor. What's the matter with you?"

Jesse shook his head. "I'll take care of it. Don't you worry about

it."

"It's my truck. Don't tell me not to worry about it. Throw that crap in your own truck."

"Relax."

Dan was checking his cell phone. The Samsung Galaxy 7, I have the same one. His had an orange OtterBox.

"You all right? Everything okay?" Jesse asked, standing behind Dan.

"Yeah, I was checking to see if Julie left me a message."

"She okay?"

"I don't know. Something's not right with her."

"What do you think is going on?" Jesse asked. Dan just shrugged, shaking his head.

"Where is she? Usually, if she's not at work, she's sitting right next to you in the truck."

"Yeah, I lost my wing-girl. She's in the house. She's acting funny about something. One minute she's okay, the next minute I can't even look at her without her getting all pissed off. I don't know what the hell is wrong with her."

Jesse tossed his garbage into the trashcan. "Well, what's going on?"

"I don't have a clue." Dan looked over toward the house before adding.

"She'll come around one of these days. She always does. It's not
like we haven't gone through this bullshit before."

Jesse looked at Dan. "What bullshit?"

I held my cell phone closer to my face to get a better look at
Dan's reaction.

"Nothing. Don't worry about it."

Dan went into the tool room, followed by Jesse and they were
both out of range.

Chapter 7

The next day, when I went to the bakery, I didn't see Lynnae. Usually when I arrived, she would be scurrying around the coffee machines, singing as loud as she could to whatever tune she had blaring on the radio. "Hmm," I said aloud, "it smells like fresh coffee."

Nothing.

I said it louder.

"I'm back here," she hollered from the office.

"Good morning," I said cheerily. "What time did *you* get here this morning?"

As I walked into the office, I saw what Lynnae had on the computer screen and collapsed into the chair next to her. She was looking at that woman's Facebook page.

"I don't care how pale your face is," she said, "you are out of your mind if you think for one second that Dan is having an affair, or anything else, with that woman. If he's having an affair – which he's not – I guarantee you, it is not with her."

I shook my head, pursed my lips, and blew out a long breath. "I know my husband."

"Yeah, and so do I. Are you kidding me?" Lynnae slid her chair backwards so fast it hit the wall. "She looks like Shrek with curls!"

She pushed her chair next to mine. "Okay, Julie, tell me something. If Dan is – and note I say *if* –he is seeing this woman…" she twirled her hands … "for I don't know whatever reason…" Her voice dropped to a near whisper. "Julie, listen to me. Dan loves you. I know this with all my heart. You have to believe Dan. You cannot freak out every time you see a piece of paper with a woman's name on it."

"Lynnae, I need to tell you something." "What?" she asked with concern on her face.

"Oh, God, Lynnae…" I thought for a moment. Remembering all the other times I suspected Dan of having an affair and had almost told her, but changed my mind, because I was not ready to go back to those memories. Not ready to talk about every painful detail.

"Julie, talk to me. I will always be here for you. No matter what."

"Thank you." I smiled. "Lynnae, we have our differences, but you're like me in so many ways. You are a good girl, Lynnae. Your momma raised you right."

"You raised me. I've learned so much from you in these past ten years. Julie, Dan has been more like a father to me than my own father ever was. I dream of having a relationship like you and Dan have." Lynnae sat back against the wall. She gave me an impish look, her eyes lighting up. "Sam's dad, Pete, asked me to marry him."

"*Again?*" I was grateful for the change of subject. "What did you say this time?"

"I told him no. Julie, Pete's a great father. I mean, he's good to *both* my boys." She looked away for a moment. "He gives me money every month, even for Max. He tells me I should just forget about Max's father. When he picks up Sam for the weekend, he wants to take Max, too. He says Max doesn't have to know that he's not his father. And when he watches the boys at my house, he cleans the entire place. Cooks for the boys. Every time he sees me, he tells me how much he loves me." "So what's the problem?"

Lynnae shook her head. "He's not Dan. When Dan looks at you, it's with desire. Dan can't walk past you without touching you. Dan closes his eyes when he's kissing you. Pete locks the bathroom door. He had a fit because I showered with the door open. Pete kisses me like I'm his sister. I'm not a little girl anymore. I want a man who...Julie, I want what you and Dan have. I wanna light up every time I see my husband. I want a husband to take care of me, the way Dan takes care of you. Dan has tested your sugar more than you have."

I shook my head. "You don't know Dan is having an affair with this woman. Maybe he needed to talk to someone. Plenty of guys come in here and talk to us."

"Yes, but I don't lie about them. And I'll have you know I check my sugar every morning."

The phone rang, and before I could get up to answer it, I heard Brooke's voice saying, "Bella Napoli Bakery, this is Brooke, how can I help you?"

"Julie, *think* about what you're doing."

I moved my chair closer to hers. Sat behind her and began to French braid her thick blond hair. "Lynnae, not one second goes by that I don't think about what I'm doing."

"Good. Care to fill me in?"

I chuckled. "When I was a little girl, I would sit for hours underneath my favorite weeping willow tree. It draped all the way to the ground. That was my secret hiding place. If I didn't make any noise, no one would even know I was under that old tree. I would take grocery boxes, line them up and open my store for business.

My customers were my Barbie collection." "All by yourself?" Lynnae asked.

"Yeah. Even as a child, I knew no one could hurt you when you're alone. You know, now that I think about it, maybe it was under that old tree that I began to believe in myself. Even as a child. As early as twelve, I would not allow anyone else's problems come between me and my happiness, or my salvation."

I wrapped the elastic band at the bottom of her braid, and kissed her on the back of her head.

Lynnae rolled her chair away from me. "I hear what you're saying. Lord knows you're a strong woman. But living alone is not the answer. That's too sad. Julie, on the weekends I'm off, my life is lonely, even with the boys."

"You'll find someone, hang in there." I touched her cheek. "I am so grateful for that willowy young girl who came to work alongside me. I love working with you." My lip quivered. I had to wipe a tear, just thinking about leaving her.

"Julie, you have taught me so much. I admire you for always doing what's right. The boys and I thank God for you every night. My God, I hope you're wrong about Dan."

"I *hope* I am too," I agreed with my whole heart, and then I stretched my neck and stood up. "I'll be fine." I reached out and touched her knee. "As long as I have my Lord and Savior with me, I will be just fine."

"I wish I had your faith," Lynnae said. "I cannot tell you how many times I say to myself *what would Julie do right now?*"

At that moment, we heard the bell attached to the front door jingle and we knew our first customer had arrived.

Most days the bakery was so busy I didn't have time to think about anything except what had to go in the oven and what needed taking out. I was thankful for the afternoons when the customers had gone about their day, the counters were clean, all was calm, Lynnae and I took a moment to share a cup of tea. It was usually only for a few minutes, but still we were both glad for the opportunity to rest our tired feet.

When we finally got a break, Lynnae brought over a plate of goodies. "Here. I picked us up a new tea from Harney & Sons. It's called Rooibos Chai. I think you'll like it; it has clove, cinnamon and cardamom in it."

"All in one tea?" I tasted the tea and it was very good. "Thank you. I like it."

We sat down on the antique sofa I had recently bought. A Victorian with mauve velvet and dark hand-carved wood. Lynnae hung her right leg over the side, leaned toward me, and handed me a plate. "Taste this."

I took a bite. My eyes opened wide. "Oh my, what is in this?" It appeared to be an apple crisp, but it was much lighter on my palate.

Lynnae nodded. "I knew you'd like it. Pear and a touch of ginger. I'm going to put a few samples out tomorrow." She took a bite of hers. "I wanted to try something different. Good, yes?"

I gave a nod, then for the first time in days, I ate everything in front of me. "What did you do this weekend?" I asked, hoping for a happy story.

She laughed aloud. "You would be so proud of me. The boys were off from school for three days, for parent-teacher conferences. Pete was taking them for the long weekend. After he picked them up, I cleaned my entire apartment." She laughed even louder. "Then

I ate two bags of popcorn and watched a movie on Netflix."

"What movie?" I asked.

"The Proposal."

"That sounds more exciting than my weekend." I rubbed the back of my neck. "Dan said he needed to cut some limbs back over on the property, but I think he is avoiding me."

"Of course, he is." Her eyes opened wide. "He knows you're upset."

"I'm sure he does. But I am not asking him about the note. So instead, I sat on my chaise lounge, reading one Nicholas Sparks novel after another. Right now, I am thankful for two words.

'Chapter One.' A book can take me places – take me far away, away from my pain and suffering. I'm thankful, because with a good book, I can go to a better place, a different place. I can't even begin to tell you how many days I've spent reading any book I could get my hands on."

"Been there, done that," Lynnae said, "except when I feel that way, my drug of choice is movies."

"Lynnae, I have to say my life has not turned out quite the way

I intended."

"Julie, Julie, Julie, does anybody's?"

Chapter 8

That night, I dreamt I left Dan.

In my dream, I ran away to Rhode Island. Of all our vacations, Rhode Island was my favorite. When Dan brought me to the small fishing town of Point Judith, he told me that I would love it so much that we would return there someday. What he did not tell me was that it would be in a dream, and in that dream, I would see my future. My safe haven.

There was something so powerful and special about REM sleep. I knew that even scientists did not yet understand the cause or purpose of dreams, but I could not help but wonder where that dream came from. I rolled over in the bed, not wanting to get up. My eyes were on the circle-top window above my chaise lounge; outside, the sky was pale blue. One thing I knew for sure: I woke up with a changed heart.

It had been a long time coming, that dream, but when it came right down to my life, just whom had I punished with that dream except myself? Seeing myself living along the ocean. Having feelings of contentment. And self-worth. Thanks to that dream, I knew how it would feel if I let myself go to another place – just for a while. My future was no longer theory or speculation. Reality was not far from my imagination. I dreamt about an inn. I was successful, surrounded by people who cared about me, and I was happy.

I used to believe, beyond a doubt, that I knew my own heart. But that, too, changed, thanks to the dream. First, I got a good look at myself and the spirit of what was to come. It made it clear – my future was up to me. In my dream, I was strong. I cared about life and about myself. I conquered my biggest fear – facing life without Dan. Even though the bitter seed of doubt existed, I still had longings and desires. "Hmmm," I said, then got up, made the bed and got myself dressed. By the time I was finished, the sky went from pale blue to fluffy white.

"Hey," I heard Dan call to me as I walked past his office, "for Easter, I'm inviting..."

"No," I said as I entered his office. "I don't want a lot of company. I'm not up to entertaining."

"I already asked Jesse. It's not a big deal," he said as I stood, stoic, in his doorway. "I'll help..."

"Ugh." I turned around and snatched my pocketbook. "I'm going to the store for milk and yogurt." "Want me to drive you?" he asked.

"No," I quickly replied.

"Lady and I are going for a ride over on the property. We'll see you when we get back."

The three of us left at the same time. Dan and Lady in the Polaris Ranger and me in my car. When I pulled into the E-Z Quik parking lot, I *saw* her. She was pushing a shopping cart that had one bag of groceries. Tagging along behind her were two small children. Each child had a Mylar balloon. As the little boy went to get in the minivan, everyone looked up as his balloon flew away.

By the time I parked, she was backing out. I sat in my car, sick to my stomach; she was even harder to look at in person. "Oh, my

God. I have to be wrong." My hands were on the top of my head. "There was no way Dan would ever...maybe I don't have to give everything up after all..."

I never went into the store. I was driving home when it hit me. As soon as I got home, I ran to my laptop and checked my Optimum phone bill. She had been calling my house! "Wait, how does she know my work schedule?" I looked at the call log again, and I noticed each call lasted a few minutes. "What is she saying to him in that amount of time?"

I wanted to scream as loud as I could. Instead, I went outside. Near the maple tree sat my favorite garden statue. Favorite, because it came apart. The hollow bottom section was my treasure chest, filled with my seven journals. I didn't have to read them; I knew what they were. A reminder of my life. Who I was – and what I had become.

I didn't know why I *had to* write it all down. It only took a few words from each journal, and I saw their faces all over again. Through the years, I had learned: it was not what you achieved in life, it was more of what you survived and overcame that made you the person you were.

I tossed the new journal and went back to the house, where I started to make myself a second cup of tea, but quickly changed it to a strong martini. Then I sat down and started writing. Before the first thoughts hit me, my hand started to shake; and once again, I was at Dan's mercy.

Journal Number Eight

My name is Julie Holliday and this is my last and final journal.

I've heard that it can be very therapeutic to write your fears down.

Well, I've been doing that for years. I have only one fear, fear of losing my husband.

The day we met, I found you to be intoxicating.

Today, I have just finished reading my third book on why men cheat. I have suspected you of adultery eight times over the past thirty years.

Comedian Steve Harvey wrote: "If a man is caught cheating and he lies and denies his behavior, it is because he knows what he has at home, and he does not want to lose it." This could be true. It could also be true that a liar and denier like you, is a repeat offender. Steve also writes, for most men, "it" was only the sex. Just a little something...to boost a man's ego. I have to ask. Is your ego bigger than your heart? Stronger than your own self-worth? Is your ego deeper than your dignity? Bottom line. Harvey says, men cheat because they can! I agree.

Women justify having an affair by saying, "But I loved him." Men justify an affair by saying; but I did not love her. Does anyone ever think about the consequences? Is a single affair more forgivable than numerous affairs? I say every one of your affairs left me feeling like Lizzie Borden with cramps!

When I was five, a man molested me. That was nothing compared to your affairs. He was a stranger. You – Dan, I thought were my best friend. When I saw you with #1, my mind and my body were in shock. Why didn't I draw the line right then and there? Do I even have a line? Then, I was confronted with #2. You said you would never cheat on me, and you wanted me back. Most men are drawn to another woman not for love or intimacy but for their own feeling of self- worth. Please explain to me, how #3 made you feel better about yourself? Oh, Dan, #4 had nothing on me. Once again, you have hit me with the trauma of another woman. I was forced to ask myself this, if you are unwilling to discuss why the affairs happened, then are you not saying our relationship is built on sand? Because having suspected you with these women was not a day at the beach for me.

It is as if I am consumed by hate. Tell me, do you really like me this way? I am constantly asking myself, why? Why do the affairs happen in the first place? Could I have done something differently? Damn it! If I stay with you, am I deliberately overlooking your affairs?

Am I strong enough now to weather another one of your storms? Or, in the end, will you make me strong because of them?

With #6, my suspicions and my actions were spinning out of control. Are you a narcissistic bastard? You have no remorse or guilt. Yet another name is dropped in my lap. Are you just incapable of empathy?

#7 shocks me into reality. That affair made everything clear. I do not know who you are anymore. Panic has set in.

Now I am thinking my heart must be made of steel. I know this to be true. I also know that you, Dan, are my magnet. Because I am humiliated by #8.

Dan, do these women even know the long line they are in?

Maybe I am wrong. Maybe my heart is so in love with you that I am driving myself crazy.

By the way #8.

So... not worth it!

I placed the last journal inside the statue, seized the other seven, went inside the house and lit a fire in the fireplace. Tossed them in and watched as they ignited, the edges began to brown and curl up and they finally burst into flames.

By the time I had finished, I had downed two martinis, a half a stick of pepperoni and most of what was left of the goat cheese. When I'd had enough, I started preparing dinner.

I stopped stirring the onions for a moment and said, "My husband is seeing a cartoon character. Oh, my God, you cannot make this stuff up." I set the spoon down on the counter and went into the pantry. Snapped up the tomato paste, crushed tomatoes and a can of sauce. A moment later, I heard Dan whistle.

"Smells great, what do ya need me to do?" He asked as he kissed me on the cheek.

I wished I hadn't drunk so much. I stared at him. He's out of his mind. Please, God, give me strength. "Where's Lady?"

"Outside peeing. What can I do?"

"Hand me a frying pan and open those cans. Please."

While Dan stirred the sauce, I rolled the meatballs, fried them and then tossed them into the simmering sauce.

"Let's go for a little hike while the sauce cooks down." Dan handed me my coat. "Come on. We'll just go as far as the old sycamore tree." He reached his hand out to me and I followed him out the door.

"You're kidding me, right?" I complained as I trudged through snow up to my derriere.

"All right, all right," Dan said as he turned back. "I wanted to show you something."

"There's too much snow. And, no, I am not wearing my snowshoes."

It was a godsend we didn't go – Dan never turned the burner down, and the sauce was boiling over.

After dinner, we watched *Casino Royale*. The entire time I kept thinking about the phone calls. I kept seeing her face.

"Are you okay?" Dan asked me as he reached for my hand.

"I'm fine." I gave him a wry grin. Truth was – it was killing me, not asking him about that damn note. About why she was calling him on a daily basis. Or if he was having an affair with her. I wasn't about to give him the opportunity to lie to me. I was going to get my proof before I said a word to him.

The next morning, I made eggs for breakfast.

"No milk?" Dan asked as he closed the refrigerator door. "I thought you went to the store yesterday."

I handed him his plate. Thankfully, he never complained.

Immediately after breakfast, I headed for the bakery. I had to talk to Lynnae. I wanted to tell her about the phone calls. When I pulled up to the bakery, there was a dark blue pickup truck in my parking lot. I approached the truck and looked inside. It was empty. Someone must have parked it there during the night. "Whoever you are, I'm sure my surveillance camera took your picture."

I headed for the coffee pots, turned on the tea urn and the cappuccino machines. Then I went into the kitchen and turned on the ovens. Pulled down the list of orders and started gathering ingredients.

A moment later, I heard Lynnae come in. "Where's my coffee?" she joked. "Good heavens, what got you motivated this morning?

And whose truck is that?"

"I don't know. It was here when I arrived. Never mind the truck for now. We have bigger fish to catch."

Lynnae poured my coffee, and handed it to me. Then she poured hers, adding cream and sugar.

I sat down on the sofa. "Hey, I saw her."

"Who?" Lynnae said as she sat down next to me.

I said her name. "She was coming out of the store." My insides were trembling. "She is worse in person."

"That's hard to imagine." Lynnae drank from her cup. "Did she see you?"

I shook my head. "She's calling my house."

"What!" Lynnae sat up straighter. "When?"

"Every day last week."

"No way! How do you know?" Lynnae finished her coffee, got up and filled her cup.

"I checked my Optimum account."

"Your phone bill?" she asked, turning to face me.

"Yes. I looked at the call log."

"How many times and when?" Lynnae asked as she sat back down.

"Lynnae, she only calls the house when I'm at work. You and I both know my schedule is never the same."

"My frigging blood pressure can't take this crap." Lynnae's cheeks were turning red.

"Dan has to be talking to her. He's the only other person who knows my schedule, besides you."

"Me?" She hitched her chin. "Brooke and Stephanie know our entire schedule. Julie, a damn monkey can figure out your hours.

Wedding season, holidays…" I lowered my voice. "Stop!"

"Julie, think about it. She calls during working hours…"

"But she *calls.*"

We heard the bell and both stood up. Brooke and Stephanie had arrived to work earlier than usual. And they were both wearing party dresses. "Well, well, where did you guys go last night?" Lynnae teased. "To the fireman's dinner dance," Brooke said, smiling. "Don't worry, we have a change of clothes."

"Hi, guys," Stephanie said. "Hope you don't mind we parked our new truck here last night."

"So that's whose truck is parked in my lot," I said smiling.

"Would you like some coffee?" "Sure," Stephanie said, yawning. "We traded our cars in for one pickup truck," Brooke said as she sat down between Lynnae and me.

"My friend Luke picked us up here last night and dropped us off. He was the designated driver," Stephanie added as she sat down next to me with her cup of coffee.

"That explains it," I said. "You both look beautiful, by the way."

We were still drinking our coffee when Lynnae demanded we all get to work. "Let's go, my beauteous princesses. There's work to be done. You can tell us all about your new truck in the kitchen."

I don't know where I would have been without those girls in my life. It was a joy to be with them. There was so much positive energy in the room. I looked around. Lynnae was mixing, tossing, and baking everything under the sun. Brooke was swaying to the music and decorating an entire tray of cookies at the same time.

Stephanie laughed, telling us about Brooke dancing all night.

"Yeah, and while I was dancing, you were flirting with Luke all night." Brooke waved her spatula at Stephanie. "How come you're not telling *that* story?"

Stephanie shrugged her shoulders. "Yep, and we're going out to dinner tonight." She smiled at me, climbed up onto her stool, picked up her drawing pencil and began sketching a wedding cake. "You go, girl!" Lynnae said as she set two cookie sheets in the oven. "I wanna find a man. I want a man in my life." She looked over at me and winked. "I want love in my life…"

The entire day had passed before I had a chance to sit down. It was late in the afternoon, almost closing time, when Lynnae motioned for me to join her in the back. "How are the boys?" I asked her while I poured two cups of tea. "I wish I knew how to help Sam with his reading. He struggles on every word. I hate dyslexia. Why does he have to deal with this bullshit? He's such a sweet boy." Lynnae set the small plate on the table in front of the sofa, then sat down with her legs tucked under her.

"I know a school that can help Sam. Lynnae, I'll pay for him to go."

"Thank you for the offer. But, umm, no." She held up her hand like a stop sign. "I'm not sending Sam away."

"Lynnae, it's not camp, or-"

"No, Julie. I won't do it."

I sat down next to her. "What's this?" I held up the plate.

She curled her lip. "Cinnamon raisin swirl buns. I made them for you. No sugar, just love." She raised her eyebrows. "And a secret ingredient."

"Butter?" I took another bite. "This is good, really good."

"Great. Then why do you look so sad? Julie, do you trust me?"

"Of course I do. What kind of question is that?"

"Then stop with the nonsense already. I'm telling you Dan only has eyes for you."

"And she has *her* eyes on my husband."

"So what?" she hissed at me and headed for the kitchen.

I got up and followed her. A half-hour later, I went home.

When I arrived, Dan was waiting for me in the living room. "When was the last time you had a good martini?"

I couldn't help myself, I smiled at his seductive tone. "Tonight?"

"Your wish is my command." He winked and then he opened the freezer and poured my martini.

When I saw the two olives in the waiting glass, I said, "Pretty sure of yourself."

Dan kissed me on my left temple and my insides became aroused. "You've been down about something. I had to find a way to make you smile again."

I held up my glass, took a sip and said, "This will do just fine."

Dan got a Corona for himself and a tray of Brie, pepperoni and soda crackers, closed the refrigerator door and said, "Bond. You can call me Bond."

"You watch too many movies. Although you do remind me of Daniel Craig," I joked.

"How was work?" he asked me.

"It was good. Brooke and Stephanie bought a pickup truck."

"A Ford, I hope." He got up and turned on the CD player. Closing my eyes, I focused on the sound of Al Green singing, "Let's

Stay Together."

Dan handed me a cracker and I ate it. When he filled my glass up to the rim, I realized I had finished the first one. I ate another cracker. My insides were hammering and there was only one way to control it. I took another sip of my drink, knowing that I had better eat soon or else. It had been weeks since we'd made love. *Lynnae had better be right about that woman. Because I don't know if I can stop myself.*

He touched me and my entire body surged, wanting him. Dan reached for me and I stood up. We were dancing to "How Can You Mend A Broken Heart". With every shortened breath, he removed my clothes. I was hungry for him and he knew it. "I'm on fire," I whispered in his ear.

Dan kissed me and then squeezed me tight. I lost my breath when he whispered in my ear, "I love you," and I felt his day-old beard on my cheek. I kissed his stubble. He reached down and touched the notch between my legs. "What do you want me to do?" "I'm not a hard woman to please…"

Not waiting for my request, he lifted me up. When Dan exploded, a second orgasm hit me like a wave. With my legs still wrapped around him, he carried me to the shower. I reached up and turned the water on.

When I looked into Dan's eyes, the pain in my heart had turned from agony to pleasure. After all, he was still the man of my erotic dreams and fantasies. Dan was playful, and sexy, an irresistible combination. Thirty years on, and I could not resist him.

When we stepped out of the shower, the house was dark. "Are you tired?" he asked me.

I nodded. "Exhausted."

Dan helped me fold the bedspread down to the bottom of the bed. Lying next to me, he reached over and put his hand in mine.

"Goodnight," he said.

"Goodnight," I whispered, closing my eyes. *Whatever made me think I could run away?*

Chapter 9

I took Dan's deposit from his desk and noticed the note was still in the same spot. I was on my third cup of revitalize tea and still was not ready for the day. When he made love to me, it was beautiful – moments that I lived for. Every day of our lives should have been as breathtaking, warm and sensual.

And seeing that damn note, I wished I could close the door on the bakery and go where no one would ever find me, but I couldn't do that to my girls. Besides, I had a special wedding cake to deliver, and to make things worse, I was allowing the bride and her bridesmaids to get dressed at my house and take wedding photos in my gardens.

I never should have agreed to that, but the bride, a friend from high school had found me on Facebook a year earlier, and asked if she could take some pictures in my backyard along the river. I said yes because of high school; in fact, I went to school with most of the bridal party.

When she came into the bakery, the idea sounded great. Designing a cake for five hundred people was an honor. Lynnae would make it and the girls would decorate it. I had been in the bakery business for nineteen years. I used to love every aspect of running my own business – nineteen years of hard work, a lot of marketing and many long hours. Never mind the long list of customers who would follow my cupcakes anywhere.

It all meant nothing to me. I'd lost my fire, my passion, my desire to bake a damn thing.

"Julie," Dan hollered from the kitchen, "can you let Lady in?"

I opened the door and in she came. Of course, she ran past me and directly into the kitchen to see her father.

"Ahh, good girl. Hey, Julie," he called, "can you give her some food and water? I have to leave."

"You're not taking her to work with you?" I asked, heading toward the kitchen.

"I have to run the excavator all day." Dan looked at me. "And Rick has a lot of woods she could get lost in." Dan patted Lady's head and moved to kiss me goodbye. He kissed my lips long and hard before he added, "See you tonight."

I stood there. *What am I doing? That damn note is driving me crazy.* Lady came over looked up at me. I sat down on the floor next to her. "You are the best dog in the world." I kissed her, got up and filled her bowl with food, filled her water bowl and promised to be back home in a little while.

When I arrived at the bakery, I was glad to see Lynnae's Jeep.

"Good morning, sunshine. You better put the top on the Jeep this

morning. I heard rain is in the forecast."

"No way."

"Okay, but if you get a wet tush going home, I don't want to hear about it."

"Never mind my ass. Are you okay?" Lynnae set the basket of coffee in the machine. "I know you're upset. I can see the stress on your face, but…"

"I don't know what to do." I tried not to crumble. "I'm an intelligent woman. I am smart enough to know that love should not hurt like this." I shook my head. "My heart feels like a target. With *no* center mass." I wanted to tell her about the hidden cameras. But I didn't. Never mind, I was no closer to catching him. Thus far, he was a saint. No calls to that woman at all. No proof of a second cell phone.

"I'm sorry. I promise to focus on the bakery, the cookies in the ovens, the…"

"Stop. I care about you, and you know it."

"Seriously, I'll stop thinking about that damn note and I'll get back into the swing of things."

"You better. Next week we have to start preparing for the Felitti wedding, and that means we have a ton of baking to do."

"Do you think I should hire someone to help out front?"

"Umm, yeah! Because you're not getting my girls. I need them. Especially this week. We have eight hundred Italian pastries to make and that's just for the rehearsal dinner."

"Oh crap. Speaking of the wedding, I have to order some flowers from Alder's."

"Who's getting flowers?"

"I want to plant some more daffodils and tulips down along the stairs, and near the weeping willow."

"For the wedding pictures? Screw that! Let her buy the flowers.

You're doing enough for her. It's her own damn fault she's getting married in the middle of April."

I laughed. "How can I help you in the kitchen?"

"You could start by baking the Bruttibonis, the cannolis and the

Sfogliatellas."

We spent the week baking our tails off. We were so busy, Lynnae and I never had the chance to sip one cup of tea.

Finally, it was wedding day. Lucky for the bride, it was 64 degrees outside. I had not seen some of those women in thirty years. I chatted with them for a few minutes – knowing they were on a tight schedule.

"Julie, thank you so much for letting us get dressed here. Your house is incredible. When I saw the photos of your gardens, I was in awe. But your home is absolutely gorgeous."

"Thank you. We're blessed, that's for sure."

"The photographer will be arriving in less than an hour; and the limo driver will be here as well. This is my third marriage; you'd think I'd be more organized."

"There's nothing to worry about," I said as I led them into my bedroom. "You're all set. If you need anything, give me a holler." The bride stopped in front of me and I almost walked into her.

"Advice," she laughed.

I heard one of the bridesmaids say, "That's how Julie does it."

"Does what?" I asked.

"A box of chocolates on his nightstand and a Bible on yours."

She was correct. The Bible *was* on my nightstand. The chocolates were something I had been doing for a long time. They were his favorite. At that moment, I had to leave; I did not wish to spoil their day. I explained myself by saying, "I'm gonna go outside and give you all some privacy."

Once again, we had people fooled. I knew it all looked good: the beautiful home along the river, several rentals, two successful businesses, and many toys in the driveway. They saw a king-sized bed where two people made love and dreamt in each other's arms. I saw long nights and a nightmare that would not go away.

I went outside and sat down under my favorite tree, the one near the stature with the hidden compartment.

Everyone came out of the house, looking gorgeous. The photographer was good. She used the river as her backdrop.

The limo driver pulled up. "Ah, right on time." I kissed everyone goodbye.

I was so relieved when they got into the limo and left.

I went back into the house, turned on the stereo and began to straighten up. I put the orange juice in the refrigerator and tossed out the remaining champagne. I was glad I had nothing else going on at the bakery for a while. I looked out at the river, under the weeping willow. I had planted English primrose, winter jasmine, snowdrops, pansy, and hellebore. Then I heard Josh Groan singing, "You Raise

Me Up" on the radio, and I started bawling my eyes out.

It was hard to be negative or mad when God had blessed me with so much. When the song was over, I closed my eyes, raised both of my hands high above my head, and began to wave them from side to side. Because I knew. He was by my side the whole time. "Thank You, Lord. Thank You for allowing me to walk beside You.

To lean on You. To draw my strength from You. Because of You, I have survived another day."

I spent that afternoon putting my winter clothes in the downstairs cedar closet, and bringing up my spring and summer clothing. Before I knew it, it was six o'clock. My head started hurting, so I sat down on the sofa. A moment later, Dan and Lady arrived. Lady stood in front of me, and Dan sat down beside me.

"Are you okay?" he asked.

The next thing I knew, he was testing my sugar. "Lady, watch her." Dan said as he went to the kitchen. He came back with two glasses of water. "Drink. Julie, take a sip. A little more."

Twenty minutes later, I exhaled. "Whew."

"Here, drink one more glass." Dan started rubbing my back. "Did you eat today? Unbelievable. How many times do I have to tell you? You have to eat. What did you eat today?"

"I don't remember."

He kissed me on my cheek. "What am I going to do with you? Julie, you *have* to eat."

"I'm okay. I'll make dinner."

"No, you won't," he said gently. "Lady, don't let her move. I'll make dinner. Pick your feet up." He set a pillow under my head. "Don't move." Then he kissed me on the forehead.

He went to the kitchen and when he came back into the living room, my heart melted. "Here eat this. This will make you feel better." He handed me a plate of Triscuit crackers. I smiled when I noticed he'd drizzled olive oil on the goat cheese, trying to be like me. "Dinner will be done in forty minutes. Pork roast, along with some fresh asparagus." "Thank you for cooking."

Dan put a CD in. I leaned back and listened to Eric Clapton sing "Wonderful Tonight," A lump formed in my throat, I wanted to cry. We ate dinner, and I have to say, I felt better. "Still wanna go hiking?" he asked.

"Oh, yeah."

We were on our way back when Dan pointed at our house and said, "See that? Tomorrow night we're staying at that inn. I'll bet they're serving your favorite fish for dinner." Then he reached for my hand. "You and me, cooking mouthwatering meals together.

Giving hiking, fishing and kayaking tours on our property."

"Sounds nice," I said.

When we got home, we curled up on the couch and watched a movie, until we both fell asleep.

In spite of my recent diabetic episode, the next day I skipped lunch with Lynnae, Brooke and Stephanie because I had to run a few errands and go to the post office. When I pulled up to the bakery, I could see cars parked bumper to bumper on all sides of the building.

"Poor Lynnae!" As I rushed past several customers, I caught sight of a woman standing behind my cash register.

"Don't mind her, she's only the owner," Lynnae said to her. "Karly, this is Julie. Julie, this is Karly, your new cashier." Lynnae raised her eyebrows at me. "Say hello! And put those packages down, woman. We have orders to take."

I mouthed *thank you* to Lynnae and extended my hand to the girl. Karly. "You'll get used to Lynnae. I did."

When things quieted down, I had a few minutes to talk to Karly.

"Are you attending college?

"Yes," she replied as she replaced the sign in front of the chocolate cupcakes with the coconut one.

"What classes are you taking this semester?"

"I'm thinking of becoming a physician's assistant. So now, I'm taking biology. But I keep changing my mind."

"It's fine to change your mind."

"Five times?" she said as she closed the door on the display case.

"Whatever it takes," I said.

"What was your major?" Karly asked me.

"I never attended college. I dropped out of high school in January of my senior year."

"I'm sorry…" Karly said as she looked at me over the tray of samples.

"Karly, there's no reason to be sorry. If your occupation requires a degree, then you need to go to college. My dream was to get paid for doing what I loved. And that didn't require a degree, it required skill."

"Me, too," Lynnae said, giving us all a little hip action and giggling fetchingly.

I picked up my packages from the floor behind the counter and went into the office. I set the box containing several tape recorders in my bottom desk drawer. And tossed the bag of new garden journals next to my pocketbook. A few minutes later, Lynnae came in. "The chick came in looking for a job. I hired her on the spot to help in the afternoon. Maybe you can take some time for yourself." She pointed her finger at me. "*After* Mother's Day, that is."

"Yes, ma'am."

Lynnae sat down in the empty chair next to me. "How's Dan?"

"He's great."

"Julie, just *ask* him about the note. How long has it been? You have to put this to rest. Where's the note?"

"Still on his desk." "It's on his desk? Seriously? Hello, because she's a customer. Julie, what am I going to do with you? No man leaves a note from his lover in plain sight on his desk for three months. Can we please focus on-?" "Lynnae, it's your babysitter." Stephanie handed Lynnae the cell phone.

"Hey, Aimee-Jo, what's up? Okay, let me talk to him. Sam, give Max his truck. Right now! No! Sam…thank you. Mommy loves you. Now put Aimee-Jo back on. You're all set. No problem."

Lynnae hung up. "I swear they turn into little monsters before you know it."

"Why aren't they in school?"

"Spring break."

"I admire you, being a single mother. I know it's not easy, Lynnae. I know how much you give up for the boys. And I know the long hours you keep to put food on the table, clothes on their backs, and maintain a good home for them. You've got my vote. I hear you turn down some sweet offers."

Lynnae rolled her eyes. "Offers. Some not so pleasurable, thank you. Remember, I texted you the other night? Cute guy moving in three doors down?" "Dating material?"

"Umm, more like asshole. Last night, I was taking the garbage out and he hollers over to me, 'How you doing? I like a girl who takes out the garbage!' He actually said that."

"Oh, no. What did you say to him?"

"I flipped him the bird. What cave did he crawl out of? Doesn't he know the difference between a girl and a woman? I'd rather live alone than have an asshole like that in my house." "Oh, Lynnae! What am I going to do with you?"

Karly, Brooke and Stephanie all had classes, so Lynnae and I locked up. "I'll see you tomorrow sunshine," I hollered over to her as she approached her Jeep.

"Arrivederci, Momma!"

By seven o'clock the next morning. Lady was lying in the old barn, waiting for her father to go to work.

Dan kissed me goodbye. "Where's Lady?"

"She's waiting for you outside."

Dan looked out the window. "I'll be home early." He kissed me again. "We'll do something special this weekend."

It was my weekend to be off. I looked around for a minute and then decided to go jogging.

When Dan and I first started taking our morning hike together, we used to see grouse, rabbit, turkey and deer. Somehow, that all changed and we seemed to be running into bobcat, coyote, bear and mountain lion. Buying the land was a good investment for us. It ensured Dan would always have his hunting rights, and I would have my hiking and jogging trail. I not only loved heading out on the trail, I lived for it. It was the only time I got to clear my head. Reflect on the previous day's events.

We knew the owner, and when the opportunity came up to buy the land, we jumped at the chance. The day we bought it, Dan asked me to name it. He giggled like a kid when I told him the name.

"Holliday's Outback Property." I chose that name because that was what I would say if someone asked where Dan was. Outback on the property. Now, we just called it "the property."

The memory of that day made me smile. I'm sure if I had written about it in a journal back then, I would have covered that day's page with hearts and flowers.

I picked up my weights. For the first time in a long time, I was on the trail alone. And it felt good. I was alone with Mariah Carey whispering "Hero" on my iPod. As I jogged deeper into the woods, the fresh breeze encouraged me pick up my pace. At the top of the first hill was the orchard. Beyond the apple trees, there was a streambed. It may have been small, but it made me stop, look and listen every time. I'd close my eyes and imagined the water was running through bamboo, instead of through the old culvert pipe. The sound was soothing, peaceful and it felt tranquil. Until the stinging horseflies appeared. Telling me to get my tush up the next hill.

At the top of that hill, something in the meadow caught my eye. Up ahead, in front of me, stood two coyotes, brown and shaggy.

I tried to gather my composure, but my heart raced. Dan would have been mad if I told him I went out on the trail by myself. The year before, we had stumbled upon two black bears. He shouldn't have been too upset with me. After all, he was the one who taught me to be observant at all times, to be aware of my surroundings. He taught me to recognize footprints, sounds, and to be cognizant of pungent smells. He said, "Your nose is your best defense. You'll smell them before you ever see them."

I knew better than to turn and run. They would have seen me as a victim, or worse yet, their prey. I allowed them to get close enough to hear me. I looked them both in the eye and hollered, "Come any closer and I will shove this weight up your ass, and this weight down your throat!"

With that, the two coyotes tucked their tails in, turned and ran back into the woods. I didn't mean to take my anger out on them, but I did.

I was a woman once full of compassion and love. Suddenly, I felt like I no longer had self-respect. Gone was my sense of control over my own life. I had no idea who I was. In an instant, I went from a woman ready to share her life with the man she loved to a woman incapable of performing the slightest task.

Chapter 10

E arlier that morning, Dan had promised me we would do something special that weekend. However, now he was on the phone with Jesse.

I was rooted to the chair, barely breathing, lest I miss a word. If it was wrong of me to be listening in on Dan's conversation, my personal stake justified it. When I heard him tell Jesse they could start at the first trestle, I could not stand it any longer. I exhaled,

"Nice."

I moistened my lips and swallowed. Tears trickled down my face. I got up and started to leave the living room. Dan hung up and said, "Where you going?"

I was too angry to face him. I shook my head. "Nowhere." I let the word linger.

Dan stared at me, frozen in a last-minute indecision.

He followed me into the kitchen. Stood behind me. His hands were on my shoulders.

I shot up one hand. "Stop. Don't touch me." I crossed my arms over my chest. I hated it when people were in my space. He was definitely in my space. I backed up and turned to face him. "Why? Why do you make plans to be over on the property every time I am home? It's not like I take every weekend off."

He mumbled something. He was standing a foot away from me, looking directly into my eyes.

"What? What did you say?" I asked him.

Nothing. Silence filled the room.

"I can't take it anymore. Julie… you need to stop this. I don't know what's wrong with you, but you better get over it."

"I better get over it?" I shouted right back at him. Lady jumped up and ran to the door. *Is this man serious? Of course he is.* "Next, you'll tell me, 'She's just a friend, a customer, someone...' Yeah, like hell she is! I *know* better."

Dan shook his head. I could barely hear him. "What the hell are you talking about?"

I went into his office, took the note and screamed, "Are you sleeping with her?" Then I threw it at him.

"Are you out of your mind?"

For thirty seconds, we did the stare down. He took Lady and went outside.

And I was glad.

The next morning, I noticed Dan had written on the back of her note. He actually wrote up a quote to remove the blacktop from her driveway and replace it with stone. Not even I believed that. Never mind the fact that she *rented* the house.

The phone rang and I picked it up. "Hey, Jesse."

"What can I bring?" he asked.

"Bring?"

"Kayaking. Never mind, I'll bring the beer."

"Kayaking? When?"

"What the hell. Dan said we were all going kayaking today."

I glanced out the window. "I may have ruined those plans. He's out in the garage, I'll tell him to call you."

Yet another Monday, I dragged myself to work, but once I got there, it was amazing how my mood improved. It had to be the aroma of baking bread and cinnamon buns.

I had just put the coffee flan in the glass case when I heard Lynnae whisper my name. I turned around and looked at her. She was standing behind the kitchen door, peeking out. She waved her hand, beckoning me to come over to her.

"What?" I whispered back.

She gripped my arm and pulled me into the kitchen as if I were on fire. "It's *him.*"

"Who?"

"Cute guy from down my street. That's him."

When I looked out, I didn't see any men, only three women sitting at the corner table, and a few others standing in the order line.

"There's no man out there."

Lynnae peeked out through the door opening. "Well, he was just there a minute ago. Didn't you see him? He's cute, right?"

"No. Sorry. I missed him. I was busy putting the flan in the case and lining the mini cakes up on the bottom shelf. Why are you hiding from him?"

"Uhh… he's hot. I wish he wasn't so damn hot."

"So that's why you're acting like a teenager?"

"Okay, okay, maybe I'm a little bit interested in him. But I would never tell him."

"Here, let me help you." I took the tray of Venetian cookies and Lynnae picked up a tray holding pecan sugar cookies. We went out to the front and set the trays down.

"Ummm," I started to say, "how did he go from ass… oh, my." He *was* hot. In fact, he was six feet tall, dark hair. Handsome. His eyes reminded me of my momma deer's. Big and alluring.

"Hey, how are you?" he asked.

Lynnae stumbled into Karly, almost dropping the entire tray.

"Okay, I guess," she managed to say.

"You work here?" "Yes, I do." She sounded rather curt.

He gave her a quick nod, tapping the counter with his right hand. "Well, it's nice to see you. You have a great day. Umm, where should I put this?" He held up his napkin and an empty cup.

"I'll take that." I reached out my hand.

When he left, I looked at Lynnae. Her lips were parted and she was rubbing her neck. "Wow. You *really* like him. My heart is racing, just looking at you."

"Not on your life. All I said was…"

"I know what you said." In my best Lynnae voice, I said, "I wish he wasn't so hhhot!"

"He's stalking me."

"He's *not* stalking you, Lynnae."

"Then why did he come in here?"

"Everybody in town comes in here," I reminded her.

Karly took the tray from Lynnae and offered to put everything on display.

"Hey, I have to tell you something," she said, pushing me toward the office. She sat down at the desk, and I sat down next to her. "Listen, don't freak, but when Brooke came into the office this morning, I was looking at Shrek's Facebook page. Apparently, Brooke knows her."

"Lynnae...did Brooke ask you why you were looking at her page?"

"No. She just told me to let her know when I was done with the computer, because she needed to post the weekly specials on our website. She only commented on the photo. Dumbass has a picture of a turkey on her wall. Who the hell posts a picture of turkey on April 29th?"

I could have said, "Someone who knows Tuesday is the first day of turkey-hunting season," but it made me sick to think about that.

I went into the kitchen and stuffed cannolis with a vengeance.

When I got home, Dan had dinner on the table. And he'd picked me a bouquet of peonies. "I bought you something today." He handed me a gift-wrapped present. When I opened it, I saw it was a book on she-shed floor plans. "If you pick one out, maybe I'll build you one over on the property."

I looked at him hesitatingly. "I've been asking for one for a long time. Why now?"

"I'm trying to be nice. I'm trying to make things right between us." Dan bent down and picked up Lady's bowl. "Maybe because I have the time. Maybe because we own the property now. I don't know. I thought it would make you happy."

I sat down. Lady rested her head on my lap. When I put my hand on her, she whined. Almost begging me to pull myself together.

It was a warm spring day in May, and for the first time in over thirty years, I was not going turkey hunting with Dan. My heart bled when he said he wanted to go alone.

Outside, the birds were singing and I could smell cut grass.

From a distance, I heard the sound of my neighbor's lawn mower. I went over to the maple tree, opened the garden statue, collected my journal and began writing. When I got mad, I wrote!

Dear Dan, make no mistake. I am all woman. Do not think just because I chose to sit alongside you at four in the morning that I am a tomboy. For thirty years, springtime meant sitting by your side, sharing a providential awakening. I've brooded over every detail. It is as if I am living in some dreadful story – the oldest kind.

There are words left unspoken between us. Words that none will ever hear, I suppose. But if they did, oh, my, would they believe me? I think not. When I started writing my thoughts and feelings down on paper, it was for therapeutic reasons. Selfish reasons? Maybe they're the same thing. Does it matter? I don't know. Now, I write to find a resolution. Words written in a leather journal. The hardest words I have ever written sealed in several journals. Thanks to you.

Last week, I was wondering if you missed all the wonderful things we used to do together. As if you were reading my mind, you asked me what I missed the most.

I looked at you and pointed toward the bedroom. You took hold of my hand. Together, you and I walked up to my lingerie chest, where I opened the two small doors, and all the drawers exposing the most beautiful clothing I owned; you said every piece was spectacular, delicate, and very romantic. When I closed the doors, you brushed your hand along its side. You bought the chest for a reason. So my lingerie would have a place of its own.

Why are we doing this to each other? Why is her name still on your desk? Dan, you of all people know how much I love a good bubble bath, followed by a long steamy night. When I said, "I miss feeling sexy..."

"I miss my wife," was your reply. Then why am I missing you?

Do you have any idea how deeply you just hurt me? It doesn't take much to make me happy. You are tearing me apart. You know how much I love turkey hunting. Loved sitting in the woods early in the morning. It felt like I was sitting in a medieval forest. The early morning birds have a unique sound of their own, and right before the sun came up...magic!

I don't know why you had the sudden change of heart.

I did notice you no longer got up at four in the morning. For some reason, you didn't leave the house until six.

I couldn't write anymore, I was done. I put my journal away. And in spite of my encounter with the coyotes, I decided to go hiking.

I took my ten-pound hand-held weights and Lady with me. The only thing we saw along our travels was a Dora the Explorer Mylar balloon. I picked it up, poked a hole in it and tucked it into my pocket.

I was sitting on our front porch reading a novel, *The Summer I Dared*, enjoying a glass of iced tea, when I saw Jesse's truck pull up to the garage. Before he opened the garage door, he called over to

me, "Hey, what are you doing home?"

"I live here."

"Funny. Why aren't you with Dan?"

"He said he wanted go by himself. Sit down; I'll get you something to drink."

Jesse sat down while I went inside to get his glass of iced tea.

"Here." I handed him his glass and sat back down.

"What do you mean, he wanted to go alone?"

"I'm not happy about it." I rubbed my neck. "What do you want me to do? Go where I'm not wanted. He must have a reason."

I needed all the self-control I possessed not to reveal how shocked I was by hearing my own words. As if on cue, one of my feathered friends began to sing.

Jesse laughed aloud. "Did that bird just say cheater – cheater – cheater?"

I cracked a smile. "Yes. Yes, it did."

Dan was turkey hunting in the field behind our home. He could have been be at her house in about forty-five minutes. We looked at each other. Jesse knew something was wrong.

I saw him swallow hard, nod several times and lean forward in his chair. "I'm gonna sharpen my chainsaws. Thanks for the iced tea. Hey, I don't know what's gotten into the two of lately." He reached out his hand and lifted my chin up. "You know I love you guys. If you need me, I'll be in the garage."

I raised my eyebrows, tucked a curl behind my ear, and glanced up at him. Jesse was not afraid to say what he felt. I watched his slow-moving pace as he made his way to the garage. A 270-pound bad to the bone, goateed, gun-strapping teddy bear...oh yeah, that was Jesse. He might have looked like a bad ass, but deep down, he was a big old softy.

I went into the house, ran downstairs to the cedar closet and pulled out my camouflage pants, shirt, hat, gloves and mask. I brought them upstairs and hid them in the spare bedroom closet, where I could put them on in the morning and get out the door in time to be in my position.

For the past twenty-one mornings, Dan left the house by six and returned at nine.

I felt confident I would have enough time to do what I needed to do. If I waited fifteen minutes after he left, it would still give me a half an hour to be where I needed to be before he arrived on foot. I needed to know one-hundred percent if my suspicions were correct.

The next morning, after Dan went out the front door, I waited a few minutes longer before I put on my gear, and went out and got into my car. When I pulled onto her road, I drove until I reached the dead end. I turned off the engine, opened and closed the car door as quietly as I could.

My heart was racing like a thoroughbred. I crawled into the woods and sat down in the bushes. I watched, observing everything around me. Listening to the sounds around me.

At six-thirty, I saw the woman's husband leave in his truck. At eight-thirty, I watched as she left with her two children. No sign of Dan.

I no sooner got back onto the main road and I had to pull the car over to the side. I spent the next ten minutes vomiting into the bushes.

The next day I decided to go back. I chose a different location. I sat in the woods where I could get a closer look. I hunkered down against a cedar tree, almost as if I wished to mold myself to it and blend in until I disappeared. A careless act had brought me to that place, sneaking around, placing myself in danger. Still I sank deeper, and I waited.

Same as the day before. Six-thirty on the nose, the husband was gone.

Two hours later, at the exact moment when I was listening to the woman hollering at her children to get their asses into the minivan, I saw a figure of a man heading in my direction. My heart hammered my ribs. "Oh no!" I murmured.

What lay between me and the figure coming at me was a huge ravine. At the precise moment he was in front of me, he dropped to the ground. It was also at the very spot where he could have seen my car.

I sat there in my hiding place for a few minutes longer, trying to figure it all out. I decided there was nothing I could do. I knew if it *was* Dan, he would be smart enough not to move. I didn't care if he saw me or not, I got back in my car and drove home.

Exactly forty-five minutes after I arrived, Dan got home. He came into our bedroom, gun still in his hand, white as a ghost, sweating profusely, and said, "You're not going to believe this, but I was all the way over on the other side of the property, and I saw ten tom turkeys."

I was sitting on my chaise lounge looking at him and thinking, Oh Dan, if you saw ten tom turkeys, you would not be standing in our bedroom! If only I could have seen your face. But I hadn't. I picked up the book, pretending to be reading.

When I did not react, question Dan, or speak, he turned around and walked out of our bedroom.

I cried, Dear Lord, who are You protecting? Her? Him? Perhaps me.

Chapter 11

"June first, and all I want to do is stay home and work in my garden. But I can't. Every bride out there wishes to get married with a summer breeze," I said as I tied my sneaker. "Did I tell you, we have twenty-eight wedding cakes to deliver this month, thirty-two graduation cakes, and then there are the people who still insist on blowing out candles on their birthday?"

"Julie, come on, are you ready?" Dan hollered from the other side of the door.

"I'm coming, I'm coming." I said and closed the door behind me. "You didn't hear a word I said, did you?"

"It's nice out this morning. Nice breeze."

I rolled my eyes. "Yes, it is nice."

Lady trailed behind us. "Come on, girl. Get up here." I didn't like it when she trailed behind me. I was always scared something would get to her before I could save her, although she thought *she* was the one protecting me.

A few minutes later, Dan stopped short in front of me, kissed me on the lips and asked, "Do you have plans this weekend?"

"Yeah. Delivering about a thousand cakes."

"I thought maybe we would go out to eat."

"To the Millbrook Café?" I asked, hoping he would say yes. I loved the Millbrook Café.

"I was thinking about this Thai restaurant down in Patterson. Jesse and I went there for lunch the other day. I think you'd like it." "Let me check with Lynnae and see if she can work later on Saturday. Lady! Stop." Lady ran past Dan and I was afraid to see what she was chasing.

"She's fine. It looks like a balloon," Dan said.

I moved past him and picked up the Mylar balloon. It was in the exact spot the last one had been. "What does it say?" he asked.

"Nothing. It's a cartoon character, Superman." I poked a hole in it and stuffed it in my pocket, same as before.

Dan and Lady left for work. He was clearing a building lot, which meant they would be gone all day. I was in my car on my way to work and I could not get the balloons out of my head. I drove past my own bakery. When I reached the traffic light, I pulled over and shut the car off.

How did two balloons land in the exact same spot? I looked up, as if God Himself would give me the answer. I started the car. Looked in my rearview mirror and pulled back onto the road. *Maybe I should ask God, how many times does a woman have to forgive her husband before she loses her mind?*

At the bakery, Lynnae was dancing, and singing so loudly she must not have heard the bell on the front door. When I tapped her on the shoulder, she jumped ten feet in the air.

I laughed so hard I almost fell into the table and chairs. "What's got you so jumpy?"

"I'm not watching any more damn scary movies with him. Last night, we watched a movie about a deaf-mute writer. Her old boyfriend was stalking her. Of course, she was living alone in the woods. Damn movie scared the crap out of me."

"I'm glad you have someone to cuddle with."

"Yeah, and *that* is all we are doing."

"When do I get to formally meet this Barry character?"

"Soon. I promise. So why were you late this morning?"

"I drove right by. Didn't realize it until I got to the light."

I looked up at the clock. Brooke and Stephanie were due any second. "Come on, we have orders to fill."

Tuesday, July 3rd, and everyone wanted the same thing – a red, white and blue sheet cake. "Good morning, Karly." "Morning? Julie, its one o'clock in the afternoon," Lynnae said as she set a cake inside one of the delivery boxes.

"Hey, it's the first time I had two seconds to say hello or see anyone. You haven't let me out of the kitchen all week," I joked.

"Not my fault, we have sixteen pickups coming in between two and five. Lynnae looked at me for a moment. "I'm sorry. Why don't we both take a break and get something to eat right now?"

"Eat. I almost forgot. I need to run home at one-thirty so I can put my spareribs in the oven. While I'm out, I'll pick up pizza for us all."

"When you leave," Lynnae said, "I'll order the pizzas." "Sounds good. Hey, can I ask you a silly question?" "Oh, boy." She rolled her eyes.

"Do you think it's possible balloons can fall out of the sky in the exact same spot, two times in a row?"

"What?" Lynnae laughed. "No way. Why?"

"This morning, Dan and I found a Mylar balloon along our hiking trail. It's the second balloon I found. Back in May, I was walking with Lady and I found a Dora the Explorer Mylar balloon. This morning, Dan and I found another one. This one was

Superman"

"Same spot?"

"Same exact spot."

"I don't know. I suppose it could happen." Lynnae rubbed her neck. "What did Dan say?"

"Nothing. I just think it's odd, that's all. Yikes, I gotta go. I'm a stickler when it comes to my ribs. Three hours at three hundred degrees or I won't eat them. I'll pick up the pizzas on my way back." "Goodbye." Lynnae waved me off.

I jumped in my car and headed to my house.

I was driving down Rte. 22 when I saw her minivan pull out onto the highway. She was five cars ahead of me. A minute later, she put her left signal on. I almost died. I backed off just enough to allow her to make the turn onto the road leading to mine.

We were both on River Road. As I went down the hill, she must have caught sight of my car. She quickly pulled into my tenant's driveway.

I drove past her. Parked my car in front of my house. Walked inside and saw Dan sitting at his desk. "What'd you do, fly down here?" he asked me.

"Not at all. By the way, what are you doing home?" Silence.

"Huh, if I knew you were home, you could have put the ribs in the oven." I took the spareribs out of the fridge. Turned on the oven and set them inside. Then I walked out the door. Got into my car, picked up the pizzas and went back to work.

If only I had gotten home *five* minutes later… I swear that man must have a guardian angel watching out for him.

When I got back to the bakery, I insisted everyone sit down and have lunch together. I did not want to be alone with Lynnae. I didn't trust myself and I didn't want to have a breakdown right there, in front of everybody. I was living such a double life. It was taking a terrible toll on me.

I'm not stupid. I knew she was going to see Dan. I knew if I asked him about her, he would have said she was probably on her way to visit one of our neighbors. I had to know…I was not imagining any of it.

When I got home, no one was there. I parked my car in front of the house. Instead of going inside, I went down by the river and sat on the bench my father had built as a gift to us. Thankfully, the bench was in the shade, because it was 96 degrees out.

I closed my eyes for a moment, wondering what advice my father would have given me. He not only loved Dan, he held him in high regard. Dan was a hard worker. Something my father understood well. I opened my eyes and looked out at the water. My mother had taught me – always do the right thing. I wished my parents had taught me how to communicate with my husband.

My heart was racing. No matter how calm and serene the water, or how the fish and the ducks tried to ease my mind, a panic attack was taking over. My hands started to shake. My insides began to tremble. My head was about to explode from the pressure. I knew what was about to happen. I slowly slid myself to the ground. A moment later, I blacked out. When I opened my eyes, a frog was sitting in front of me. It was inches away from my face. I was still looking at it when it headed in the other direction.

I sat up and looked up to the heavens. "I promise you both, I will not make the same mistake twice."

Wednesday morning, Dan and I stumbled upon *another* Mylar balloon on our hike. *What do they mean? Do they have a purpose?* Even Dan was suspicious about where they were coming from. He picked it up, said, "Cars," and handed it to me.

We hiked every day. Ate breakfast, cooked and ate dinner together, and we watched movies as if our lives were perfect. *Seven months of driving myself crazy and for what?* Seriously, was I supposed to give up my bakery? My home? My lifestyle, over another woman that I thought... my husband was having an affair with?

"Lord, I could use some help here. A little guidance would be nice."

"Are you talking to me?" Dan asked. "No. Just talking out loud to myself again." I tossed the throw pillows on the bed and moved past him.

"Okay. See you tonight," Dan said as he headed for the front door.

A few minutes later, I drove to work. Before I knew it, it was eleven o'clock. I was standing in the back of the bakery. I could smell fresh bread baking in the ovens. Only for a half a moment, I closed my eyes. Despite the tension rising up inside me, I smiled – there was nothing like the smell of bread baking. I followed the scent all the way into the kitchen.

We were at the worktable when Karly called for Lynnae to go out to the front.

"Oh, my goodness!" I heard Lynnae say. "Are you kidding me? Thank you."

I went out to the front and saw this enormous floral arrangement sitting on the counter in a blue vase. "They're beautiful."

Lynnae was blushing. "I'm in trouble. I'm in big trouble. I let him play with the boys the other night and I..." "Oh, my..." I said.

"Who are they from?" asked Stephanie.

"My neighbor, Barry, and he's a sweetheart."

I'd been waiting a long time to hear her say those words. To find a decent guy. I was so happy for her. Lynnae deserved to have a good man in her life. "I thought you have been acting funny lately."

Lynnae smiled and rolled her eyes.

I pointed my finger at her. "More like a tired wench, you mean..."

Brooke and Stephanie both laughed and then went back to the kitchen.

"Okay, so I haven't been getting much sleep lately. We love watching scary movies together. What can I say?"

"Nothing." I hugged her. "I am so happy for you." In perfect unison we both said, "Tea time!'"

"How did it happen?" I asked.

"Let me check the ovens and grab my cup." Lynnae ran into the kitchen. "Brooke, keep an eye on oven number four. They're almost ready to come out. Julie." She pointed her thumb at the couch.

I sat down with my bottle of water and watched as Lynnae filled her cup with hot water. "This tea bag has been in my cup since nine o'clock this morning."

Lynnae sat down next to me. "Ah... oh, Julie. Where do I begin? July Fourth weekend, I went home and Barry was in one of my trees. Sam had climbed way up the tree and was refusing to come down. Apparently, Max got away from Aimee-Jo long enough to go and knock on Barry's door and ask for help. Barry is amazing with the boys. They have so much fun with him. Wish I could say the same for me."

"What do you mean? You just said he's amazing."

"He is." She rolled her eyes. "Except he won't sleep with me."

"Maybe he took an oath. You know, a virginity pledge."

"Yeah right. No, he says it has to be special. Our night. Just the two of us."

"He's *that* romantic? Wow!"

"Yeah, okay. Thank God for my rabbit sex toy."

"Oh, Lynnae. TMI!"

Her voice was tight and her eyes were shining. "The other night, he asked me if we could take the boys to the drive-in together." She sat up and moved to the edge of the sofa and added, "My heart's in trouble. Right?" "Oh, yeah."

After I left work, I stopped at the grocery store to pick up a loaf of Italian bread. Dan was making mussels marinara for dinner. I was sure my heart was made of brick and mortar. My mind, well, that was another subject. I used to believe that I could do anything, as long as I had my Lord and Savior watching over me.

When we were together, he was the perfect husband.

I went into the house, and Lady rushed over to me. Suddenly, my life didn't seem so bad. I could smell the marinara sauce cooking on the stove. As I went into the kitchen, I began to laugh – Dan was wearing my apron.

"How was your day?" he asked me.

"It was good. Lynnae has a new friend. His name is Barry."

"Oh, yeah? Is he a keeper?"

"I think so. She said the boys love him."

"Hmm, that's good. We got a movie from Netflix today. *Iron Man.* What do you say we go for our hike as soon as we're done eating and then watch it?"

"Fine by me."

After dinner, we cleared the table, rinsed the dishes and put on our hiking shoes. "Hang on, Dan; I want to take my cell phone in case I see momma deer." Actually, I was preparing myself for the next Mylar.

We were heading down the hill when Dan asked me, "Is that another balloon?" That balloon was not where the other Mylars had been. It was at the bottom of the hill. Lying between the rocks. I moved past Dan and picked it up. That one had writing on it: You're #1.

Unlike the others, that balloon was not a cartoon character. I stood there for a moment, to purposely block the spot so he and Lady wouldn't step on it. When Dan went ahead of me, I waited for Lady to follow him. Then I took a picture of the footprints in the sandy soil.

Chapter 12

Seven a.m. and the sky was the color of hot flames.
When I got to work, everyone was there: Lynnae, Brooke,
Stephanie and Karly. I opened the door and the entire bakery was
decorated for Halloween. "It's only the first of the month." "Hi,
Aunt Julie," Sam said, running up to me.

"Hey, Sam, hey, Max." They both hugged me at the same
time.

I held my hands up. "Fee Fi Fo Fum. I smell the blood of a
little boy." They both ran to the back of the bakery.

"Pete's coming in twenty minutes to pick them up. Sam, Max,
get your coloring books and…"

"Mom, we know…"

"Customer," Lynnae said. "Behave, boys."

"Hi, welcome to Bella Napoli Bakery," Karly said to the
women coming in the front door, "What can I get for you today?"

I made my way into the kitchen. "What can I do? Oooh,
something smells delicious."

Lynnae pointed to the bowl. "Pour the snickerdoodle cobbler
into the pans and then you can start on the churro bowls."

"You got it."

Brooke took hold of a tray of something that smelled
wonderful, and I had to ask about that as well.

"Pumpkin gingersnap icebox cake. Carol Higgins ordered it.
She'll be here in a little while to pick it up."

After a long day at the bakery, I was ready to go home, put
my feet up, and drink a cup of tea.

I collected my cell phone, sat down on the front porch and
waited for Dan and Lady. I looked up and saw a red sky. "Sailor's

delight. And hopefully mine as well." A moment later, Dan pulled his truck into the garage.

"Look at that sky," he said and then reached for my hand.

For dinner, we ate leftover vegetable beef soup and French bread *crostini*. Afterwards, we headed outdoors for our evening hike. The day before, we had seen the most amazing buck. He was quite majestic. Standing all by himself along the edge of the corn, as if he belonged there.

When we got back to the house, Dan said he would be home late tomorrow night.

"Call me," I forced myself to say, "when you are on your way home and I'll start dinner."

"Okay, but make sure you eat a snack," he said. "Don't wait until your sugar is out of whack."

Eat something, I want him to say, I love you, I'll never let you go, you're my life, my love, forgive me, I promise... and all he says is eat something?

"I'll be fine," I replied.

That was how we were living, parallel lives, not touching on an emotional level. A stagnant pond. Afraid to break the surface to see what lay below.

Behind his back, I would do little things that I knew would please him. And he would leave me special gifts to find. Just so we didn't have to question our reason for being nice. One day, he left me a bouquet of flowers in a little vase on my vanity. The next, I found twelve bottles of Glucerna in the refrigerator with a loving note.

When I got to work, I didn't see Lynnae's car. I was just about to turn the key when she pulled into the parking lot. Her wet hair was hanging down her back. I went inside, closed the door for a moment, turned the alarm off, and opened the door for her. "Good morning."

She just looked at me. I set my bag down behind the counter. Lynnae was heading for the coffee station. She wrapped her hair up into a tight bun, and started turning on the coffee machines.

"Oh, that man. He has got to stop working so late every night." I went over to help her. "Huh, that's not good."

"Tell me about it. By the time we eat dinner, I'm exhausted." She stretched her back. "I'm so tired."

"Go home. Take the day off."

"No!" She insisted and proceeded to make the coffee.

"Lynnae. I insist. Now go." I pointed toward the door.

"Stop it. I'm not going anywhere. Seriously, two cups of coffee, and I'm good to go." She held her hand on my shoulder. "How's my best friend in the whole world?"

"I'm fine. As good as can be."

Lynnae smiled warmly. "Last night, Barry told me that he cannot imagine his life without me and the boys."

"Oh, Lynnae, you just made my day. I am so happy for you."

"I told him that if he wanted to have a life with me, he'd have to ask you guys for permission first," she laughed. "I mean it."

"You let me know when you want to come over to the house and we'll make dinner for all of you. Let's go in the kitchen and start the muffins. I want to ask you something before the girls get in."

"Okay," Lynnae said as she set two cups of coffee and followed me. She started the recipe for the blueberry muffins and I started the sour cream coffee ones.

"Remember, I told you about the balloons falling in the same location?"

"On your hiking trail? Yeah?"

"Well, three balloons have somehow fallen in the exact same spot and now another one has fallen; in a different spot, but still along our hiking trail."

"Four balloons? Four Mylar balloons?"

"Yes, four. You can ask Dan. He's seen three out of four."

"What are they? Is there any kind of connection?"

"A Dora, a Superman and a Cars. All in the exact, same spot. And now this one. It had writing on it."

"Someone *wrote* a message?"

"No, printed on. It said, *You're number one.*"

Lynnae stopped mixing the ingredients. "Like you're number one? Or Dan is? Who do you think put them there? Never mind. Don't even answer that."

I took out my cell phone and showed her the picture of the footprints.

"There's two sets of footprints in this photo... Oh, my God! It's the footprints of a woman and a child. Shrek has children, right?"

"Yes, and stop calling her Shrek. Twins. You know that, from her Facebook page."

"Julie, think about it. Why would she only take one child with her? Don't look at me like that! Fine. Have it your way. But I'm telling you, Dan is not having an affair with that woman."

"What am I going to do?" I rubbed my face. "I've tried just about everything to catch him..."

"Stop! Wait. I've got it," she said. "Tell Dan that you're going to color your hair."

"What? Why? Dan knows I would never dye my hair. I love my hair."

"I want to prove to you that he is not having an affair with her. If anything, *she's* toying with you."

"And he's letting her?"

"Stop it, she said. Tell Dan that you're gonna...umm? No, wait, I know! Tell Dan you're having hot flashes. Obviously. A thirty-three-year-old isn't having hot flashes."

"Oh, my goodness, I'm so confused. What is that going to prove? And how do you know she's thirty-three?"

"Facebook. Julie, trust me. Just tell Dan that you think you're experiencing hot flashes."

We both heard the bell on the front door. "Okay. I will. But what... oh, I get it. You're a genius."

Every time I looked at Lynnae, she smiled at me and I winked back at her.

The next day, I waited until we were out on our morning hike.

"I think I'm having hot flashes. Last night, I was burning up."
Dan said, "What do you want to do, move to Alaska?"
When I got to work, I told Lynnae that I had done exactly
what she told me to do. Lynnae ran to the office, turned to the
woman's Facebook page.

Nothing. "I told you so!"

I just looked at her and walked away. "Whatever, Lynnae."

I worked Saturday and Sunday mornings at the bakery.
Lynnae was home. It was her weekend with the boys. She said
Barry was building them a tree fort. Complete with stairs.

Monday morning, Lynnae was in the office when I arrived at
work, sitting quietly at the computer, biting her lip. "Sit down."

I walked in and she pulled up a chair next to hers. "Look at
this," Lynnae said as she pointed to the computer screen. The
woman had written on her Facebook page, "I don't know if I'm
having hot flashes or if it's the weather. Maybe, "I" should move
to

Alaska."

At that moment, I knew for her to write my words – exactly,
could only mean she wanted me to know that she was indeed
speaking to my husband. It might be all fun and games to her, but
for me, it was my life.

"How did you know to look at her page?" I asked, with barely
a breath left in me.

"I've been looking at her page every day since you told me."

I had to make a decision. And I had to make it soon. It was
almost Thanksgiving and I was still singing the same old sad
song. *I cannot go on like this for much longer. I have to stop
torturing myself.* Why did I even give that woman a second
thought? From that moment on, I was only worried about myself.

I refused to give up my morning hike. I didn't care if Dan was
with me. I focused on my animals. Momma, the rabbits, and my
Lady running in the open field.

That night, instead of watching the movie with Dan, I sat in
his office and ran the numbers. First, I needed to make sure

Lynnae would accept my offer. Paul had asked to buy my other commercial piece of property numerous times. I hoped the offer still stood. Between Lynnae and Paul, I would have enough money coming in every month to live comfortably... anywhere I want.

As for my four rentals, I'd have to sell them in order to have the funds to make my next purchase. Even after I satisfied the two small mortgages, there would be plenty of money left over. "Hmmm," I said, "I need to start looking at where I want to live."

"Hey, are you done yet?" Dan hollered to me from the living room. "You're missing a good one. It has your favorite actor in it." I wasn't deaf – I knew exactly what he was watching, *Tall Man Riding,* with Randolph Scott. I looked at the clock. It was 8:39. "I'll be there in a minute."

My heart was bleeding. It would not be easy, and I knew it. I had to be strong. In my heart I knew what Dan wanted. I was certain of it. It had to be, right? All I ever wanted was for him to be happy. Nothing else ever mattered to me. Our dream home – the one we built together, was his now. Even the gardens I loved so much. He could have it all.

I put my head down. I would miss our dog. Lady was like our child. I remembered the day we thought she had fallen in the river. We ran up and down, screaming her name. When we went back up to the house, there she was, lying on a pile of hay in the old barn.

Dan said, "There she is, lying in a manger."

If my walking away gives him the life that he truly wants, I have no other choice... but to leave. I swallowed hard in order to remove the lump forming in my throat. When the telephone rang, I picked it up before I realized it was Jesse calling for Dan. "Hello." Trying to sound like myself.

"Hey, what are you doing?" He always said that to me. "I'm working on a few things. What's up with you?"

"Nothing, just calling to see if he still needs me tomorrow. Hey,

I like that Thai restaurant you told Dan about."

"Me?" I thought for a moment. "When did you go?"

"Today. We had lunch there. He didn't tell you? We dropped off his estimate, and Dan said you loved the food there. So we went there today for lunch."

I glanced down at his calendar and noticed he had an appointment in Patterson.

"Julie?"

"Yes, I'm sorry. I'm here, hang on, I'll get Dan."

Dan picked up the phone and I sat in his office in utter despair. I couldn't even tell you what he said to Jesse. I sat there feeling devastated. Remembering that I suggested the Millbrook Café for dinner *two weeks ago*, but Dan had told me that he and Jesse went to the Thai restaurant and that I would like it.

After Dan hung up, I went into the living room and said, "You told me that you took Jesse to the Thai restaurant. Well, he just told me he went there today for the first time. Damn you! Who did you go to the restaurant with?" I shouted, "Who did you take to lunch, Dan? Because it wasn't Jesse!"

Dan was shaking his head. I could hardly hear him. "I called you at the bakery that day. I had to meet with the landowner one last time before he flew to Tahoe. I thought I'd introduce you to him, and take you out to lunch while we were down there. I wanted to tell you about the land-clearing job I acquired, because it was good money. I always celebrate big jobs with you, but you said you were busy and we should talk later. I was starving, so I went there alone."

Dan stood up, coming over to me. "Julie, if I told you that I went there alone, you would have accused me of lying. I didn't want to start an argument." He touched my shoulder. "It was one-thirty, I

was hungry. I was by myself. I'm tired, Julie. I'm going to bed."

Chapter 13

December 24th was a cold and bitter morning. The only place I had left to sell was the bakery.

I had to let it go. My heart was sad, broken. Nothing held my interest, not even my love of baking. In my gut, I knew Dan would be happier without me. But in my heart, I still wanted him. Needed him.

When I woke up, Dan was in the other room. I snuggled in, trying to capture the same sort of delight that I had felt as a child. Christmas Eve was better than Christmas morning for me. What excited me most was all the preparation, cooking, setting the table, putting out the fruit bowl, the nuts, and the alcohol, exactly the way my mother used to do.

I closed my eyes, remembering Christmases past. I used to spend days preparing appetizers in anticipation of our guests. Although my mind remembered, my heart still refused to make the sound of Jingle Bells.

I thought about Dan, sitting in the living room. He was out there waiting for his cup of coffee. I was feeling melancholy. Longing for someone to take away my pain. I needed to be held. I wished for the old Dan. The old me. Before…he would come back to bed with me. I missed so much about him. The way he would tickle my foot with his own. Hold me in his arms. Talk in my ear until I drifted off to asleep.

I could take off my pajamas and change into something sexier. Just one more time. I certainly had enough to choose from; the blue lace halter usually did the job. He would not likely complain or yell for help.

I closed my eyes. Lord, this is not fair. Please help me. Help me to stop dreaming about him. Thinking about him. Why do I need him so?

"Coffee's hot. I sure could use a cup. How about you?"

I stumbled out of bed, heavy-hearted, and poured two cups of coffee. When I sat down next to him, I thought, *how sad it was not seeing a Christmas tree.*

Normally, Dan would have turned the tree lights on before waking me up. He'd seen the child in me come to life…many times. He used to love that. Thirty years of memories. I glanced at the snow outside the windows and thought, *it shouldn't be like this.* And for a moment I wished I had just put up the damn tree.

Then I remembered that he was the one who left the note for me to find. New Year's Eve, Dan insisted on cooking prime rib for dinner. He asked if I was up to entertaining. Normally, we would have had dinner guests. Or an intimate party with a few friends. But each time he asked, I declined.

It was just Dan and me. After dinner, we curled up on the couch and watched *American Gangster.*

"See, this isn't so bad. Who needs a bunch of people? We can have our own party," he said. Then he tossed the blanket over our legs. I thought about the old wives' saying: Whoever you are with on New Year's Eve will be the people you will be with all year long.

January 2nd, I drove up to the house after work and I saw Jesse's truck in the driveway. I pulled the car into the garage, not knowing Dan and Jesse were in there, working on one of the plow trucks.

"Hey, my sunshine is home. Do you want to stay for dinner?" Dan said to Jesse.

Thankfully, he was going out for dinner.

I said hello, took my bag, and started to head over to the house.

Before I got to the door, Dan called to me, "Where do you want to go for your birthday?"

"I don't need to go anywhere. We'll have dinner at home."

I saw Dan look toward Jesse. Then they were both staring at me.

"Why don't you want him to take you out for your birthday?" Jesse asked.

"I don't feel like celebrating, okay?"

Suddenly, Jesse lashed out at me. "Let me tell you something! This man has never cheated on you. I've never heard him talk about another woman. You are the only woman he talks about. He sings your praises every day. You need to stop this bullshit, Julie, I'm telling you!"

I tilted my head, as if to say, *seriously.*

"Julie, I would know. I'm his best friend, for chrissake. Trust me, I would know if he's cheating on you. And he's *not.*"

I went into the house. Ate a bowl of Cheerios and went to bed. By the time Dan came in, I was already asleep.

The next day, I skipped our morning hike and went to the bakery early. I brewed a whole pot of coffee just for Lynnae and me. I was ready to let everything and everybody go. I just want to be alone. Even if it meant for the rest of my life. Sat down and wrote up a contract of sale for the bakery.

Lynnae wasn't in the door two seconds when I said, "Lynnae, I need to talk to you about something. Before everyone else gets here."

"You look like crap. What's up?"

We went to the back of the bakery, and I pointed to the table with the pot of coffee.

"I'm just going to come out with it. I would like to know if you're interested in buying the bakery."

Lynnae's eyes opened wide. Her jaw literally dropped open.

A few seconds passed. Lynnae took a sip of her coffee. When she set her cup down, I thought she was looking into the cup for the answer.

"Lynnae, I can't do this anymore."

"Do what…?" She drank from her cup. "You're *selling* the bakery? No. Oh, Julie, what am I going to do with you?"

"It's not about Dan anymore, it's about me."

"Oh my God! Are you *kidding* me? I thought we were past all this crap. Julie, you are so wrong. Okay, no, I'm not doing it." She tossed the paper onto the floor. "I am not going to let you walk away from everything you love. If you really believe this nonsense that is all in your own little head, then make *him* go."

I picked up the offer and set it back on the table. "I cannot stay in that house, cook in that kitchen with his ghost – every room, every dish, meal." I sighed. "Every morning. Every evening…"

"Julie, I would *love* to own the bakery. But no, absolutely not, even if I had the money. You are *not* going anywhere."

"Lynnae, try to understand. Do this for me, for the bakery." I looked at her with pleading eyes. "I'm trying to save the bakery."

"Julie, if it means saving the bakery – and saving you…" Tears filled my eyes.

"Please don't cry. Whatever you do, don't fucking cry. I would love to buy the bakery." She set her cup down. "But I can't. You know I don't have that kind of money. Between the boys eating me out of house and home, and needing clothes every other month and…"

"Lynnae, you don't need any money. I am not asking for any cash up front. You are a great baker. You have a good head for business. Listen, I ran the numbers. I'll sell you the business and the property, and I'll hold the mortgage on both. It's a piece of cake." I handed the paper to her. "Lynnae that was a joke." "What was?" she asked.

"The cake joke. So? What do you think?"

"First of all, why? Why now?" She took a quick look at my offer. "Second, no. Julie, you could get triple that amount for this property and we both know it."

"Yeah, and then what? Lynnae, you do the books. You know you can do this. It will be a good living for you and the boys, and I can sleep at night knowing…"

"Where are you going?" Lynnae blew her nose on a napkin. "So that's it? You're going? You're leaving?"

"Listen to me. I have to take care of a few things first."

Lynnae stood up, wrapped her hair up, and then sat back down.

"So, what are your plans, really?"

"With the money I have from selling my four rentals, I should have enough money to buy something nice for myself. I'll have a monthly income coming in from both you and Paul."

"You sold your rental properties?"

"Yes, for close to a five million. Don't worry, I won't spend it foolishly. Seriously, I put the money in a money market."

"Julie, you know you could get another million for this property. Why would you sell it to me for so much less?"

"Because, you're all I have. Lynnae, I trust you to love it the way I do."

Lynnae stood up, turning away from me. "I'm worried sick about you."

"Don't worry about me. Between you and Paul, I'll have about five thousand a month, plenty for me to live on. Besides, if I'm living in the woods, I won't have Internet access to Amazon," I joked.

She sat back down. "Oh, so you're planning on living in the woods? What, in a tree fort, I suppose. What about twenty years from now?"

I tried to smile. "I'll be old enough to collect social security."

"Not if they do away with it. Julie, ten years ago, when I drove by your bakery and saw Dan hanging the "Now Hiring" sign I *knew*

I was seeing my future. When you hired me, you were all the teaching I needed. You taught me…" She rubbed her face several times.

She may have been crying. I wouldn't know. I had never seen her cry.

"Why are you doing this to us?" In a quieter voice, she said, "You are my mentor. You are the only woman…person who has ever believed in me. Cared enough about me to teach me to believe in myself. You told me to live my dream. That it was okay to live my life my way. When I got pregnant, you told me to hold my head up high."

I swallowed hard.

She got up and went outside. I never moved.

Ten minutes later, Lynnae walked back into the bakery singing,

"Who Knew."

When she stopped in front of me, I had no idea what she was about to say. She put her hands on her hips, looked to the right, bit her lip and said, "I'll take your offer."

Chapter 14

It was February 5th. A year and four days. My world had changed dramatically. All because of a single piece of paper.

Well, no. Because of many things, over the years. But finding that note opened my eyes. Made me ask myself some tough questions. Like why did I love him more than I loved myself? Why after all those years, did I stay? Why couldn't I leave?

Once Lynnae agreed to buy the bakery, I had nothing holding me back. Lynnae and I left the lawyer's office as different women. Lynnae was so happy she wanted to celebrate. I agreed to go to the Millbrook Café for a quick lunch. I was excited for her. Glad she agreed to buy the bakery. But I was still sad my bakery was gone.

We sat at my favorite table – the one near the grill, away from the bar.

"Julie, I want you to promise me something."

"Anything."

"Promise me you won't leave us. Julie, you and Dan are perfect for each other. I've never known a couple so ideal. He loves you so much."

"Lynnae, I…"

"Listen to me. Dan's human. If he did it, he did it. We all make mistakes. Tell me you're not leaving and that you'll forgive him if he…"

"I know no one is perfect. Relax, I'm not going anywhere right now," I said, motioning to our server for the check.

Her cell phone rang. "Just a few minutes more, Brooke. Okay. Thanks." She set her phone down on the table. "I'm sorry. I have to get back."

"Believe me, I totally understand."

After she left, I sat there wondering, where do I go from here? What am I supposed to do with the rest of my life? Surely, this is not it. I am not ready to settle down. Stop working. Sit idle. I've worked my whole life, I love working.

I waved goodbye to their chef and thanked our hostess and drove home hoping I had done the right thing, selling my bakery.

When I pulled up to the house, Dan was sitting outside. Of course, Lady was right next to him. I parked in front of the house and by the time I opened my door, Lady was there to greet me. "Hello. How's my girl today?" I patted her on the head, fighting tears. "How'd things go?" Dan asked.

"It went well."

"You weren't there very long."

"We only had to sign a few documents."

"You know, when you said you were selling the rentals, I was glad. And when you told me that you were selling your commercial property to Paul and holding the mortgage for him, I understood. It meant you would still have an income coming in but with no expenses. It was a good deal. But selling your bakery?" He stepped down off the porch. Moved past me. He was standing with his back to me and I heard him say. "You've got it all figured out, don't you?"

Before I could say anything, Dan opened the garage door. Two seconds later, he left in his pickup truck.

It was sad. So sorrowful how our lives had turned out. We were both just cardboard cutouts. Living in the same house. One day, we were fine and the next, were throwing daggers at each other.

The next day, before Dan left for work, he asked me, "How long are you going to keep this up?"

"What? Keep what up, Dan?"

"Julie, I love you. But I don't know who you are anymore. What are you doing? What are you trying to prove? You know I never stopped you when you wanted to invest in your own real estate transactions. I supported you when you said you wanted to run your

own business. I never said no, don't do it. Did I?" I shook my head.

"I stood by you in every way I could. There isn't anything I wouldn't do for you – give you. But if you think I'm going to stand back and watch you throw everything away..."

"I'm not..."

Dan started crying, and I lost it. I reached for him, but he turned his back and walked away. I wanted to die.

What if he's right? Maybe I was destroying everything, and us. I didn't know anymore. I had no clue what to think. I spent a good part of my day cleaning the house. Wandering from room to room. Trying to get my mind off her. I should have asked him about her, and her stupid Facebook comments. About the phone calls. But I didn't. Wrapped up in trying to catch him, I lost sight of everything.

Dan was right. I had turned into a crazy person. Hiding tape recorders under my bed, in his office, trucks, anywhere I thought he would talk to her. So I could know without a doubt that my suspicions were correct.

I sat on my chaise lounge, trying to figure out where my life was going. Then I began searching online for investment properties. When I stumbled upon an old farmhouse for sale not too far from where I lived, I thought about calling the real estate agent, but decided against it.

This went on for several weeks. My cleaning every room, searching online for... what? I didn't know.

I was bored out of my mind. I could not sit still. I needed to work. But something mindless, something without pressure, where I could do a good job. I read many want ads, online, in the local papers. Nothing appealed to me. What did I like to do? Clean.

Organize. That's what kept me sane. Finally, on a whim I ran an ad. *Meticulous housekeeper seeks employment.*

Two days later, a headhunter from Long Island sent me an email. By the end of the month, I had two cleaning jobs. I went from sitting idle all day to working six days a week. It *was* mindless, cleaning other people's houses. It was just what I needed.

Three days a week, I worked for a family close to home. He was so neurotic, his wife had to shoot whisky on a daily basis, but I didn't care. Their five-year-old daughter stole my heart. On Wednesdays, I worked for a teacher in Rhinebeck. He was so nice I didn't mind traveling. I actually enjoyed the hour ride to and from his house.

I was just about to get in my car to go home when my cell phone rang. Lynnae.

"Hey, Cinderella," she said, "how come you haven't come by? How's it going?"

"I'm great. Is everything okay?"

"Yeah, everything and everyone. I haven't heard from you in a few days; I needed to hear your voice, and share something with you. I got a call from Sam's teacher. Apparently, he's been saying 'shut the front door' a lot at school," she laughed and added, "No, he didn't get it from me. There's this girl he's been playing with on the playground and it's her favorite thing to say."

My eyes welled up, hearing her voice. "Are you sure she's not yours?"

"Ha, ha. I miss you. Where are you?"

"I miss you too. I'm on my way home from one of my cleaning jobs. Can I call you in a little while?"

"Sure," Lynnae said, sounding disappointed.

I stopped at the store, then headed home. When I arrived, Dan wasn't there, but Lady was. She was lying in the old barn – her favorite spot, sound asleep. Apparently, she didn't hear my car pull in.

I went over to where she was. Sat down on a bale of hay just as she opened her eyes. I looked back over my shoulder and glanced at the new garage. "Out with the old and in with the new."

Thursday morning, I stopped by my favorite bakery, Lynnae's Hot Buns, to see how the girls were doing. It was hard, but I had to do it. I missed Lynnae so much. When I saw the new sign, I thought it was perfect. Under the name, she had a photo of a hot cross bun. The colors on the new OPEN flag I bought her matched the sign – brown, tan, ivory and burgundy letters.

When I went inside, Lynnae ran to greet me. "I miss you so much! Everyone is asking for you."

Stephanie, Brooke, and Karly were all wearing denim skirts, white T-shirts, cowgirl boots and red bandana's tied in their hair.

Lynnae pointed over to Karly. "She makes the best cake pops in the world. It was her idea to give them away today."

"You look fabulous! I love the sign. It came out perfectly."

"You better. The name was your idea. That's what I tell everyone."

"You can tell them whatever you want. It's your bakery. I love the tan checkered tablecloths! Nice touch! How are the boys doing?"

"They're wonderful. They keep asking when they are going to see you. Come sit with me for a minute."

I saw she was busy. "Hey, how about I make lunch for you and the boys on Sunday? I'm sure Dan will be over on the property. We can catch up." For a moment, I did not wish to leave. I wanted to sit in the back. I just wanted to have one more cup of tea with my dear friend. When I felt the lump in my throat, I knew I had to get out of there.

Lynnae looked sad. "Sure. I'll be there. About noon okay?"

"Perfect."

Three days later, on a gorgeous snowy Sunday afternoon, I made a pot of chicken and dumplings for Lynnae, Sam and Max. I was sitting in the living room next to a roaring fire, with the book I picked up at a library event, *Take Time for Your Life,* by Cheryl

Richardson, in one hand and a cup of red raspberry tea in the other.

At quarter after one, I went over to the door. Just when I was thinking they weren't coming, I saw Lynnae's Jeep pull into the driveway. When I saw only Lynnae getting out, I hollered to her, "Hey, where are my boys?"

She rushed up to me and hugged me. She was still hugging me when she said, "The boys are with Barry, they're going tobogganing. I wanted to spend this time with you alone." Then she squeezed me even harder. "I want you all to myself."

"Would you like a cup of tea?"

"Actually, I could go for something cold. How about a beer?" Lynnae sat down on the sofa and I returned with two Coronas. When I handed Lynnae hers, she laughed, "Is that a pickle in your beer?"

I raised my eyebrows, nodded, and asked her if she wanted one.

"Sure, I'll try anything once."

When I opened the fridge door, I heard her holler to me, "I wanna read this." When I turned to face her, she was waving my book in the air.

I handed the Corona to her and she tasted it.

"This *is* good."

"Dan says 'the pickle is your reward,' but I think it just makes you want to drink more."

"Well, it's different, that's for sure." She took a few more sips of her beer. "Ahh, peace and quiet." She was staring out at the river.

"I love being near the water," I said, feeling good for the moment.

"It is breathtaking, that's for sure. You're so lucky to have this view."

"It looks crisp," I said.

"Crisp? It's pretty cold out," Lynnae said jokingly. "And from where I'm sitting, the air looks mighty cold especially coming off that water. Hey, you look better." She patted my knee. "How's Dan been? What's going on lately? I'm hoping, with you being away from the frenzy of the bakery, the two of you have worked everything out by now."

I didn't say a word. I just stared at the black water snaking along the large rocks, around the bend, mostly unseen under the ice.

Lynnae reached into her bag. "Julie, before you say no, just listen to me. I found a really good therapist." I pursed my lips.

"Stop. I know you told me you can walk this journey of yours alone, but I think you should talk to someone."

"I have you."

"Will you at least consider it?"

"I *will* consider it. Lynnae, you need to understand something; it wasn't the thought of Dan having an affair with her that made me realize I needed to make changes in my life. It was what I saw with my own eyes that made my heart stop."

My hands were limp in my lap. My heart was heavy. I took a long deep breath. I glanced into the fire. "I was standing in front of the mirror, putting on my lipstick, and for the first time in my life, I disliked the woman in front of me. I just stood there staring at her. Wondering how I allowed this happen. Why the hell I didn't draw the line when he…"

Lynnae started to say something. I held up one finger. "I worried about you, and your boys. Seriously, how can I tell you to be a strong woman and live life to the fullest, when I was holding myself back? How many times can I pull myself out of the foxhole? I wasn't living my own best life. Not by any means. I was allowing myself to question everything Dan did. I had to start somewhere. I have to start over."

"That's why I want you to call the therapist. Julie, please do it for me. She's local. You won't even have to drive far."

I finished my beer and looked out toward the river. I thought about her request for a moment. Thought about my life. Writing about his affairs opened my eyes, and it made me confront some tough questions about my marriage and about myself. I realized for so long I was waiting for someone to show up and save me, but in the end, I needed to find the courage to save myself.

"I promise you, I will call her. Now tell me about your man."

"He's wonderful. He surprised me with a trip to the Hero Inn in Vermont. Just the two of us. We spent the entire weekend in our room. It was so romantic. We were on Lake Champlain, drinking wine, laughing and oh, Julie, Barry was so worth the wait. He took his time..." She seemed unable to finish the sentence.

"Nobody deserves it more than you."

"Julie, my wish has come true. Since Barry has been spending so much time with Sam, his reading is getting so much better. He's good therapy for all of us."

"I'm so happy to hear that. And Max, how is he doing?"

"Barry reads to them every night and when he's done, Max *reads* to Barry."

"Max is reading? That's so cute."

"Barry's something else. He found out that if we use a sans serif font, in bold, and double-spaced, Sam doesn't have as much trouble identifying his letters."

"That is such great news."

"I know, right? Wait until Sam reads to you." She sat back, rested her head on the sofa and sighed.

I looked at her. "What's the matter?"

"Julie, where's Dan?"

"Over on the property. He's plowing our walking path with the tractor."

"Plowing a path around one hundred acres?" A wry smile crossed my face.

"Julie. In the summer he mows, because he's afraid you'll get another tick bite. Now you're telling me he's plowing a path for you. Please go and talk to the therapist. I'm begging you." She sat up straighter. "I want you to tell me what *you've* been up to. Right now, tell me."

"I am slowly putting my life back together and making plans for *my* future."

"Here, right?" Lynnae asked, drinking the rest of her beer.

I got up and grabbed two more bottles. When I handed Lynnae hers, she said, "To the future."

I tapped my bottle to hers. "To the future."

After Lynnae left, I was microwaving a cup of tea and then I remembered – I had forgotten about the recorder plugged into Dan's office line. When I looked at, it was flashing red. I played the calls.

She called him again. This time I heard her voice. "Call me." My blood surged. I heard the microwave beep several times. I unplugged the recorder and brought it downstairs.

I drank my tea and made a list of what we needed at the grocery store. It seemed we were out of everything. I had been working six, sometimes seven days a week. Dan and I hadn't gone grocery shopping in months. I needed to stock up my pantry.

At the grocery store, my cart was overflowing. I almost hit the floor when I saw the total amount. "Four-hundred and seventy dollars?"

The cashier twisted her mouth to the right and said, "Yep."

I set the last bag in the car, closed the hatch and saw her pull into the parking lot. She sat in her minivan, staring at me. I approached her vehicle. She was quick to hit the door lock. I tapped on the glass. "Someone needs to teach you some manners. Call my husband again and I will beat you so bad, your mother won't recognize your fucking ass!"

She looked at me and said in this squeaky high-pitched voice,

"I don't know who yur' tawking 'bout." I wanted to vomit… all over her.

By the time I reached my car, my hands were shaking and my heart was pounding. I was proud of myself. Not happy with my language choice, but glad I'd said it. I knew she got my message, because she never got out of her minivan. She was still sitting in it when I left the parking lot.

During dinner, Dan was extremely quiet, and I wondered if she had told him what I had done. I decided to break the silence by asking him about his plans for next weekend.

"Dan, what are you…"

He became extremely angry. When he stood up, his chair fell over backwards. Dan flipped his plate over, food went flying and his glass fell over! With blue fire in his eyes, he said, "The last person

I fucked was…" He said her name.

That was barbaric.

I remembered it only too well. I had all I could do not to scream.

"Julie, that was *ten* years ago."

The arrow had hit its mark. For thirty years, I had only asked for the truth. After all those years, he had given me exactly what I had been asking for: proof.

Only someone you loved with the purest of intentions could hurt you that deeply. It might have been ten years ago; it felt like yesterday. *Twisting the knife… still hurt.*

"Julie, I'm tired of this."

I didn't move. Dan got up from the table and turned the TV off. We sat in silence for what seemed like forever before I heard him say, "I am *not* cheating on you."

In spite of his confession, as crazy as it was, a part of me still wanted to curl up in his arms. I hated, truly hated needing him. I also hated myself for wanting healing from a man who inflicted so much pain; but Dan was the only person who could make me feel better. *That's what happens when a woman worships the ground her man walks on.*

"Julie, I love you," he said, but his words rang hollow. "You're making both of us crazy. I am not having an affair. Or anything else.

I swear to you."

I moved to the living room, sat down and stared at him. I'd never seen a broken man in my life, but I do believe I was looking at one that evening.

"You swore to God... ten years ago."

"Julie... please?"

The next morning Dan left me a note on the coffee table saying he was sorry, that he would bring home dinner – my favorite. Swordfish.

I got up from the couch feeling empty. Nothing to keep me there. I wasn't about to wait ten years to learn the truth about number eight.

I went into my closet, secured all I needed and stuffed it into a carry-on. Called Enterprise, asked for an SUV and instructed them to pick me up in front of the local deli in one hour. I knew what Lynnae would say about everything, but I didn't care. *It's one mistake, you have to forgive him.* Well, I *did* forgive him. I had to let go of him. It was time I gave my husband his freedom.

I sat down and wrote my letter:

Dear Dan,

You are my one and only true love. You were my life. You were my every dream, desire and prayer. I'll miss our morning and evening hikes together. Cooking, laughing, and creating so many memories. I'll be missing you every day, evening and especially at night. I could only pretend for just so long. Now, I know the truth –

I am not crazy. You're free now. Free to be with whoever you want. From this day forward, you are in God's tender, loving and forgiving hands.

With all my heart... I will always love you. Julie.

Then I prayed for myself. I asked God to place a shield in front of my heart. To place a hedge of protection all around me.

PART TWO

Life is not measured by the number of breaths we take, but by the moments that take our breath away.

Maya Angelou

Chapter 15

B ecause of my separation anxiety, it took me three agonizing
days to drive from New York to Rhode Island. I felt horrible
the entire way. I drove on back roads, knowing that I would have
to make numerous stops. I was glad I rented an SUV. The first
thing I had done was to put the second and third row seats down.
I just wished I had thought to bring a blanket. Every time I got
sick, my body shivered uncontrollably. Several times, I had no
time or place safe enough to pull over to the side of the road. I
vomited into a bag, right there in the car.

At the first motel I stopped at, I vomited in their lobby, all
over their tan and brown carpet. I was so sick, I couldn't fall
sleep. I sat on the floor in the bathroom the entire night.

I tried to think about anything other than Dan. I thought about
the three houses I had seen online. Unlike the home in Georgia or
the one in Maine, the house I was going to see had a lot of
acreage. Two-hundred and thirty acres of vacant land. I had mixed
feelings. I wanted to start a new life, one with no worries. But, I
also wanted my husband by my side. We had done everything
together since I was a teenager. I couldn't believe how much I
missed him.

I thanked the Lord for not allowing hatred to enter my heart.
"Thank You for Jesse. Please, Lord, I pray You were with Jesse
when he went to see Dan."

That was my prayer because on my way to the corner deli, I
had stopped by Jesse's house – I wanted him to find his letter
before Dan found his. I knew Dan would immediately call the
cops and I could not let that happen. I was going to leave Jesse's
letter in his mailbox.

When I saw his truck was still in the driveway, I set his letter on his seat.

Dear Jesse,

Thank you for being a true friend to both Dan and me. Jesse, I need you to be strong. Not for me, but for Dan. I have decided to leave Dan. In my heart, I know Dan is not happy with me. I know he sees other women.

I'm not asking you to take sides. I know you are Dan's best friend. Please, Jesse, I'm begging you to make sure Dan does not call the police. I'm going to be just fine.

Jesse, please take care of Dan and Lady. And take care of yourself.

Love you, big guy! Julie.

Lynnae's letter was not as easy to write. It took me many tries before I could sign hers. At five a.m. I got up, showered and left the motel. In addition to a generous tip for housekeeping, I left a note apologizing for the odor left behind.

Two hours and twelve minutes later, I crossed into Rhode Island. The moment I saw the sign, I started to cry. I was elated and nervous at the same time. It was a huge milestone for me. An awakening. Entering Rhode Island was step one for me. I didn't have to stop the vehicle, I was able to continue driving. When I reached Shelter Harbor, I stopped at a little store for a box of saltines and some ginger ale. An hour later, I stopped at the first *Vacancy* sign I saw. A small bed and breakfast. When I entered the front room and read the check-in sign – 3 p.m. – my heart sank. I hit the bell on the desk anyway.

"Morning, can I help you?" a man asked me as he set a stack of newspapers and magazines down on the corner table.

"Good morning. Your sign says you have a vacancy. By any chance do you have a room ready?"

"I have two rooms available. Would you like a view of the ocean or of the neighborhood?"

"The ocean. Please. Can I check in early and pay cash? I'm exhausted."

"Not a problem." He held a pen out to me and I signed the registration form using my maiden name.

"Thank you so much."

He handed me a key. "Do you need help carrying your luggage?"

I thought for a moment. *Luggage?* "No thanks. I can handle it." He pointed to the staircase. "First room on the right."

My room was perfect. King sized bed, lamp, wingback chair, desk and chair. I dropped my overnight bag on the floor and for the first time in three days, I fell asleep.

Before I could open my eyes, I felt a warm breeze. I could smell the scent of salt water coming in from the window next to my bed. I opened my eyes, looked around the room and thought, *this does not look anything like my bedroom.* But the moment I looked out the window, I remembered exactly where I was. Point Judith, Rhode Island.

I showered, went down the stairs, and headed out into the sunlight. I was not dreaming. I was on Sand Hill Cove, and around the corner, waiting for me was my new favorite fish market and restaurant.

One thing I knew for sure, I was starving, and definitely no longer tired. "I made it!" My stomach growled. I practically ran down the street.

The diner was full to capacity; nearly every seat taken by what appeared to be local people on their way to work. It looked like most people ordered the house special – pancakes, bacon, eggs, and home fries. Not me. I was eating healthy from that moment on.

As I looked around the room, I noticed one empty booth and a few empty stools at the counter. Not wanting to engage in much conversation, I quickly made my way to the empty booth. The server must have spotted me, because she was hot on my heels with a pot of coffee.

"Good morning. My name is Kelly. Coffee?"

"Yes, please. I'm ready to order as well. Can I have wholegrain toast, spread with peanut butter, and a piece of whatever fresh fruit is in season?"

"We have berries."

"Perfect."

"Okay, I'll be right back with your order."

After I left New York, I stopped at a Verizon store and purchased a new cell phone and a tablet. I had to have access to the Internet. Waiting for my food, I closed my eyes, wondering, hoping I had done the right thing. Praying I would not be tempted to log on to the security system website. When I opened my eyes, in the next booth, a little girl was smiling and waving to me. I blew out a breath, gave her a wink and smiled back at her. I noticed the décor on the walls. Nautical. My new favorite.

I could always spot the tourists in the room; they were the ones wearing the new T-shirts and sweatshirts with the name of their most recent vacation. Block Island seemed to be the clear winner.

It was only my first day in Point Judith; for me, it felt like a completely new world. I was convinced the small town was going to be the perfect little hideaway. There was something special about living next to the water.

Sadness took over. I looked away from the décor and tugged on the hem on my dress.

Every meal we ate, we had a view of the Ten Mile River.

Breathe…I looked up. I'll never make it, if I keep thinking like this.

Before I knew it, Kelly came back with my breakfast. "Here you go. If I can get you anything else, just let me know."

"Thank you, Kelly."

Kelly was adorable. Short brown hair, big blue eyes and a smile that didn't stop. I enjoyed my breakfast and thought the morning seemed to be a day made in heaven. The sun was shining and there was not a cloud in the sky. The temperature was supposed to get up to seventy degrees. Perfect for walking the property. The real estate agent said she would meet me there. When I spoke to her yesterday, she said she had several homes besides that one for me to look at.

"More coffee?" Kelly asked with her big smile, as she picked up my empty plate.

"No thank you. Just my check, please. I'm in a bit of a hurry. I'm meeting a real estate agent this morning to look at some property on Mallard Way."

There was a slight pause. "Do you mean the property that belongs to Mr. Adams? I *know* that property." She hesitated for a moment. "Did you know, after his wife became ill, they stopped selling their vegetables? As soon as she died, he sold everything, even the furniture." Kelly shook her head. "They were nice people. Are you going to have a farm on the property?"

I raised my eyebrows, and shrugged. "I haven't even seen the property yet. I guess I'll just have to wait and see."

"Well, I'd better get ya your check. I don't wanna make you late."

I paid for my meal, leaving Kelly a generous tip and leaving myself plenty of time. I knew the property was twenty to thirty minutes north, outside of town. As I stepped out of the diner, I was reminded of the beauty a small town had to offer. I took a deep breath, exhaled slowly and said, "I'm here. I'm really here. I can't believe it." I walked away. Or should I say ran away, from everything I loved. I felt terribly sad about leaving Lady. She was my baby but she was her father's dog. And even though Dan loved me, I knew this was best for both of us.

When the lump appeared in my throat, I sensed it would only get worse from there on in. I looked up toward the sky. "Stay with me, Lord. Don't leave me now. You are all I have. Walk with me.

Talk to me, Lord. Please help me get through this day. Amen."

I had parked my rental car in a different parking lot at the end of the block, near some large rocks, far enough away from the bed and breakfast and the diner so no one would see me – paranoid, I suppose.

I didn't care; I had to be cautious about everything, especially my heart. Before I reached the car, I turned around to make sure no one was behind me. Point Judith was a small town, but not that far away that I couldn't run into someone vacationing from back home.

I sat in the car for a moment, watching two boats. One was leaving the harbor, and the other one was just pulling in. The sound of their horns could not have come at a better moment, or sounded sweeter to me.

Before I backed out of the parking lot, away from the rocks, I glanced into the rearview mirror. "This is it," I said. In my heart, I knew there was no turning back. I looked in the mirror again. "No more panic attacks, no alcohol, no pills, no overeating, no unhealthy eating at all. And no nervous breakdowns." I closed my eyes, "This is for you, Dan. This… is how much I love you." Opened my eyes and smiled. "This is for me, too."

I left his note on his nightstand, next to his chocolates. I wished I had written:

I am genuinely sorry that I could not make you happy.

I began to pull away from the only thing separating me from the ocean floor. I had to, or my entire body would have started shaking, and I would have lost control. "Like I used to. Right Lord? Lord, I am going to be happy, too. Right?"

I shook my head and turned my attention back to the reason for my being in Rhode Island. I was driving toward my future, knowing that I was finally conquering all my fears. I was not in a hurry; I was eager to start healing.

When I called the real estate agent, Geri, to get the details, she said the five-thousand square foot house might need a little cosmetic work; however, the floors and walls all seemed to be in good condition. I asked Geri about the well, septic and foundation. She assured me both the building inspector and the engineer had given it all their stamp of approval.

The last few months, I had spent more time reading articles about where to live than I did reading romance novels. When I'd researched Rhode Island, every article had read the same: "Point Judith best known for its beautiful beaches, quiet days by the ocean, and its many small fishing boats. People arrive from all over to fish for cod, flounder, sea bass and bluefish. From May to October, visitors are able to get on quaint charter boats, usually carrying four to six people, and fish the entire day."

I had read: "People taking rides on party boats, known as a head boat, with fifty or more people hoping to snag the day's big catch.

You'll find the captain eager to share in the history surrounding the many anglers before you. Always something to do in Rhode Island!"

It had all sounded so good to me; I had photocopied the entire article, hoping to use it to entice my guests to stay at my future inn. There I was, driving toward my dream.

On my way to the house, I passed through beautiful countryside. I had always had a passion for the outdoors and for fishing; thanks to… I couldn't even say or think his name. Two seconds later, a lump formed in my throat, I had to pull over to the side of the road. The lump was no longer in my throat. After ten minutes of vomiting, I forced myself back into the car, remembering the rest of the article. I closed my eyes for a second, imaging myself taking the ferry from Point Judith to Block Island. When I felt calm enough to drive, I put the car in motion.

I turned off the radio and looked at the clock. I was making good time, in spite of my pit stop. When Geri said the house was twenty or so minutes outside of town, at first I didn't think twenty minutes was far enough away. But just a few minutes into my drive, and I began to appreciate the wide-open parcels of land, along with the occasional home. Surprisingly, even being sick, the drive gave me a peaceful feeling and the exact amount of privacy

I was looking for. I hoped some of Rhode Island's tourists would feel the same way, and want to stay at my new inn. "Lord, I can do this, right?"

On the right side of the road up ahead, I saw the private road sign for Mallard Way. Once again, I needed to stop the car and pull over to the side. Thankfully, my stomach was empty. I tossed a mint into my mouth and drove down the driveway.

Geri had described it perfectly. The driveway was about two miles long. The fields on both sides of the road were overgrown. But that was okay, I knew how to take care of that. And as soon as I went around the bend in the road, the house appeared before my eyes. The house was a typical Victorian. It had three stories and a tower. It was even more spectacular than the computer photos.

A woman, neatly dressed, was standing on the front porch holding a clipboard. I recognized her from her photo. Petite frame, white hair, crystal blue eyes. As soon as I parked my car, Geri stepped down off the porch and walked over toward me. "Well, hello, I'm Geri, you must be… Julie?" She tilted her head.

From that day forward, I was on a first name basis with everyone. I extended my hand out to her. "Yes, I'm Julie. You were right about the drive up here. It *is* worth the trip; and just as you described, the house *does* appear before your eyes, once you're around the bend."

"Oh, good. I'm glad you like it. Shall we take a look inside?" Geri said to me as she stepped up onto the porch and opened the front door.

"Please, then can we take a walk around the property?" If Geri only knew how important the land was to me. My gardens were everything, and 230 acres was a lot of garden space. I read that if you focused your attention long and hard enough on one thing, eventually your heart and your mind would be in line with one another. My mind and my heart needed to be awakened by something other than Dan. I coughed so loud Geri spun around and I almost bumped into her. "I'm sorry," I said.

"Are you okay?" she asked.

"Yeah, I just have a lump in my throat." My throat was sore from the past few days.

"Are you sure? Can I get you a glass of water?" "I'll be fine."

She nodded. "As you can see, the house has been totally remodeled inside, with an open floor plan, allowing every room to flow nicely into the next. I think you'll appreciate it once you see the entire house."

"I can't wait. Geri, why is the house listed as a farmhouse? Clearly, from the outside, it's a Victorian."

"Deed restrictions. The original house was a farmhouse. The home was originally built in the early 1900s. Mrs. Adams loved Victorian homes. In 1981, Mr. Adams had the tower, the porches and the third floor built for her. Rumor has it she wanted numerous children. I guess they intended on turning the third floor into bedrooms."

"I see." Once again, I coughed. More like barked.

Geri stepped to my side. "There's a drugstore in town. Perhaps, you should stop in and get something for that cough."

"I will. Thank you." I followed her from one room to the next and with every turn, my heart beat faster and my stomach surged and plummeted.

"There are two formal rooms, one on each side of the spacious foyer; a very nice, open staircase leading to the second floor bedrooms. Come, I can't wait for you to see the large country kitchen."

She led me to the back of the house.

"There is also a small laundry room, and one full bathroom on the main floor," Geri continued. "Upstairs, there are five lovely bedrooms and two full bathrooms."

"Sounds great. When did the engineer see the house?" I asked.

"The same week I listed the property. I'll give you a copy of his report if you're interested."

I practically ran through the house. Mostly because I was feeling nauseous. I needed to get outside. Geri tried to keep up, but as we came down from the attic, she sounded as if she was out of breath. At the bottom of the stairs, she took a deep breath. "Okay, the basement is right this way." She pointed toward the door.

After seeing the entire house, I knew someone had loved it. The home was immaculate. "Can we walk around the land?"

"The fields have become overgrown during the past few years, and the brush has literally taken over what used to be beautiful farmland. I'd be more than happy to drive you around the property.

There's a utility vehicle in the tool shed."

"Umm, I wanted to walk the property."

"I'll take you around the entire parcel. I'll stop whenever you ask. I'm not that fond of ticks myself, let alone snakes."

I followed Geri out to the larger shed. "Geri, is there any water on the property?"

"Yes, actually there's a small pond and a stream that runs through the property at the lower end." Geri opened a folder attached to her clipboard. "Here, you can have this." She handed me a map of the property.

She opened the door to the shed, drove the Kubota out and said,

"I wish he would have sold that old truck. It's such an eyesore. Shall we go?"

We rode around but I wanted to see more. I needed to take my time. I wanted to see every sunny spot and shady location. I didn't want to be rude or pushy, so it would have to wait another time.

"Would you like to see anything else?"

"No thank you. Can you send over the engineer's report to my room at the bed and breakfast on Bleaker Street?"

"Of course. I know the owner, Sal. I was the listing agent for the sale a few years back. Owning a bed and breakfast was part of Sal's bucket list."

"Part?" I said out loud but did not mean to.

"Yes," Geri replied as she closed the shed door. "And living near the water so he could fish every day. I like Sal, he's a nice man.

We go to the same church." She paused. "I'll have the report to you this afternoon. So what do you think?"

"I think I'll need some time, and I'll have to see the entire parcel, before I make any decisions."

"Julie, I don't mean to be so blunt. However… are you a developer?" she finished with a glance.

"No," I said quickly. "Absolutely not."

"Although farmers' markets are on the rise, farming is not. I'd hate to see…"

I didn't want to share my idea with her, but I understood why she needed to know. I too had a love for the land. "Geri, I'm thinking about opening my own inn."

She sucked in a breath. "Wonderful!" she exclaimed and touched my arm.

We said our goodbyes and both got into our cars. On the drive back to town, I could not get the stream out of my head; I had to go back. I didn't care about ticks. I already had Lyme disease and snakes didn't scare me. I turned the car around and headed back to the farmhouse. "Lyme disease, haven't thought about that in a while."

When I drove around the bend, the view astounded me all over again. I could feel myself getting excited about what lay ahead.

I got out of the car and went to the back of the house. "This is where the outdoor dining patio will be. And over there, lots of flowers."

I hiked down toward the woods. Over the past thirty years, I had learned how to navigate the woods extremely well. Turkey hunting had its advantages.

The property was a rectangle – deeper than it was wide. As I hiked farther, I *could* hear the sound of running water. Geri was right. There was an old streambed. It ran down from the nearby hills. I hiked, hoping it ran a long distance. It actually got wide enough in many places to create some beautiful water gardens. The pond *was* small but expandable.

When I got back to the house, I wished I had brought some paper and a pen; I had so many ideas. For the first time in a long time, I had something to look forward to.

I got in my car, turned the ignition and the radio came on. "Seriously?" I sat there listening to Al Green singing, "Let's Stay Together." The last time I heard that song, Dan said, "It's still our song…"

I could not listen to the end. I opened the car door and spewed all over the door, my leg and the ground. It was a good hour before I had the strength to drive away.

Chapter 16

When I got back to town, I stopped at the local drugstore to purchase some drawing paper, scissors, glue, a box of pencils, six bottles of ginger ale, and four boxes of saltine crackers. At the bed and breakfast, I asked if a package had arrived for me. It hadn't.

In my room, I had mixed feelings, from feeling excited to an overwhelming amount of fear building up inside me.

I had so many ideas running wild. I started writing them down. On a separate piece of paper, I began to draw. By the time I was done, I had consumed an entire box of crackers and one bottle of ginger ale.

The engineer's report arrived at noon, as promised. "Wow," I said, seeing the expanded septic system and the three artesian wells.

With all the new ideas in my head, I went back to the diner and sat at the same booth, hoping that Kelly, the chatty server, would be there. I liked her very much. She seemed to talk to everyone with the same amount of enthusiasm and compassion. She had mentioned the property owners, so I wanted to hear more about that.

"Would you like to see a lunch menu or dinner menu?"

"Hi, Kelly. May I have turkey and cheese on whole grain bread with mustard?" I smiled. "Oh, and a glass of iced tea, please."

Kelly smiled back at me. "Sure you can. I thought I recognized you when you came in. So how did your appointment go?"

"Very nice. The property is exactly what I am looking for."

"Did you buy it? Are you going to live there?" Kelly asked.

"I'm thinking about it. Kelly, do you know any local contractors? Someone who knows a little history about this area?"

"Sure, but why does he or she have to know history to fix a house?"

"I would like to use material native to Rhode Island, if I decide to buy it, that is."

"I know exactly who you should call: Frank Freeman. I'll go and put your order in and get you his number."

Kelly came back to the table with my lunch in one hand and a list of local contractors in the other hand. She had plumbers, painters – even a person to mow the grass – on her list.

"Thank you so much. I knew you were the right person to ask." I decided to leave a little something extra for Kelly. I didn't see her when I left. Perhaps she was on break, or in the kitchen. Not a big deal. I could thank her when I saw her the next time.

First, I moved the lamp closer to the desk, then I turned on the two lamps on both sides of the bed. I started cutting, pasting, and followed my drawing to the letter. I wanted to have every detail complete before I spoke to any of the contractors. The main building would be in the shape of a square "U." The inn would have twentyfive guest rooms, all suites, and every room would have a view of the gardens.

The two new side wings would be two stories high, the same as the original house, and each side wing would consist of five guest rooms on each level. I'll use the space in the attic for staff living quarters. I needed a meeting room, and at least five bedroom suites.

As for the original part of the house, there was not too much that needed to be done there. One of the living rooms would remain as the library and sitting room; the other living room was large enough for billiards, along with a few smaller tables for chess, checkers, or a game of cards. The laundry room was small, but large enough to take out the old washer and dryer and add two sets of stackable industrial washer and dryers. The kitchen was plenty big enough for any chef. Maybe, if the budget allowed, I thought about buying all new appliances, and a walk-in cooler.

That left the two dining rooms; they were perfect just the way they were. Besides, I'd have dining on the porch. And an outdoor eating area on the new patio. Just thinking about it, I got butterflies.

After careful planning, I felt ready. All I had to do was call Geri, sign the papers, and contact my contractors. At two a.m., I turned out the lamp, and by the light of the stars, I fell asleep. When I wokeup, I emailed Geri the details and said a prayer. I thanked God for blessing me for the past thirty years, for Dan and for the life that we shared. "Lord, I need you more than ever."

At the realtor's office, I was somehow calm, confident, and eager to begin my new adventure. At least I looked like I was.

"No financing and no contingencies. I'll be paying cash for the house. I would like to close as soon as possible, if that is okay with Mr. Adams?"

"He would love that. I'll have the papers drawn up, and ready for both of you to sign by next Tuesday."

"Thank you, Geri. Would you like earnest money today or should I give you a certified check when I sign the paperwork?"

"When you sign will be fine. Thank you and congratulations!"

"One more thing. I'd like to buy the F100, if it's still available."

"That old rust bucket?"

"Yes, and I'll give him his asking price."

As I walked out of her office, I smiled, knowing how many flowers I could put in the bed of the truck.

By selling the four houses, I had enough money available to finance my entire project; and by holding the mortgage for both Paul and Lynnae, I had a guaranteed monthly income coming in for the next twenty years. All I had to do was stay within my budget. Which meant no ordering online. *Ahh, I'll be fine.*

Ten days after the closing, I stopped at the hardware store, and at the grocery store for some saltines and more ginger ale. When I walked past the ice cream parlor, I caught sight of my reflection. My shorts were practically falling off me. My separation anxiety was not getting better. At any moment, I could click on the security site and see Dan. I could also log on to the security system at the bakery and see my girls. If not for the inn, I would toss the tablet. It was killing me not to see him or to hear Lynnae's voice. After an hour or so on the bathroom floor, I headed to the house.

I took the yard stakes out of the car and started to place them in the ground where the new addition would go. It was perfect, as if the whole parcel was waiting for me. I took a deep breath, a sigh of relief, and for the first time in a long time, I allowed myself the kind of smile that rose from within. I allowed it to linger. I knew I'd made the right move. Somehow, I knew in my heart that I could make it on my own.

My life was about to reveal a brand new chapter. The beginning of a new adventure – one that I did not intend on missing. I had to admit, at first I was scared, but then I remembered my life book; someone must have written the words *Rhode Island* in it.

I sat down on the front steps. "I can do this," I said as I looked around the property. *My* property. "I hope Dan is happy. Lord, I mean that with all my heart."

I got up and turned the key. When I stepped inside for the first time, my heart raced. I suddenly felt alone. I made myself go into every room. I ran my hand along the kitchen countertop. Touched the four stools. When I went upstairs, I imagined myself leaving a tray of tea and cookies at a guest's door. I stood at the top of the stairs for a moment. "You can do this. Come on. You're strong. Breathe. Julie, breathe."

I drove back to Sal's Bed and Breakfast, wondering how long it would take me to find the courage to sleep at my own house. I thought about the old truck and possibly getting it restored.

The next morning, I woke up when it was still dark outside, got dressed and quickly got in my car. Around five-thirty, I pulled up to the house, went to the backyard and stood under the tall trees, staring at the back of the building. I loved to see the morning come to life. The woods took on a completely new feeling early in the morning. It was when the birds woke the ground creatures, when plants came to life in anticipation of a new dawn. If I had it my way, I would live in the forest. *But that's not reality. Turning a home into an inn, that's my reality.*

As the sun began to rise, I had to stop myself from remembering – remembering when I used to get up at four in the morning just to sit by Dan's side in a turkey blind.

"Stop," I told myself. "A name." I closed my eyes. "What shall

I call you?" My eyes opened wide. "The Inn in Rhode Island." I liked that.

Watching the sunrise, I knew exactly where I wanted to plant each of the gardens. The herb and vegetable gardens would need to be close to the house, with full sun. The rose garden and all the perennial gardens would go throughout the property.

Moments after the sun came up; I went over to the car and got a few items. I went into the house and set my drawings on the kitchen table. I purposely set the model up on the counter near the east window, hoping it would catch the sun's rays.

With chalk in hand, I climbed the stairs up to the attic. I wanted to measure and draw a rough sketch of the rooms on the floor with the chalk. I chose the southeast corner for my sleeping quarters. My bedroom suite didn't have to be larger than the rest of the staff; it just needed to be a little more private. Next to my room, I'd have the meeting room, and then continue down the space with the rest of the staff bedrooms. *Staff?* I hoped someone would be willing to stay in this big house with me.

I hoped that whoever was across the hall wouldn't mind if I snored, because I do.

The attic was large enough for five bedrooms, leaving about 200 square feet for the meeting room.

I could hear a car approaching in the driveway. I was hoping it was Frank. Before I reached the bottom step, I heard his voice. "Hello? Are you in here? Miss Julie?" Frank yelled.

"Good morning, Frank," I called down to him from the top of the second floor staircase. "I'm coming down from the attic." When I reached the bottom step, I extended my hand to him. "Hi. It's nice to meet you."

Frank looked at me and pointed back toward the front door. "The driveway really opens up as you approach the house."

"Yes, it does. In fact, that's one of the features I love the most about the place. Frank, I would like to give you a tour of the existing house. Then, I'll show you my plans. They're in the kitchen."

"If that's what you'd like. I've never been up here before. I've heard of the farm stand, but never had the time to come this way.

How much land comes with the place?"

"A total of two-hundred and thirty acres," I replied.

"That's a big parcel of land for one woman to take care of all by herself." Frank stood still for a moment. Rubbed his chin and added, "You're a brave gal, doing all this by yourself."

"I will have plenty of help. I'll hire people." I quickly started my tour. "This is one of the living rooms. I'm planning on leaving the entire downstairs as is. I may make some changes in the kitchen, but I won't know what I'm doing until I find a chef."

"A chef? Will he know how to cook collard greens and catfish?"

"*She* might, but I do, and if you give me a good price, I'll cook them for you every day."

"I like you already, young lady."

"Frank, I am hoping to run my own business – an inn, to be exact."

"Sounds like a nice idea… don't know too many inns around here."

I smiled, thinking there must be ten on Block Island alone.

"This is the other living room. Let's go upstairs, so we can talk about what needs to be done up there."

He huffed and puffed up the stairs after me.

"Up here I would like to take this wall out, and have a bathroom adjacent to the bedroom. Then I would like to have three more bathrooms added to the other bedrooms. Small but elegant *en suite* bathrooms. Do you think that can be done?"

"Don't see why not."

"Great. I would like to show you the attic next."

Frank followed me up the stairs. Every now and then I would hear him let out a little, "Hmmm."

I was hoping he was thinking about the project. And not whether I could pull this off. I liked him. He had a sweet Deep South way about him.

I was headed up to the attic with Frank when it dawned on me.

I needed to do a quick search on the name, "The Inn in Rhode Island" and file the papers for a DBA. *The Inn in Rhode Island,* "Yeah, I like that," I said under my breath.

"You say something?"

"Just thinking out loud again." I looked back at Frank and raised my eyebrows. "You'll get used to me. Up here, I'll need five bedrooms with their own bathrooms and one room for my staff and me to conduct meetings."

"That can be done, too, if the foundation is strong enough."

"Can you tell that by looking at the engineer's report?"

"By the looks of the foundation I don't think it's gonna be a problem. Besides the engineer's report, the town's gonna want to see a set of plans drawn up by an architect."

"Oh. Okay, how long will that take?"

"A few weeks. Don't worry, I know the gal who grants all the approvals." Frank winked at me. "You know, some old farmhouses were built using cement and bricks. Luckily for you, this one was built using concrete blocks."

"I'm glad to hear that." Frank's eyes were on me and I thought he wanted to say something. When I looked into his eyes, he didn't say anything, he just inhaled. "Let's go down to the kitchen so I can show you the rest of my ideas." This time, I walked a little slower down the stairs; Frank was a bit older than I expected.

As soon as we approached the kitchen, Frank headed for the model that I had constructed. "It's not quite a true scale model, but I gave it my best."

Frank looked back at me. "It works for me." Then he moved to his left and picked up my drawings. "You did these? They're pretty good."

"Thanks." He looked at them while I explained, "I would like to have an outdoor patio off the kitchen, along with some gardens, so I will need the building on both sides to have sufficient walkways and proper overhang."

The thought of lush hanging baskets made me smile. "Oh, and I would also like to extend the front porch from the main house to continue down along the two new side wings."

I stood back and watched as Frank looked over the plans. "This is a pretty big project. Do you have a time frame in mind as to when you would like to open this inn of yours?"

"When you're finished. Do you know how much time it will take?"

"About eighteen months or so. First, I'll have to have the architect look at the engineer's report. Then I'll have the architect draw up a set of plans that I can take to the town hall." He looked at me. "They'll need to be stamped before I can start."

At that point, I was a little nervous. "That's fine. Do you think we can build it for this amount?" I pointed to the top of the paper entitled budget. When Frank shook his head, I was even more nervous.

"I can't answer that. You'll have to sit down with Gina Marie, my project manager, and go over your ideas with her. She's extremely accurate when it comes to actual expenses. I'll have my design team look at your plans. Call the lumber yard for actual cost, draw up a cost analysis and give it to Gina Marie along with your budget of four million."

With plans in one hand, Frank extended his other hand to me. "I'll send Gina Marie over to see you tomorrow."

"Frank, thank you, and thank you for taking on my project. Wait, one more thing: do you require any money up front?"

"No, I'll pay for everything out of my business account. It's easier for me to submit a bill to you weekly for the material and for my labor. Besides, I have a good feeling about you, young lady."

"Thank you."

After Frank left, I knew I hired the right person.

Chapter 17

F eeling confident, I called Enterprise and told them where to pick up their vehicle. I drove into town and parked the vehicle in front of the ice cream parlor. I left my car in New York because I didn't want to apply for a Rhode Island driver's license, or have to register a vehicle every few years. My plan was to get settled in at the inn and stay there.

Before I contacted the local taxi service to bring me back to my house, I bought some smoked trout and seafood salad from Ferry Wharf Fish Market to eat later that day. The driver never made it to my driveway. I vomited in my mouth. I had to get out of the car and walk the rest of the way. My separation anxiety had kicked in. I wanted to go home to Dan and Lady.

As soon as the driver was out of sight, I started to cry. "What is wrong with me?" I looked up at the sky. "Walk with me Lord. Stay with me. Please don't leave me."

An hour later, I reached the house. I still felt sick and yet I was starving for the smoked fish. I needed to eat something, so I ate a few crackers.

I went into the tool shed and made a list of the garden tools hanging there. When I turned around, I bumped into the Kubota and immediately thought about Dan. I closed the door, latched the shed, went back to house as the sun started going down. Sat on the front steps, ate my fish, and researched auto restoration places. I found two close by to the house. I decided to give Classic Restorations a shot.

Frank never told me what time Gina Marie was coming, so I slept on the floor in the hallway at the top of the stairs. When I woke up, I went downstairs to wash my face and brush my teeth.

Thanks to my separation anxiety and uncontrollable vomiting episodes, I never leave home without mouthwash, toothbrush and toothpaste.

At eight o'clock, I was sitting on the floor in the room that was going to be the library when I heard a knock on the front door.

I got up and opened the door. "Good morning. You must be Gina Marie. Come right in."

"That's me, Frank asked me to stop by to go over your budget." "I can't tell you how nervous I am right now."

She grinned. "Don't be nervous. Frank knows what he's doing.

He's been in the construction business for fifty-seven years."

"He must have started when he was young."

"He was fourteen when he started. He worked for his father and two uncles down in Georgia. Been on his own ever since he moved to Rhode Island, back in the early eighties."

I looked at her. She reminded me of Lynnae. Same happy-golucky attitude. "You're wearing the same boots as Frank." I had no idea why I said that.

She flashed her boots at me. "Every contractor's go-to gear – Carolinas. Frank insists we all wear steel toes."

"There's a couple of stools in the kitchen we can sit on. Would you like a cup of coffee or tea?" I asked her.

"No, thanks," she said.

"You sure? I purchased a Nespresso and a One Shot. I have plenty."

She shook her head. "I'm good."

"So, you're the project manager who's going to keep me in budget?" I turned to face her, rolling my eyes as we entered the kitchen. "Okay."

"Are you not happy that I'm a woman?"

"Oh, for heaven's sake, I'm not at all worried about that. I like the fact that a woman will be working on my project. I'm worried about my budget."

"We'll take good care of you. Umm, there's four of us. Jessica is the team leader in charge of the electricians and painters. And there's two other women who work directly under Frank."

"I really like Frank. I like the way he thinks."

"We do, too. You won't be disappointed. He's a perfectionist."

"I'm glad to hear that. Are you sure I can't get you something to drink?"

"No. I drank a cup of coffee on my way over here. Let me ask you something – is there any chance you're going to want to build more than the twenty rooms?"

"No." I rubbed my temple. "Why do you ask?" I said, making myself a cup of Nespresso.

"The ceilings are ten feet. The existing house downstairs has five-and-a-half inch crown molding and I'm sure you'll want to continue that throughout the addition. That's going to be expensive to match."

"How expensive? Like over budget expensive?"

"Yeah. Ten feet requires three sheets of rock, more tape, spackle and a few more dollars in labor cost. I suggest you go with an eight foot ceiling and four inch molding in the addition."

I thought for a moment. "That will work for me."

"Good. Otherwise, I think your budget of four million is workable"

"I have to stay within budget…"

"Don't worry. Hey, did Frank tell you his goddaughter, Sabrina Abrams, is the architect who will be working on this project? And he knows all the right people at the town hall. So it won't take long before we can get started."

"That's good to hear. And you should know I'm not in a hurry." "Good to know," Gina Marie said.

"It sounds like an almost all-women crew."

"There's a few men. Rhode Island is an equal opportunity state. You know Rhode Island is the only state that banned slavery before there even was a United States?"

"I didn't know that."

"Don't feel bad, Frank didn't know it either until I told him. All right. I'll go back and let Frank know we're set."

I walked Gina Marie out to her truck and thanked her one more time. I sat down on the porch steps and thought about how much

Sal's Bed and Breakfast was costing me.

Later that morning, Frank sent me a text message saying he would be ready to start construction in three weeks.

Until his text, I hadn't thought about buying food or furniture for the house. I called the taxi service and asked if they could pick me up at the end of my driveway. I was starting to enjoy my little two-mile hike.

The smoked fish was good but not enough to hold me over. I was hungry, so I had the driver drop me off at the diner. After breakfast, I strolled down to the beach.

I thought about buying a bicycle. I wished I knew how to swim.

Just walk. Lord knows, I've hiked further.

Strolled on Sand Hill Cove, past George's of Galilee, and of course, I remembered Dan and me eating dinner topside. We'd laughed so much that night. I wished we had taken more vacations, but Dan had been afraid the phone would ring and he would miss a big land-clearing job. I continued down the street, stopped and bought a large hat from a small boutique. Up ahead, on both sides of the street, there were a few more shops.

The sign out front of Elliott's Antique Shop read: "Free coffee and cookies. Proprietors, Kevin and Kourtnee."

I stepped inside. Their shop was as neat as a church pew. Everything was in its place and dust free. They had some nice antiques, but mostly what they had were items given to them by local people on consignment. I asked how long they had owned the shop and if they enjoyed running their own business. The man picked up a small table and said, "Too long," under his breath, before going into the back room.

"We don't make a lot of money," Kourtnee said, "which is why

Kevin has to work a lot of side jobs."

"What kind of side jobs does he do?" I asked.

"He mows lawns."

"Does he like doing that?"

"He does. When he works on big jobs, I go with him. I pull the weeds but I don't mind. I like being out in the sun. It gets me out of here for the day. And it's relaxing."

"I agree with you. Gardening can be very therapeutic. You certainly have a lot of merchandise in here. How on earth do you keep it all so clean?"

"Believe me, it fills my day, cleaning, dusting, never mind changing the displays so it looks like we have new items."

"Well, you do an excellent job. I'd like to buy this." I held up a small wine rack. The tag read: "Point Judith Pickers."

"I'll put it in a carry bag."

"Thanks. I'm sure I'll be back. It was nice to meet you."

After I left their shop, I strolled down the street, stopping at a few other shops. I thought about going back to see Kevin and Kourtnee but it was hard for me to see George's restaurant and not think of Dan. I was too upset to think about lunch. Yet I had a craving for something. Maybe after dinner, I would head over to the bakery and treat myself to something sweet. I was sure they would have something tasty, without all of the sugar. Speaking of sugar, I needed to pick up testing supplies. I'd used my last testing strip that morning.

I was looking up at the sky in admiration. Rhode Island was so beautiful. I inhaled the sweet salt air. Suddenly, a man ran past me, nearly knocking me off my feet. I watched as he and his family boarded the Point Judith ferry. On the spur of the moment, I boarded the ferry and spent the rest of my day on Block Island.

I stopped by The Blue Dory Inn and The Avonlea. Both inns had an old world charm. I spoke to the owner, Ann Law, for a bit. I *wanted* her look. Her face was glowing with pride, contentment and the satisfaction of working for herself. Ann told me that she loved every aspect of running her inn. Before I left, she said, "If we didn't have the storms, we'd never get to play in the waves."

On the ride back to Point Judith, I thought about what Ann had said to me. Dan had always said, "We're strong enough to weather the storms. As long as we're together." He would tell me that *every* time I spent more money than I should have.

I looked out at the ocean. *I miss you so much. I miss the way you...* I looked up at the sky. *I will always love you, Dan Holliday.* When I stepped off the ferry, I headed for the diner; I didn't see Kelly, which was a disappointment. I ate my dinner, thinking about Kevin and Kourtnee; they remind me of a country music duo. Tall, handsome man with dark hair and eyes. She's just as tall, but with long straight blonde hair and blue eyes.

After I ate, I wished I had just one of Lynnae's sweet treats. I was going through cinnamon withdrawal. Before I went to the local bakery, I went into the drugstore and purchased some testing strips, just in case my sugar levels rose. I had to learn to take care of myself.

I was standing in line at the counter waiting to pay for my supplies, and I suddenly heard this beautiful, harmonious sound coming from aisle number four. I went to investigate and found a woman who was pure sunshine. She was humming my favorite hymn, smiling as if she was a lottery winner. I introduced myself, and she told me her name, Teresa. She appeared to be about my age, with shoulder length golden blond curly hair and the most beautiful blue eyes. For such a petite woman, she had some voice on her. I liked her very much.

I was glad I chose Point Judith. Everyone I bumped into seemed to be courteous and friendly. At the bakery, they had sugar-free chocolate croissants, so of course I bought two, one for at night and one for the next morning. I also noticed the aroma, sweet and homey.

I couldn't resist, I had to ask the woman behind the counter about the bakery. She was more than happy to chat. The bakery owner, Mary, had been in the business for just under twenty years.

"We make the best wedding cakes, birthday cakes, and the pies on the East Coast." She smiled with pride. "Every Fourth of July, other bakers enter their pies in the local bake-off contest, just to come in second to ours."

"That's nice to know," I said, paying for my croissants.

I looked at their berry pie and noticed it had four different berries in it.

Pie.

I felt a lump in my throat.

Looking at the pies reminded me how I'd always baked Dan's favorite – apple, just for him. I couldn't even go into a bakery and not think about Dan. *Oh, Julie...* silently, I yelled at myself. Then I had to rush out of the bakery as the tears ran down my face.

As I walked away, I tried to turn my thoughts to the inn, but then I thought about Lady.

I didn't go into any more shops. I called for a taxi to take me back to Sal's. The entire way, I tried to focus my attention solely on my plans for the inn.

As soon as I got to my room, I looked online for local furniture stores. An hour later, I started to draw and sketch each of the gardens. Every garden would be different and unique in its own way. The inn would need an herb and vegetable garden for the kitchen, a cutting garden large enough to supply fresh flowers for all the guest's rooms. A lots of aesthetic gardens – gardens just for pleasure. And my favorite – rose garden full of David Austin roses. I could not get the couple or Teresa out of my head.

I made a list: Someone at the front desk to greet my guests. A chef. Someone to serve the guests. A property maintenance worker, and a meticulous person to assist me with all the cleaning.

I wrote the ad. But then decided not to run it. I was still scared, confused and needed to be sure no one would find me. I didn't want to hear about how happy Dan was with his new girlfriend.

I wished Lynnae were with me. She would tell me to snap out of it and be real. She would also tell me to come home. My heart hurt thinking about her. I felt guilty leaving her. Leaving the way I did. I missed them. I especially missed Dan.

Of course, I was awake most of the night thinking about Dan. Wondering if he cared about where I was.

I was sitting in the wingback chair next to the window, watching the sunrise, enjoying a chocolate croissant. I took a hot shower, dressed, and opened my notepad. I decided to make a list of each of the rooms. I wanted every room to have its own theme. In the Americana room, the color scheme would be cranberry red, slate blue, and creamy white. I assigned each room with a name, not a number. Besides, no one wanted to sleep in room number 13 on a Friday night.

I went downstairs for a cup of coffee, toast and eggs. Afterwards, I headed over to the fabric shop.

As soon as I opened the door, I heard, "Good morning. May I help you?"

"Good morning. Yes, I would like to see some fabric books, specifically the ones that refer to an American theme, nautical, and let's say natural or nature in design." I nodded, feeling sure of my choices. "Please."

"Okay, follow me over to the tables and have a seat. I'll get you started with a few books. Either you must have a big project, or maybe you're not sure which design to go with?"

"No, I'm pretty organized. I'll definitely need quite a bit of fabric. Oh, and I'll need to buy a sewing machine. I'm making curtains for about thirty rooms."

"Thirty? Will you need assistance? I could help you. My name is Molly."

"I appreciate the offer…"

"I'll give you one of my cards in case you change your mind." She handed me her card, along with a piece of paper and a pen.

"When you see something that you like, write it down and I'll see if it is available, and get you a price. If you have any questions, just holler, I'll be in the next room."

"Thank you, and thanks for offering to help me. I may take you up on your offer after all." According to Molly's business card, she was an interior designer. Graduate of the Rhode Island School of

Design. "Hmmm." I put her card in my pocketbook.

I sat in the fabric shop for more than four hours. With every decision, I wished Dan were there to give me his opinion. Designing our home together was a memory I would always treasure. I thought twice about buying a sewing machine.

I handed my list to Molly, took her up on her offer, and instructed her to make all the substitutions herself. "If a fabric isn't available, you have my permission to exchange it with something similar."

In addition to each room's interior, making a statement of their own, the gardens outside were just as important to me. The inns on Block Island had the ocean to enjoy. So, my inn needed to step up in some way, if I intended on competing with those waves.

I needed to walk the property one more time to confirm my vision for each of the gardens and their placement. I hailed a taxi and once again had the driver drop me off at the end of the driveway.

I imagined how perfect the driveway would look in a few short years, lined with red maple trees on both sides. "After all, they are the state tree."

It took me three hours to hike the entire parcel, all 230 acres. With sketchpad and pencil in hand, I went around the house to the backyard. I began visualizing each garden, until the noise distracted me. I had to go inside and investigate. I followed the sound all the way to the attic.

"Good afternoon, young lady. Want to see your room?"

"My room? You're kidding me, right?"

"I would never kid you. Come with me."

I walked past nine or ten, maybe twelve workers. "Frank, I heard about some of your workers, but I didn't know you had this many people working for you."

Frank made a familiar noise.

There were two-by-fours everywhere. Frank had the entire third floor framed out. He even had all the holes drilled out for the electrical lines, and for the plumbing pipes. He had a team of five women and six men scurrying around.

Frank led me down the long path between all the standing wood, and pointed to the room at the end.

"Frank, it looks as if there are three rooms framed out in here." "I thought you might like a walk in-closet."

"You're the best. I cannot believe you have all this work done. And this is only the first week. Oh, Frank, this is fantastic."

He smiled. "When I get started, I don't stop." He waved his hammer in the air.

"Well, I better get out of your way, and let you get back to work."

On my way down the stairs, a thought struck, and I quickly turned around. "Frank, do you suppose you could give me a fivefoot opening and fill the closet with shelves? I'm not much of a

clotheshorse; but I do enjoy reading."

"Sure, I'll take care of that."

"Thank you."

I walked away hoping I had not made things too hard with my change of plans. Honestly, how was he supposed to know that I hadn't even taken up a third of the closet I had shared with Dan.

Seeing the living quarters almost complete, I knew it was time to start thinking seriously about finding my staff. As I stepped out of the house, I knew it was really happening. I had so many mixed emotions.

I didn't even make it off the front porch. I had to sit down. My heart was heavy. No tears, just sadness. My head fell into my hands.

Why am I here alone? How am I supposed to get through the next thirty years… without you?

"Why do I want to go home?"

Chapter 18

It was early Saturday morning, none of the shops would be open yet, so I decided to go for a stroll down the beach. But it was like strolling down memory lane.

Every time I went past George's of Galilee, I remembered telling Dan that it was my favorite seafood restaurant. He told me that he would bring me back the following year.

A year later, when Dan turned fifty, he bought a beautiful black AC Cobra and promised me we would go back to Rhode Island in his new car. "This is not my mid-life crisis. This is our get-out-oftown-car." He said it with kisses and promises.

I wandered down the beach for an hour. I couldn't take my eyes off the number of people windsurfing. When I stepped on the edge of a conch shell, I noticed a silver charm lying in the wet sand. It was an anchor. I looked around but no one was close enough to ask. I picked it up, and the shell and carried them both. Headed to the diner, and had breakfast, before going to the antique shop.

"Good morning, Kourtnee. Is Kevin here?"

"He's in the back sanding down a chair. Should I get him for you?"

"Please. I would like to talk to the two of you, if you both have the time."

Kourtnee went into the back room and returned with Kevin by her side. When he wrapped his arm around her, I wanted to die.

"Hey, Julie, what's up?"

"I'm preparing to open an inn, and I'm going to need help managing the place. I have a few positions that I would like to offer the two of you."

"Positions?" Kevin held his hand out, palm up.

"Yes. I was thinking, you could tend to the mowing and assist me with the gardens. Kourtnee, I think you would make a great assistant. You could assist me with the books and on occasion in the dining rooms."

Kourtnee answered me immediately, "Oh, hell yeah."

"Wait a minute, Kourtnee. What would we do with the shop?" "Umm, we could give the consignment stuff back and then have a tag sale? And if nothing sells, we could give it all away to someone else, like everyone does to us. Kevin, we're not making any money here, and we still get to work together. Never mind the property owner just raised the rent on us. Come on, let's try it."

Kevin twisted his bottom lip. "Yeah, well, I think it depends on the salary we're being offered, don't you think?" "I was hoping the two of you would live at the inn for no cost. Collect a salary a few dollars over minimum wage each, and receive bonuses as soon as the inn starts earning a profit."

"Seriously?" Kevin said but I wasn't sure if he was talking to me or to his wife. "Yes," I replied.

"Kevin, we can give up our apartment and the store." Kourtnee glanced over at me and then stared back at Kevin. "Kevin, please?"

"Come on, Kourtnee. No, don't you think we should talk about it first?" He turned to me. "When do you plan on opening this inn?"

"You have a few more months to wrap things up here. Then we can start working on the inn together. It's my intention that everyone have a hand in things from the beginning."

"Thank you for remembering Kevin and me."

"Kourtnee, the two of you were first on my list. That's if the two of you are both saying yes." I looked at Kevin.

Kevin was nodding. "I suppose we can give it a try."

"Sounds good. If you're not happy…"

"We'll be fine. Right Kevin?"

When he smiled at her, my heart melted.

My next stop – the fabric store. One thing I knew for sure, I was a good judge of character. As I turned the corner toward the shop, a red cardinal landed on a fence post directly in front of me, and I knew someone was watching over me. I was so distracted; I walked right by the shop.

"Hey, Molly, how are you today? Oh, busy, I see."

"Busy with your order; this is the fabric for the kitchen curtains." "I see my little rooster hens. That is one of my favorite fabrics. Molly, if I am not being too personal, how much does your boss pay you?"

"She doesn't pay me," Molly laughed. "It's my sister's shop. I'm just covering for her while she is recovering from hip surgery. Why?"

"How would you like to earn a substantial living, and have no living expenses?"

"What do you mean?"

"I would like you to live and work for me at my new inn."

"Wait, what exactly would I be doing?"

"Molly, I think you should be the inn's decorator."

"Seriously?"

"Once the rooms are complete, your job will include planning the inn's activities, seeing that all the rooms have fresh flowers and things like that."

She bit the inside of her mouth. "Um, I can't take the job. I can't move. Not right now. My father has Alzheimer's. I have to be with him in the evening. As much as I need a job, I have to be home at night. I…"

"I'm sorry to hear that about your father. Really, I am. The job is still yours if you want it. You don't have to live at the inn…"

"Thank you. I can work every day til four. That's when my dad's caregiver goes home."

"You can leave whenever you need to."

"I love flowers," Molly said, sounding happier.

I was standing outside a flower shop when I heard someone singing, "How Great Thou Art." *It can't be.* I listened for a moment. It had to be her. I stepped inside grabbed a bouquet of snapdragons.

Two houses down from the flower shop, I saw her. Teresa was out in the front yard watering flowers and singing like a songbird.

"Hello, you sound wonderful today. These are for you." I handed her the bouquet.

"Oh, my, good afternoon. What did I do to deserve these?"

"Teresa, do you have a few minutes to talk to me about my new inn?"

"Sure, I do. Come on in." Teresa held open the small gate. "I have some lemonade in the fridge. Have a seat on the porch, and we'll talk out here." As she went up the stairs I heard her say, "It's gorgeous out today."

"I agree." I sat down and waited for Teresa to return. When she came back out, she had two glasses of lemonade and handed me one, thanking me again for the flowers.

"Teresa, I would like to offer you a job."

"A job?"

"I'd like you to consider working for me. I am prepared to pay you..."

"Pay me?"

I smiled. "Yes, plus bonuses, and a place to live."

"Are you kidding me?"

"No, not at all. Teresa, the day I saw you in the drugstore, I knew you were perfect for the inn. I would like to offer you the receptionist position. You will be the first person to greet our guests and assign them to their rooms. Does that appeal to you?"

"It sure does. You have no idea how much rent these people are charging me. When do I start?" she laughed, "Never mind I'm running out of merchandise to sell." "What do you sell?" I asked, thinking I would buy something.

"Oh, just this and that. Mostly whatever I find on trash day in Newport. I'm a picker."

"Are you...?"

"Point Judith Pickers. That's me."

"I bought one of your pieces. A wine rack."

"Thanks. Gosh, you have no idea what good timing you have." "I'll take that as a yes. The staff's living quarters will be ready in about a month, so you can give plenty of notice to your landlord and pack up whatever you would like to bring with you. Your room will be about two-hundred and fifty square feet. Oh, and you will have your own bath. Teresa, you are going to love the others; they're all wonderful people, just like you. I look forward to having you join our team and I'm very excited you said yes."

We chatted for a short while then I excused myself, not wanting to take up her entire day.

I was so glad I went into the drugstore that other day.

I looked up toward the sky. "Thank You for walking with me today."

Another week had gone by and I needed to work on the gardens. First, I had to gain control over my vomiting. I literally spent an entire night lying on the floor in the bathroom. One day, I was fine and the next…?

Before I went downstairs to say goodbye to Sal, I ordered a bed, set of sheets, pillows, towels and a wingback chair for myself, to be delivered that afternoon.

Then I called the taxi service. I smiled when I saw it was the same driver as last time. "Mallard Way?" he asked.

"Yes, thanks."

Once again, I walked down the driveway. When I reached the house and turned the key, I said, "Home." But as soon as I opened the door, I closed it.

Sadness took over.

I wanted Dan to be inside waiting for me. But he wasn't. A moment later, I opened the door and stepped inside.

I was headed to the kitchen to make myself a cup of mint tea when I heard Frank's voice. I threw on some lipstick, turned around and smiled back at the sweet man.

"It's nice to see you, young lady. I found the note you left for me. When do you come out, in the middle of the night?"

I laughed. "Only when the stars are out. Actually, from now on,

I'll be sleeping here. So you're going to be seeing a lot more of me."

"Sounds good. Come outside, I want to show you what we did out on the front porch."

"Frank, the ceiling fans look wonderful. I'm so glad I decided to hang them on the porches."

"I agree," Frank said as he turned to face the driveway. "Well, it looks like you have company. I better let you go."

"Frank, wait. I'd like to introduce you. They're going to work here."

"Hey, Julie," Kevin shouted.

"Hello. Let me introduce you to Frank, our contractor."

Kevin shook Frank's hand. "We've heard a lot of good things about you."

"It's very nice to meet you," Frank said. "And you." He nodded toward Kourtnee. "As well," Kourtnee replied.

"I'm so glad to see the two of you. How is the liquidation coming along?" I asked hoping it was going well.

"Coming along? We're done. Kourtnee had a tag sale. She got rid of everything. Okay she gave it away."

"I only gave back the consignment stuff. Actually, we got good money for the stuff we owned." She shrugged her shoulders. "So, we thought we would help you, if you would like."

"Kourtnee, that's so sweet of you. But first, let me give you guys a tour and show you some of Frank's work."

"Heard that. Back to work," Frank said as he turned up the corners of his mouth.

Kourtnee and I followed the men into the house.

Kourtnee chose the bedroom suite across from mine.

"Julie, Kourtnee thinks she needs to watch over you. She said you need protecting."

"Kevin! Men, I swear," Kourtnee snapped. "I had a dream that you were in the witness protection program. I don't think you need to be protected at all. It was just a dream."

"Well, thank you, I feel much safer now." I changed the subject and took them outside to show them where some of the gardens would be going. "I'm thinking we should have the herb and vegetable gardens close to the kitchen. What do you think?"

"Makes sense to me. By the way, how many gardens are we talking about?" Kevin asked.

"Lots, all around the property, mostly on the nature trail to the pond."

"There's a pond on this property?" Kourtnee asked.

"A small one. We're going to make it a little bigger. I thought I would rent a bulldozer and start digging it out this fall. I plan to dredge out about forty acres for kayaking, or swimming, or we can just float around the entire pond, until we fall asleep. Kevin, can you run a bulldozer?"

"Are you kidding me? Sure, I can. In fact, it's a dream of mine to get back on one. I used to run one on my grandparents' farm. I can't wait to see this place when you're finished." I was glad Kevin was excited.

I placed a hand on each of their backs. "You mean when *we're* finished. Kevin, I can't do this alone. So if you ever have an idea or thought, I want to hear them. This is our inn." I smiled, "I would love to go shopping for some of the plants. Any chance you could drive me to a nursery?"

"Sure."

"Good, and on the way I'll tell you about some of the other gardens I have in mind."

"Great, we have all day. Kevin and I had planned on spending our day washing walls or something."

"Not at all, Kourtnee. I'm telling you, the house was in excellent condition the day I bought it. All we have to do is dress it up."

"Julie, it's kind of nice that you always say 'we.' It's as if we have an interest in the place, and it's our inn too,"

"Kevin, I want each of my staff members to feel like this is your home. I want every one of you to take pride in the inn. Remember, this will be our home, and our workplace, as well as our place of enjoyment. The inn will belong to all of us. It is my intent to see each of you share in whatever profit the inn may have. That's why at any time if you have an idea to make this a better place, I want to hear those ideas."

I looked over at the tall herbaceous peony. "Kevin, do you know where I can buy a new lawn mower?"

"Sure, it's actually on the way to the garden shop. We're going to need a pretty big machine with all this property."

"I know it's a lot of lawn, but remember, there are going to be a lot of gardens, too. When we plant the flowerbeds, I want them planted in big clusters."

"Just how big will these clusters be?"

"The first perennial garden will start with a row of peonies six feet wide by one hundred feet long."

"Now that's a flowerbed," Kourtnee said.

"Yes, and right behind the peonies, we'll be planting the iris in the same fashion. Did I mention that I love flowers?" They both laughed.

"I want to make the walk on the property feel both relaxing and invigorating for our guests. The gardens are the most important part of the inn for me."

We drove to the garden shop and stopped at the mower shop.

After a long day of shopping, both Kevin and Kourtnee were starving. They decided to go out for dinner. I declined their invitation by saying that I needed to check up on Frank and look at my garden sketches one more time. When we pulled up to the inn, there must have been twenty additional pickup trucks in the driveway.

"Good evening, Frank. Are you having a party?"

"No, these are some of the men I help out from time to time.

We're part of the same barn raising team. I want to get the living quarters done for everyone. I see the staff is starting to arrive."

"Oh, you mean Kevin and Kourtnee; yes, they're so excited. We just purchased all the plant material and a garden tractor."

"Oh, yeah? What did you buy?"

"Every plant under the sun, all perennial of course. I'm going with all low-maintenance gardens."

"That's nice. What kind of tractor did you buy?"

"We purchased a John Deere Two Track with a sixty-inch mower deck, and two forty-eight inch side decks. Do you think that's big enough?"

"That's a nice tractor; it'll do the job just fine. I met the gal who'll be at the front desk. She stopped by while you were out."

"Teresa came by?"

"She wanted to see the progress and say hello. She said she would come back tomorrow to help you."

"That was nice of her. I'll have to go and see her later."

"By any chance, you got room for another pretty face? She's real smart. Could use the work."

I thought for a moment. "I could use help in the dining room. Do you think she'll be willing to seat the guests and help me serve food?"

Frank reached in his pocket. "Why don't ya ask her yourself? Tell her Uncle Frank recommended ya give her a call." He handed me a small piece of paper with her name and phone number on it. "Bea Freeman. How is she your niece?"

"She's my youngest brother's daughter. First year in college. You'll like her."

"I love her already! I will give her a call right now. Thanks, Frank."

Frank winked at me. "Well, I figure I better get those bedrooms finished, or you'll all be sleeping downstairs. Would you care to see the finished project?"

I followed Frank up to the third floor. I was amazed at every turn. "Frank, you're doing a fantastic job. Thank you."

An hour later, Frank and his friends packed up their tools and left for the evening. Fearful Frank's friends cost me more than I could afford, I Googled "barn raising" and realized it was common in the 18th and 19th century rural North America. Community members *helping* other members. "Thank God."

I was glad for the opportunity to be alone. Spending the day with Kevin and Kourtnee made me feel a bit sad. Anyone could see they were both happy and in love.

I remembered feeling the same way. I remembered looking at Dan with that same deep passion.

I suppose it was all just an illusion.

I wish I could erase those memories forever.

I was sitting on the front porch when I felt a gentle spring breeze. In front of me were two re-blooming lilac bushes. I closed my eyes and took in their scent. I felt stronger, more powerful than ever before. Four days had gone by without one episode of getting sick. "Home." The inn was starting to feel like home to me.

My stomach growled and I thought about what food I had in the kitchen to cook. "Cook! I had better find a chef." Finding a knowledgeable chef would not be so easy. I needed someone capable of changing with the seasons. I wanted a professional chef who would *never* require my assistance.

When I closed my eyes again, I saw Dan's face. His smile. My heart started pounding. Our kitchen served as a playroom for Dan and me. We had just as much fun in that kitchen as we did in any of the rooms. I swallowed hard.

In my bedroom, I'd be able to close my eyes, and pretend that Dan was still by my side, but in the kitchen, I'd be missing him.

The next day, I needed to see Frank. He had a way of making me feel better.

I could only imagine some people thinking I was running from memories of the world I had just left behind, or they might believe I was simply there for the sake of a new journey. Any way they wanted to look at it, I didn't care.

When I entered the foyer, I met Frank coming down the stairs.

"I was about to call for you," he said.

I smiled graciously. "That's why you were on my mind."

"Gina Marie is on her way. We're ready to start the new addition."

At that moment, I was suddenly scared to death. I wanted to tell

Frank no. Stop everything. I couldn't do it. I was going back home.

But I told him, "Of course."

When Gina Marie arrived with Sabrina, Frank gathered his entire crew and we all stood at the back of the house. Gina Marie handed me a bottle of honey whiskey and said, "Here's to building your dreams," then she explained every detail to each of the department heads. She went over the timeframe and all the work details. I stood there amazed at how smoothly she orchestrated the entire project. Listening to Gina Marie and Sabrina speak, I knew the inn would be ready to open the following spring.

Chapter 19

K ourtnee was ready and willing to do whatever it took to get the inn prepared. I was so grateful; I let her take over the office. She ran the ad and a week later, on a warm spring afternoon, an outdoor dining room had been set up in preparation for chef number one. Both chefs were arriving on Wednesday. Each person would cook lunch for the existing staff and the workers. We set up tables and chairs out on the rear patio.

The first chef, Michael, was in great shape, and he was a little mysterious looking. He stood about five-feet-ten inches tall, with jet-black hair and dark brown eyes. When he spoke, his voice sounded both calming and alluring. He promised to excite everyone's pallet with his flair for herbs. Michael had studied at the Culinary Institute in Hyde Park, New York. After graduating, he had worked in several of the finest restaurants throughout the south, near his hometown.

Michael said he enjoyed preparing both Northern and Southern dishes. He loved to use local produce and fresh garden herbs. He enjoyed cooking healthy dishes that were tasty and fun to eat. For lunch, Michael prepared chilled curried zucchini soup, asparagus wraps, and veal and prosciutto bundles. Orange glazed baby carrots on a bed of chopped baby greens and radicchio, along with a fresh strawberry – rhubarb sorbet.

Right before Michael served his creation, he extended his hand out to everyone. While still holding my hand, he made eye contact with me, leaned in very close, and thanked me for allowing him the opportunity to prepare the day's meal. I only smiled back at him.

Any other time, my heart would have skipped a beat. Michael was very attractive. Too bad my heart was both cold and heavy, like steel.

I heard Molly as she whispered, "Ooh la la!" I *thought* Molly was my wild one.

I leaned over and asked her if she noticed how every word seemed to come from his heart, especially when he was describing food.

Molly tapped me on my leg. "I like standing next to him. I can feel his energy."

We both agreed: Michael was intoxicating and electrifying.

Not surprisingly, everyone enjoyed the meal, starting and ending with a cold dish.

The next day, Chef Stefan arrived. Stefan was a large man. Not heavy, just big. He chose to serve buttery leek soup, swordfish *beurre blanc*, roasted mixed vegetables with orzo, mixed salad and fudge rum chocolate cakes for dessert. The staff agreed with me. It would not be an easy choice.

"Hey, Julie," Kevin said, "I was thinking maybe we should set up for dinner out on the back terrace. That way we can all watch the sunset together."

"What a great idea, Kevin." I smiled. "I'll go and inform Kourtnee right now."

Kourtnee had crystals hanging from fishing line in every tree along the terrace. At the base of the trees, she set tea lights. While Teresa, Bea, Molly, Kourtnee, and I set the tables, Kevin began to light the many tea lights. Kevin lined up all the chairs facing the gardens, leaving everyone's back to the main building. Kourtnee said she wasn't sure if he wanted everyone to see her twinkling lights or his gardening expertise. I knew why Kevin set the chairs up that way.

Since we just couldn't decide between the two, for dinner, there was going to be a cook off, where both chefs cooked the same meal. What they didn't know was I would be choosing the menu. Black bean chili, jalapeno muffins, short ribs, game hens and apple pear crisp.

Chef Michael had taken upon himself to serve his version of macaroni and cheese to go along with the short ribs. He also picked up a loaf of country bread from the local bakery, and brushed it with olive oil and herbs from our garden.

Chef Stefan took no chances or risks. He only served what I asked of him. Leaving me to think long and hard. I needed creative thinkers. People who understood the meaning of attention to detail. At my inn, you only got one chance to prove yourself, and you had better get it right the first time. Or the guests would not be coming back.

I knew Stefan was an excellent chef; perhaps he would be better suited cooking at his own restaurant. I decided on Chef Michael.

"Thank you. Julie, I won't disappoint you." He added, "I'll fly home tomorrow, gather my belongings and start cooking for you on

Saturday."

Before leaving for Florida the next morning, Michael served us a breakfast we would never forget. He started us off with fresh strawberries, blueberries, and red currants with a grand marnier sauce. When Michael served his homemade orange pecan waffles, I knew I made the right decision. Michael left us wanting more. We could not wait to see his many talents and taste his creations.

"Kevin, are you happy with my decision regarding our new chef?"

"Actually, Julie, I think both chefs were great cooks. Michael, however, was the best choice, considering his personality. I think Michael fits right in around here. The question is, are you happy with your choice?"

"Absolutely. I think Michael is creative, talented, and a great chef. Besides, Michael assured me he could run the kitchen all by himself. Above all, that pleases me. Michael has passion, real fire.

He's true to those around him." "Wow, you like Michael?" "Shall we plant a few more plants?" I quickly added.

"Julie, wait, it's raining," Kevin pointed toward the window, "and it's a little early in the season to be planting..."

"Kevin, the best time to plant is in the rain. And just so you know, I like Michael as much as I like you."

Kevin nodded. "Got it."

"Wonderful, I'll get the herbs, and the vegetable plants. You grab the shovels, please."

"One question, if we're not opening the inn until next spring, why are we planting vegetables now?"

"Kevin, we have to eat, don't we? Besides the best gardens in the world are well tested. Relax. It's just a little garden."

"Where would you like for me to start digging?"

"How about in the center? Here, I drew a chart for us."

"I should have known. You're incredible; it's to scale, and in color." Kevin turned around abruptly. "Whoa, is that an AC Cobra pulling in? Check out that car."

My heart started racing, but I did not dare turn around and look. It was the moment I prayed for, and yet, feared the most. What if it was Dan, and he was looking for me? I'm wasn't sure how I'd react. "Kevin, I have to go. I'll be right back." I ran toward the garden shed, and when I felt safe, I turned around and it was a red Cobra, not black.

Days turned into weeks and before I knew it, the house started taking on a new appearance.

With Frank keeping his promise to finish the construction by spring, and with the completion of the pond expansion, I really had my hands full.

By purchasing all the furniture the same day from Cardi's Furniture in Wakefield, I was able to lock in a huge savings. I scheduled the furniture for the twenty new rooms to be delivered the end of April the following year. However, the furniture for the main part of the inn had arrived a month after I ordered. I was thankful

Frank sent over his two friends to help Kevin and Michael lift the heavy pieces. As much as I needed Michael's help, I was worried about him hurting his hands. We waited for the professionals to set up the pool table, before we set up our bedrooms, the library, billiards room, dining rooms, and the five guest rooms on the second floor. I was glad I purchased two more wingback chairs for the library. I planned on reading many novels in those chairs.

"Hey, Julie, all the wicker and rattan furniture needs to go in to the Jamestown room, and all of the oak furniture goes to the Galilee suite, right?" "Yes, Kevin, that's correct." I looked at Molly for assurance. She shrugged her shoulders.

"Why? Where did it get put?" I asked.

Kevin cocked his head to the right. "In the Newport." "How does it look?" I asked.

"I think it looks fine, but you better come and see for yourself, before the guys leave."

We all gathered in the doorway. "I have to say, I simply love it; all the dark wood with the light blue fabric is stunning." When I looked at Molly, she was holding two thumbs up.

"It's gorgeous. Leave it," Molly said, smiling at me.

"Thanks so much for helping us today. We couldn't have done it without the two of you." I handed the two men each an envelope.

"Any time," they both said.

"Okay, let's make the beds," I said, clapping my hands.

"I think it's beer-thirty," Michael shouted.

So Molly, Bea, Teresa, Kourtnee and I started making beds. Before we knew it, it was past midnight, and we were all exhausted. I sat down on the floor, then Molly, followed by Bea, Kourtnee and Teresa. Actually, we collapsed. And for some reason we all just started laughing. We were giggling like schoolchildren. It was at that moment I knew my wish had come true. I had friends in Rhode Island.

Everyone worked in great harmony, and it showed. Twenty-one months after I met Geri and saw the house for the first time, the inn was ready. Frank finished a few weeks behind schedule. However, he completed the entire project under budget. The inn would be open in time for summer. In fact, I was taking reservations for Memorial Day weekend. No task had been left unattended. We'd had a few minor hiccups, but nothing to scream and shout about. It was incredible how a small inn out in the middle of nowhere could fill such a void in my life.

I was standing on the front porch watering the flowering baskets when a car pulled up and parked in the guests parking lot. When the two couples got out of the vehicle and pulled out their luggage, I knew my first guest had arrived. I was so happy I started to cry. Before I could set my watering can down, another car approached. I was still standing in the driveway when two more vehicles rolled in. The inn, my inn, was buzzing with excitement.

And for four straight days, I never had a chance to sit down. I was elated. Every time I walked by Teresa, she smiled and winked at me. When I went into the kitchen on Tuesday morning, I hugged Michael and said, "We did it!"

As I entered the lobby, I could hear Teresa on the phone. As usual, she was smiling. When she hung up, she grinned, "Julie, a couple from Philadelphia just booked a three-day weekend every season for the next year, so they can see how the gardens change. Can you believe it?"

"Teresa, you have no idea how much that pleases me. Thank you for sharing that with me. My gardens are a big part of my life.

I'm so glad Kourtnee included garden photos on our website."

I went into Kourtnee's office. "Kourtnee, would you schedule a meeting? I would like to speak to everyone before next weekend."

"Sounds good. I'll inform everyone and schedule it for Thursday at nine a.m. Hey, should I call Frank and ask him to attend?"

"No, thanks."

"Hey, wait a second. Everyone has a backstory." Kourtnee paused, looked down at her desk and for a minute, I thought she would change the subject. "Can I ask, what brought you to Point Judith?"

"I just needed to start over, that's all," I said rather sharply.

"I'm sorry. It's none of my business."

"Kourtnee, I didn't say it wasn't any of your business. It's just as simple as, I needed to do something differently. So, I thought I'd try Point Judith for a while. Not that I wasn't happy where I came from. Believe me, I was. In fact, I never thought I would leave. It was a beautiful small town. I used to think there was no place in the world more appealing."

"Julie, I'm glad you made the move to Rhode Island." "Me, too." I slipped out of her office.

Wednesday morning, I met with Frank. "So, what are your plans now?" I asked.

Frank pursed his lips. "What do ya have in mind?"

I chuckled, "Well, since you're under budget." I raised my eyebrows. "How about you build me a small day spa? Your niece, Bea, my little fashionista, has all my girls getting their nails done every Saturday. And rumor has it the young lady working there would like to run her own spa."

Frank kissed me on the cheek. "I'll apply for the permits. Where?" he asked.

I pointed to the east yard.

That evening, the staff celebrated Frank's completion with a celebratory dinner for his entire crew, including all his friends on the barn raising team.

Thursday morning at nine a.m., I stood in the library before my staff.

"Thank you for coming this morning. I promise I will only call a meeting when I have something important to share. I could not have chosen a better staff. You are all very dear to my heart. I was extremely proud of everyone when you all lent a hand to the other person to ensure that every job was completed.

"When I hired you, I said that you would share in the profits. Well, Frank completed the inn under budget. I have a check for each of you for $2,500. It's my way of saying thank you. Job well done."

The look upon their faces was that of astonishment. Then, the room erupted with loud cheers.

"Well, good. You can all start your very own 401K retirement plans, or hell, celebrate."

Michael spoke up first. "Julie, I don't know what to say. Thank you."

"Michael, the food you prepare is phenomenal. Every dish is delicious. Masterfully prepared. With all my heart, I thank *you*."

I looked around the room. "I need to thank each of you, Teresa, Bea, Kourtnee and Molly, the four of you know exactly what I am thinking before I do. I trust all of you. I trust you with the inn. I know that if I could not be here, the four of you could run this place with no problem. Kevin, I could not have created the outdoor look without you. Your long hours, dedication, and hard work show in every garden, and in all the beautiful landscaping. With that said, I have asked Frank to come back and build us a day spa." "Is Cathy going to run the spa?" Teresa asked. "Of course, she is," I said knowing how much she wanted to become a part of my team, and run her own salon.

Chapter 20

T he following day I went into Kourtnee's office and asked her
to transfer money from the money market to the checking
account. I felt like celebrating. Ever since I moved to Rhode
Island, I had been good at not spending money. I only purchased
exactly what the inn needed. I gave Frank a budget of thirty-
thousand dollars for the day spa. What I really wanted was a
swimming pool, but the spa would make a wonderful amenity for
my guests.

"Kevin, hey, do you have time to take me shopping?"

"Sure." He closed the door to the shed. "Now?"

"If you have the time."

"Let me wash up. I'll meet ya out front in ten."

We got in his truck and headed down the driveway. "Where
to?"

"I want to look at swimming pools."

"A pool?" He almost snapped his neck to look at me.

"I just want to get some prices. I'm thinking of putting one in
next spring."

Kevin and I both loved the idea of a granite pool with a
Jacuzzi built off the side.

"Kevin, what are your ideas for the backdrop and landscaping
around the pool?"

"How about we keep everything as close to nature as we can.
For instance, let's use all-natural material like bluestone for the
patio, and great big rocks surrounded by evergreens."

"I love it already. I can see it now. An oasis out in the middle
of nowhere."

We were on our way back to the inn when Kevin asked me why

I didn't drive.

"I have you. That's why."

"Huh. But you had a car when I met you."

"A rental. I don't like to drive." *When did I become a liar?*

"Hey, what about the pool guy's suggestion for an outdoor kitchen and a fire pit?"

"I'll have to see what the budget looks like. For now, let's just stick with the hope of a pool. Okay, maybe a fire pit."

"This year? Or next year?"

"We can build the fire pit this year."

"How about some outdoor furniture? Never mind, we'll sit on the ground," he said, chuckling.

"Kevin, I think Molly, Kourtnee, Bea and Teresa might like that task. They did such a good job setting up for the cook-off. They can go to Lakeside Trading in Narragansett and buy some nice outdoor furniture."

"You're the boss. Boss Lady," Kevin said as he pulled his truck up to the inn.

I shook my head. "I'm going inside. I have to make a call. Boss Lady? You kill me, Kevin." As I went up the stairs, I was not only thinking about what Kevin called me, I was thinking about my new pool and went upstairs without saying a word to Teresa. Before I picked up the phone, a book caught my attention. I was glad I asked Frank to build me a bookshelf in my room.

"Hello."

"Frank, hello."

"Good morning, young lady. How's my gal?"

"I'm fine, Frank. How are you on this fine day?"

"I'm doing well. Is everything all right?"

"Yes, everything is perfect. Frank, if you have the time, I would like to talk to you about a project I have in mind. Can you be here sometime this week?"

"I can be there tomorrow. Eight o'clock?"

"Sounds wonderful, I'll see you then. Goodbye."

The next morning before heading down to the kitchen, I decided to take a few minutes to read from the novel I had purchased from the local bookstore. Even more than gardening and kayaking, reading had to be my deepest passion. A book could take me places, allow my mind to explore new adventures, and give me something to hold onto.

Michael was already in the kitchen when I went downstairs.

"You're up early, Michael, are you feeling okay?" I asked because no one is ever up before me.

"I feel fine. I just couldn't sleep last night. Julie, I've been thinking. We've been buying all our desserts and pastries, and we're not making any money on them. What if we made our own desserts in-house?"

"Go on... I know that head of yours has yet another great idea. Michael, I am always willing to hear your ideas, you know that, right?"

"I know, and I am thankful for that. Julie, you've allowed me to run this kitchen my way, and I appreciate it. Heck, you even let me pick a few herbs myself."

"Wait a minute; you go out into the herb garden without me?" We both laughed.

Michael poured me a cup of coffee, and for the first time, he sat down next to me. "Julie, the other day I went into the bakery, and there's this new girl working there. Believe it or not, she had free samples on the counter."

"She did not! Where were the owners?"

"I don't know, but they weren't at the bakery. Julie, this girl can bake. I tried all five of her samples. I'm telling you they were all good. She made the best lemon tart, with fresh blueberries, and topped it off with a homemade blackberry yogurt."

"Sounds nice. Go on, tell me more." As I sipped my coffee, I was thinking... *Michael is in love and it has nothing to do with a pastry.*

"Well, I was thinking we could hire her part time. She could do all the baking, and we would make money."

"Michael, if you think she is worth a shot, then so do I. Would you like for me to talk to her?"

"Julie, you won't be disappointed."

"Michael, with you, I am never disappointed. I have to meet with Frank this morning, then I'll go into town and, hey, what's this gal's name?"

"It would be nice if I told you her name, wouldn't it now? Her name is Christine."

When I walked out of the inn, I made a mental note to take some time to finish the book I was reading.

I spent an hour in my kayak. Then, I headed to the herb garden. After I showered, I went back to the kitchen, poured a cup of coffee for Frank and a cup of tea for myself. I was sitting on the side porch for not more than two seconds when I saw him pull in. "Good morning, Frank. I have a cup of coffee for you."

"Good morning. So, I hear you have a new title, Boss Lady."

"Yes, thanks to Kevin, or should I say Kourtnee and the rest of the ladies? They watched a DVD the other day – *Australia,* and in the movie, the little boy called Nicole Kidman 'Boss Lady'. Frank, I would love a swimming pool. Not now. I'm thinking next year. If I can afford it. How much do you think it would cost to build a pool house to go with it?"

"How large of a building will you need?"

"A small sitting room, one bathroom, a men's dressing room and a ladies'."

"That's fine. But what about the chemicals, and the pump? Where are they going to be housed?"

"I guess in the same building, except, can they be two separate spaces?"

"Sure, I think I know how I'm going to design it. You just leave it up to me."

"Thank you, Frank."

"I'll be back tomorrow with a rough sketch. I like you, you have vision."

As Frank walked away from me, I thought about my finances.

For a moment, I had hoped I wasn't falling into the same old bad habit of spending. But I needed to come up with ideas to keep my mind busy. I had to, or my mind would have gotten the best of me.

I sat down under a maple tree, remembering the movie, *Valentine's Day*. Dan and I had watched a while back. After the movie was over Dan said, "Our love is strong enough." He was referring to the scene where the woman, Estelle, confessed to her husband after fifty years of marriage, that she'd had an affair. Her husband told her, "When you love someone, you love all of them. You gotta love everything about them, not just the good things but the bad things too. It's how you find forgiveness."

I was thinking… I could have forgiven Dan, but how was I supposed to forget?

Like many of the inns in Rhode Island, we were booked solid for the summer. For them, it was business as usual. But for me, it was a turning point in my life. It meant I had accomplished something wonderful. I had set out to build a new life for myself, one that would satisfy my need to keep myself busy and support me financially.

On my bookshelf, wedged in between my books I posted a note: "Be Strong Enough." And every time I chose a new book, I reminded myself to be strong enough for whatever came my way. I didn't have to be stronger – just strong enough.

Every morning I checked the daily roster to see where my guests were coming from. It amazed me when I saw that someone had traveled more than ten hours just to stay at my inn. *My inn.* I still loved the name, The Inn in Rhode Island.

I learned so much from the experience. I was proud of myself for sticking to my budget. I was glad I'd hired mostly local people.

I wanted my guests to feel like they were staying with family.

Kourtnee possessed the heart of an eagle. Kevin, on the other hand, carried a gentle soul. When they stood together, they were just beautiful to look at.

Teresa had the voice of an angel. I could have listened to her sing hymns every day for the rest of my life.

Molly became the inn's cheerleader. She had a ton of energy and everyone loved to be around her.

Michael turned into the rock that held us all together, and Bea was becoming more and more like a daughter to me.

On a gorgeous sunny day, Kevin and I planted four-hundred Nikko blue hydrangeas on the west side of the pond. When the sun reached high noon, it was amazing how the water took on the color of blue from the hydrangeas' reflection. I was glad they turned out so beautiful, because with every hole Kevin dug, he asked, "How many more?"

At five o'clock Wednesday morning, I sat in my room watching the sun rise over the rose garden. Cabbage roses were my new favorite. I used to love Vendella roses – creamy white roses that smelled like vanilla, but ever since Dan had confessed his affair, they reminded me of him, our anniversary and my birthday.

I shook it off, smiled and told myself that I had taken an old farmhouse and turned it into one hell of an inn.

I had decided to open the inn for three-hundred and thirty-five days a year because asking the staff to work as hard as they did, meant they deserved a little time off. Therefore, the inn would be open from January 2 to November 30. I priced the rooms according to my competition. The five *ensuites* priced at nine-hundred and forty-seven dollars. The twenty *ensuites* priced at eight-hundred and forty-seven, because guests had to go outside and enter from the porches.

Besides, I needed to be alone during the Christmas holidays. The sun had risen, enticing me to get down to the pond and my awaiting kayak.

I kayaked, picked herbs, showered and was ready for my day. I picked up the tray of flowers from the hallway and brought them to the dining room. I was headed to the lobby to ask Teresa about her plans for Sunday brunch when I overheard her speaking to the other women about our guests.

"Hey, on Labor Day, we have guests checking in from every state on the East Coast. We have a big group from New York that booked the entire main house for the whole weekend. Can you believe it? Julie will be so happy." "What are you all talking about?" I asked as I walked closer, making sure I heard her correctly.

"We were just saying how amazing this place is, that's all, and wait 'til Teresa tells you..." Kourtnee looked at me. "Julie, are you okay?"

"I need to see you in your office."

I followed Kourtnee into her office, shut the door and asked her about the guests from New York. "Did you run the credit card yet?"

"Yes. They're staying for four days."

"Can you please give me the zip code?"

Kourtnee wrote down the zip code and handed the paper to me. My hands started trembling.

"Is everything okay?" she asked.

"Yes, of course. I just need a bite to eat, that's all."

"Wait for me out on the patio, I'll get us a snack." I sat down on the lounge chair, wondering what to do.

Kourtnee set the tray down in front of me. "I got us each a glass of Michael's fresh brewed iced tea. Decaf. Some of Christine's sugar-free Italian cookies from your recipe box. Julie, the guests are all from that same zip code. You know, I am here for you. If you need me to do anything. Just tell me." Kourtnee sounded just like my Lynnae.

I looked at the receipt again. I didn't recognize the name but I didn't want to take the chance. I took a sip of the tea, and swallowed hard. "Kourtnee, I need to go away that weekend."

"Okay. Would you like one of us to go with you?"

"No. Thank you. That's very sweet. I'll only be in town. I just need to take care of a few things."

"I'll tell everyone you're out looking for a new project. Julie, you don't have to say anything if you don't want to. I'll always have your back. I'll take care of things around here."

"Thank you," I said but then wondered if Kourtnee knew more about things than she let on. "Hey, Kourtnee. Julie, I'm sorry to interrupt you," Teresa said. "I just received a call from a woman named Jan Sydrak from the Block Island Fire Department's Ladies' Auxiliary. She'd like to know if you would host a garden tour, and allow them to have their annual meeting in one of our gardens. She thinks our gardens should be on the cover of garden magazines everywhere. Come on, I think it will be fun watching you walking around with one of those pointers. You can say this perennial garden is…"

"Keep it up, Teresa, and you'll be the tour guide," Kourtnee said in a stern voice.

"Yes, Teresa, that's fine. Please tell Jan thank you for asking," I said.

"You know what," Teresa said. "We could do an inn of Rhode Island calendar, with a different garden for each month."

"Good idea," I agreed. We chatted for a few minutes longer and then I went up to my room.

I sat in the chair next to the window, looking out at the rose garden. I was glad I could see the flowers from my room. Oh, God, I miss him so much. I miss our hiking together. Dan stopping along our path just to kiss me. I even miss the way he always had a way of fixing things. Dan knew how to make things better.

Once again, I had to force myself to stop thinking about him. I bowed my head. "Dear Lord, did you fix him yet? Did you open his heart, his eyes? Does he even miss me?"

Chapter 21

For some reason, I was not as eager to go downstairs the next morning. When I looked at the clock on my desk, I realized it was almost nine o'clock. I set the book I was trying to read on the bed, sat up, stretched, and looked out the window. It was a calm morning. The sun was shining, and there was not a cloud in the sky. Although I didn't see anyone, I was sure someone was looking for me. I had to do something. But what? I sat in my chair for a few minutes. I needed to call Frank.

After I hung up with him, I jumped in the shower, and headed down to the driveway. I wanted to talk to him before anyone else had a chance to see me.

I leaned against the trunk of a maple tree and waited patiently for his truck.

Frank stopped the moment he saw me. "Good morning, young lady."

"Good morning, Frank. Thank you for coming today. May I get in?"

Frank put the truck in park. "Here, let me get that door for you."

"I'm fine." I opened the passenger door and climbed in before he had a chance to open his door. "Where are we going?" he asked and put the truck in gear.

"Can you drive the truck on the grass and park down by the pond?"

"I can. Is there a problem?"

"No, not at all. I need to ask you something. Frank, I'm thinking about building a small cottage for myself, in the woods down by the pond. I love the inn, but sometimes I like to be alone for a few hours."

"I hear ya. I like to go out into my workshop and be alone for a while myself. You know, young lady, it seems everything you touch turns to gold."

"Thank you, that is so nice of you to say." *I wished it were true for my marriage.*

"You're welcome, and very deserving. When do you want me get started on this little cottage?"

"Tomorrow?" I jokingly replied.

"For you, tomorrow will be just fine."

"Frank, am I your only client?"

"No." Frank gently touched the side of my face. "You're my favorite client."

I gave Frank a kiss on his cheek. "Thank you so much for making the time for my projects."

Five days later, I went into town and checked back into Sal's bed and breakfast. Except this time, I never left my room. I thought the peace and quiet of being alone for three days would do me some good, but I actually missed the inn and my staff.

I missed Kourtnee's smile. How Molly always made me laugh.

I sat in front of the window, watching the rain come down. I had become friends with my entire staff, especially with my new tea partner, Teresa. Evening time, we would sit and drink a cup of tea out on one of the porches. Sometimes we would take our tea and walk through one of the many gardens. We often spoke about God, music, and about whatever novel the two of us were reading.

When Teresa spoke about God, I could imagine her having a schoolgirl crush on Him. She lit up and her every word became eloquent. I could tell she read her Bible. I was embarrassed to tell Teresa how I used to read my Bible only when I had a problem, or during a situation that I could not handle. The way a person pulls out their spare tire. Only when they really need it.

I got up, opened my luggage and took out my Bible. Sat back down in the chair, closed my eyes and asked for a number. Fortyseven came to mind. I opened my Bible to Psalms 47. I stopped reading when I heard a knock at my door.

"Julie, it's me, Teresa."

Carefully, I opened the door, surprised to see her.

"Teresa, is everything okay?"

"Julie, Sal told me that you were staying here. He said you haven't left your room since you checked in."

"I'm sorry. How did Sal…?"

"Well," Teresa blushed, "he's my new boyfriend. We met at church." She gave me a crimson smile. She paused for a moment. "Julie, please, let me help? I know something's wrong. I can feel it. Why else would you be here? I've prayed about this. I know God has put you on my path for a reason."

"Teresa, I believe that as well; but I assure you I am fine."

Teresa's voice became tight. "Please let me come in." She reached out and touched my arm. "I'll order a pot of tea for us."

That made me smile. I opened the door a little wider. "I'm sorry, please come in." Teresa was such a joy to be around; she literally lit up the room. I closed the door. "I'm afraid we'll need more than a pot of tea for this one. Teresa, I came here this weekend because I didn't want the guests from New York to see me."

"We all figured that." Teresa took a deep breath and slowly exhaled. "You are in the witness protection program…"

"No, I'm not. I…"

"Julie, that's a joke. What are you doing here…"

"I love to be near the ocean."

Teresa was shaking her head. "No, why don't you want them to see you?"

"Teresa, I'm not going to lie to you. The guests are from the area where my husband lives. I didn't want anyone to recognize me." There it was. I let it slip. Opened the box.

Teresa reached out to me with both of her hands. "Was he mean to you? Did he hit you?" I stepped back. "No! My God, no. I would never stand for that. It was just time to give him his freedom. Apparently, he and I have different values when it came to fidelity. After thirty years of trying it my way, I stopped trying."

"I don't understand. His freedom? What do you mean...?"

"Let's sit down."

Teresa called Sal and asked him to send up a pot of hot tea, and then she sat down on the edge of the bed. I pulled the chair closer to where she was sitting.

"Teresa, I thought I was doing everything right. I loved my husband with all my heart. But not even my love was enough for him. He cheated on me, so I left."

"The divorce was hard on you, wasn't it?"

"I wasn't strong enough for a divorce. I never would have made it through the whole process. Honestly, I think he would have fought it. I guess you could say that I loved him enough to give him exactly what he wanted. When I first met him, I thought he was a gift from God. That's why I gave him back to God."

Teresa's voice was trembling. "You still love him, don't you?"

"Please don't cry. Yes, with all my heart. I was married to a man who cheated on me, and there was nothing I could do."

"No wonder you left him. Good for you. I'll bet you were a wonderful wife." Teresa let out a sigh. "Julie, I'm very proud of you for finding the courage to leave."

For a moment I could not speak. My heart ached. "Believe me, I don't feel very good about what I did. I was so upset the day I left, I almost didn't go. I had plans for the two of us. I just didn't plan on all those other women. He didn't care enough about me to stop. I had to let him go. My spirit was gone. My mind would not let it go.

I was killing everything good about us."

At that moment, I felt numb. Too numb to continue. Thankfully, our tea had arrived.

"Julie, you don't have to tell me, but how many other women were there?"

"If you don't mind, can we talk about this some other time, please?"

We drank our tea and spoke for several hours that afternoon. I promised Teresa that I would open up and explain everything to her someday. I was already feeling very sad about being away from everyone and the inn. We talked about Kevin and Kourtnee, how they made a great couple. It was nice to see a couple who actually wanted to work together every day.

"You know Michael and Christine are dating, right?" "I know they are," I said.

"I hope Michael and Christine find the same happiness, love, admiration, and respect that Kevin and Kourtnee have for each other."

"I do too, Teresa. Tell me about Sal."

"He's great. We're taking it slow. I've known him for a few months, but we just started seeing each other. He goes out on his damn boat every day. He knows I work for you but that's all he knows."

"God's little creatures may have St. Frances to watch over them, but I'm glad I have you watching out for me." For a moment, I was lost in thought, gazing out the window. "Teresa, Kourtnee knows nothing about my past. I only asked her to take care of the inn. You are the only person who knows I am married." "Your secret is safe with me." She smiled. "I've got your back. Speaking of back, I have to get back. I asked Bea to cover the phones for me."

"Thank you for coming and checking up on me. Mostly, thank you for being a good friend." I hugged her goodbye. "I promise you, we'll talk again."

After Teresa left, I was thankful for the visit, but at the same time, I was scared to death knowing... I had just opened Pandora's Box. My backstory was no longer a secret. I sat down in the chair next to the window – drifting in and out of sleep.

Tuesday morning, it was raining but I didn't care. I wanted to go home.

I paid the taxi driver, and headed straight for the herb garden. I stood there for a moment, allowing the scent of every herb to welcome me home. I was soaking wet when I went inside.

"Hey, stranger, we missed you. What were you doing standing out there in the rain? It's September, not July, woman. What are you trying to do, get sick?"

"Oh, Michael. I missed you all more than you will ever know. Is my list ready?"

"On the counter."

"Thank you. I'll be back in an hour."

As I was leaving the kitchen, Kevin approached. "Hey, you," I said and quickly headed up to my room. I stood in the shower for a long time. By the time I'd dried off, the rain had stopped. After breakfast, I was going on a tour of my gardens.

Often, I would pretend I was a guest staying at the inn. I would take my time and look at every detail as if I were paying for the pleasure. It seemed like the gardens all knew of my arrival. Every garden was in perfect form and in grand style. There's a bench by the reflecting pond on the way to the bigger pond that always seemed to be occupied by someone.

It pleased me to know that my guests took the time to enjoy all the work Kevin and I had put into the grounds and the gardens. Whenever I saw someone strolling along, I was reminded of just how special the place was.

When I went back, Teresa and Kourtnee were both assisting Bea with serving lunch. "Need any help?" I asked.

"I think we have everything under control. Did you eat yet?" Kourtnee asked.

"No, I just got back from taking a hike around the property. But if Teresa stays out here and helps you, then maybe I will go and get a bite to eat."

"I'm okay. I have my phone on my hip." Teresa pointed to her right hip, then gave me a nod. "Go eat."

I hadn't even swung open the door or stepped inside the kitchen when I heard, "There you are. Sit down, I made you something special for lunch." Michael pulled out a chair for me. "Hey, I need to talk to you about something."

"We have no more rooms on the third floor, so if you want to hire anyone else, Christine is going to have to move into your room." He raised his eyebrows. "Here, try this." Then he sat down next to me. "Listen, you know I think the world of you. I know you like your privacy, but you're not sick or anything…"

"No, I'm not sick. Why would you ask me that?"

Michael touched my arm. "How about your Lyme disease? Or your diabetes? Are either of them bothering you?"

I sat the fork down, "Michael, I assure, I am not sick. I feel fine."

"Okay, I'm just going to come out with it. Julie, you're a wonderful, loving and giving woman. Wouldn't you like to share all this with someone?"

I knew the questions would come. I never expected them to come from one of the men. "Michael, I have all of you. Now please." When Michael put his arms around me, I held back my tears.

"Hey. Hi, is everybody okay?" I was so happy to hear Christine's voice. "Julie, I made you a special dessert. A sugar free peach tart."

"I'm content," I whispered into Michael's ear. "Thank you, Christine. I'm going to take it with me, so I can leave you two lovebirds alone."

I took my peach tart and went out to the backyard. "Is that for me?" Kevin asked me. I nodded and handed it to him.

"Hey, I heard Frank is almost finished with the cottage. Want to take a look with me?" he asked.

"I would love to. My goodness, he's so quick."

"He should be. There were about twenty people down there this week."

"It's called a barn raising." I looked back at him. "Seriously, I looked it up."

When we got down there, everyone had left for the day. Kevin was correct. The cottage was 90% complete. It consisted of four rooms: a large bedroom with an adjacent bathroom built for a queen, a small gourmet kitchen, an oversized living area with fireplace, custom bookcases, and under every window, a seat complete with its own storage compartment. Out on the front porch, there were two rocking chairs and a small café table for two. I was not expecting many guests at the cottage.

Molly chose French-country fabrics with warm shades of cream, green, and beige. Kourtnee purchased four crystal vases, placing one in each room. I promised her I would keep them full of flowers from my new garden. Teresa framed some of my favorite scriptures, like Matthew 19:26. My cottage was perfect.

Chapter 22

On a gorgeous Rhode Island day, Kevin and I started planting the perennials in my new garden all around the cottage. "This garden will serve as my very own cutting garden."

"Like you don't cut from the other gardens?"

"Kevin, those flowers are for the guests. These flowers are for my pleasure only."

"All right, and what type of flowers give you pleasure?"

I looked at him. "Getting personal are we?"

"Hey, I'm just the guy who digs the holes, and yeah I'm a little curious to know if there's something else that gives you pleasure, besides the inn."

"I do love the inn. Mostly, I love Rhode Island. Being surrounded by wonderful people and gorgeous flowers, well, that doesn't hurt either."

While Kevin finished planting the last flower, I took one more look at my new lodging.

"Good night, Boss Lady."

I turned back around. "Good night, Kevin. Kevin, thank you." A few minutes later, I traipsed up to the inn. I was rubbing my neck the entire way. "Kansas, maybe I should have taken my butt to Kansas." I was glad I built the cottage. I certainly couldn't keep hiding in town.

I looked up and saw Teresa sitting on the front porch. On the side table next to her, she had a pot of tea and two cups. "Well, if you aren't the best thing I've laid my eyes on all day. How did you know I was ready for a cup of tea?"

"I saw you coming up the path from the cottage and rubbing your neck. Thought you could use a cup of relaxation."

My back was screaming out for a hot bath. Every muscle in my body ached. "Teresa, you are the best. I have to say, keeping up with

Kevin is not an easy task some days."

"You do love your gardens, don't you?"

"Teresa, it's my fire."

"Your fire?"

"Yes. Everyone needs to find that one thing in life that brings out his or her passion. I bet far too many people die with a heart that has gone flat and full of indifferences. Life will offer us amazing opportunities; we just have to recognize them. You'll know when it happens. Just don't ignore the signs. Open your mind and explore them. Hell, fan your flame."

I was so thirsty; I drank almost the entire pot of tea. "Teresa, I'm tired. If I don't go upstairs right now, I'll never make it up those steps. Good night, sunshine. I'll see you in the morning."

"Good night, Julie."

After working in the garden for so many hours, I was more than ready for a long hot bath. First, I submerged my whole body in the water. As I lay there, with every breath I took, I could feel my muscles ping and pang. Finally, I was able to stay in one position for a while. Solitude was something I favored. Most people seem to be afraid to be alone. I was getting good at weighing the odds: suspecting my husband of having an affair *or* spending the rest of my life alone.

After my bath, I immediately went to bed. Once again, I thanked God for the pillow pressed up against my back. It did not take long for me to fall asleep.

The next morning, I woke up and forgot all about my aching muscles. It was a colorful October day and I had the perfect plan. After my daily ritual of kayaking and herb picking, I was going to find my book and head to the library, toss a log on the fire, sit down and read.

Eight a.m. I lit the fire, opened my book.

"Good morning, Julie, can Christine and I have a word with you?"

"Absolutely, Michael, come on in."

"Julie, I've asked Christine to marry me and she said yes." I jumped up and hugged him. Kissed Christine on the cheek.

"Congratulations!"

"Thank you," Christine said.

"Julie, we would like to know if we could have our wedding here at the inn."

"Oh, Michael, I would be honored if you got married here. Do you know how many guests you will be inviting? When? My goodness, when?"

"The first weekend in May. We would both like to keep it just family and close friends. So we're thinking around a hundred people."

"Sounds great. Give the date to Teresa and I will block the inn off for that entire weekend. Your guests can stay with us. It will be my treat. We'll make it a weekend wedding no one will ever forget."

"Julie, you're incredible. That is above and beyond…"

"You're welcome. Now go before you make me cry."

I went into Kourtnee's office and informed her of the news. "I'm going to let Molly know right now."

As I approached the lobby, I overheard Teresa calling out to Molly.

"Molly. Molly, come here. I just booked a room for Hugh Jackman. Okay, he looks just like the actor. His name's Chad Claremont, but I'm telling you, this guy is to die for."

"Great. Now he comes along," I heard Molly say. "I just starting dating Brad and oh, my… goodness. You are right about one thing,

he *is* to die for. Has Julie seen him yet?"

"No, he's just checking in."

I stood in the hallway and listened. I heard a man's voice.

"How late is the dining room open?"

Both Teresa and Molly said in perfect unison, "Nine." He probably heard them both say, "Ahh," because I did.

Sounding excited, Molly asked, "What room did you give him?"

"Are you kidding me?" Teresa replied jokingly. "I told him to go to the third floor last room on the right, my room." I heard them both laugh.

"You should have sent him to my room," Molly teased.

"I gave him the Jamestown suite, directly under Julie's room. Maybe he'll send some of his passion up to her and she'll fall in love again," Teresa said.

"What do you mean again?" I heard Molly say. "Do you know something I don't?"

Teresa told Molly to get to work. After Molly left, I let Teresa know about blocking the rooms off the weekend of Michael and Christine's wedding.

The next morning, I was in the garden on my knees, picking the last of the basil, parsley and rosemary when I noticed a strange man meandering along the path. He was talking to himself. "She said the smell of fresh herbs would awaken my senses. I must be getting close."

It was still early morning, and from where he was standing, the scent of dew-kissed lavender was strong. When I stood up, I realized he had not seen me.

"Good morning. My name is Julie, and your name is?" Even though I had already heard all about him.

"Chad Claremont. The receptionist said I would find you out here."

"Well, Mr. Claremont, it's nice to meet you. Are you enjoying your stay?"

"Very much – so much that I was wondering if I could talk to you for a moment about my staying a little longer than usual."

"Certainly. Can you give me a few minutes? I need to bring these herbs to the kitchen. We could talk in private over there on the resting bench." My hands were full, so I hitched my chin toward the bench.

He pointed to the area and said, "I'll wait for you over there."

"May I bring you a cup of coffee or something else to drink this morning?"

"No, thank you."

I could not imagine how long he intended on staying; however, any time spent at my inn was all right by me. I had not seen anyone that handsome in a very long time. He appeared to be about six-three, dark brown hair, with the dreamiest dark brown eyes, and he was in great shape.

"Here are your herbs, Michael." Michael gave me an unusually big smile. You know, the smile only a cat wears when he is caught eating a canary. "Are you smiling for any particular reason?"

Michael shook his head, giving me a child-like pout. "No, no, not at all."

Men. They are always up to something. I headed back to the garden to see this Mr. Claremont.

I stood between the chamomile and the sage, looking at him for a moment before I asked him, "Mr. Claremont, how long are you intending on staying with us?"

"I need to stay for a few months. I'm a private pilot and I have to be in the area for a while. I was thinking you must have higher rates during your busy season. I'm prepared to pay you your highest rate for the whole time, if necessary."

"It sounds as if you would be better off renting a house or an apartment, wouldn't you? Besides, we close the month of December and the staff–"

"I know," he said interrupting me. "Your receptionist explained that to me. I looked into apartments, but there's not much available.

I promise I'll be out of your hair as soon as my assignment is up. I saw a few of the motels in town, along with the local bed and breakfast. Nothing compares to your inn. The staff made me feel welcome the minute I arrived, and my room is incredible. Plus, I've been told you have an excellent chef."

"You drive a hard bargain. I'll have to speak to Teresa to see if we can accommodate you the entire time. Is it okay with you if I get back to you by the end of the week?"

"That would be great."

During the next several mornings, I noticed Mr. Claremont regularly out on the side porch, eating his breakfast.

I could not stop thinking. Wouldn't it be cheaper to rent a small house in town? How much money did he have to burn? I knew my inn was worth every penny, but that man wished to take up permanent occupancy. I went to see Teresa about the rooms. "Teresa do you really think it's possible to accommodate Mr. Claremont?"

"Oh, Chad? Very handsome, isn't he, Julie?"

"Chad? Very friendly…"

"Julie, he insists we call him by his first name."

"It's fine, Teresa. I'm just saying, maybe you fancy the guy." "No, everyone can see he has eyes for you. Haven't you noticed the way he sits out on the side porch and watches you every morning when you come back from kayaking?"

"Really, Teresa? I didn't notice. Just how long has he been watching me?"

"A few days now. He just seems to smile more when you appear, that's all. Maybe he's a gift from God."

"Teresa, enough. Let's find out if we can accommodate the man. Check the schedule for the upcoming season, so I can get back to him by tomorrow, please."

I decided to do a search for Chad Claremont – pilot. I discovered that he was born in South Carolina, and that he graduated from a nearby flight school. He appeared to be legitimate. I decided to keep a close eye on ol' Mr. Claremont. Closer than the eye he seemed to be keeping on me.

When I went downstairs, I saw Kourtnee and Bea setting up the dining room. I stood close to Kourtnee and whispered, "What do you think about our guest, Chad Claremont?"

"He's nice. Extremely handsome. I know he's a pilot and apparently he is working on assignment for some big shot. Why?"

"Just checking, that's all."

She tugged on my arm. "Julie, trust me, when I saw him checking you out, I immediately went online and did a Google search. I assure you, he's just a pilot. Oh, and he's extremely wealthy."

I laughed. "You're something else. I just went online and checked him out, too. Okay, I guess I'll go and see what Teresa has to say."

As I left the dining room, I thought how easy Google made our lives. Before I could say a word, Teresa was waving at me with something in her hand.

"Julie, I have the schedule for the next year. We can accommodate Chad, if we can move him from room to room. I don't think he'll mind, except Molly says he has a lot of maps all over his room."

"Thanks, Teresa. I'll speak to him this evening. I'll tell him it will be his responsibility to roll his own maps up."

The dining room was full to capacity. I looked for Chad, but he was nowhere to be found. Perhaps he had already eaten. Then I noticed him out on the side porch. He was sipping an after dinner drink. "Good evening. May I call you Chad?"

He stood up. "Of course." Then he pulled a chair out for me.

"May I buy you a drink?"

"No, thank you. I don't drink." I sat down across from him. "Chad, we can meet your request; however, we will have to move you from time to time."

"That's no problem. I'm just delighted that I get to stay. Julie, thank you. You don't know what this means to…me."

"You're welcome. See Teresa in the morning and she'll give you your room schedule. I just hope we can live up to your expectations."

Chapter 23

A fter a few weeks passed, Chad had become extremely close to both Kevin and Michael. The three of them began hanging out, playing billiards and cards. It almost seemed as though he was a part of the gang.

"Good morning, Julie, have you seen Kevin?"

"Good morning, Kourtnee. I did. He left with Chad about five minutes ago."

"That's nice. I wanted him to take me into town this morning." "I'll go with you. I need a few items myself." We got into Kourtnee's car.

"Thanks for going with me. I only have to pick up a few things.

Hey, did you hear Christine is done with the wedding plans?" "I did," I said, buckling my seatbelt.

"Julie, I always thought we would have your wedding here."

"*My* wedding? Don't I need a man first?"

"What about Chad? He's great looking, has a career, and..." "And, what Kourtnee?" I interrupted.

"It's just that Kevin says he likes you. A lot. Please don't tell Kevin I told you. Kevin thinks I am being over protective of you, and that Chad should be allowed to make his moves without any of us interfering." I could feel her eyes on me. "He reminds us of that actor..."

"I know," I said. "Come on, Kourtnee, I'm not dead."

"You should have watched that movie with us." "What movie?"

"Australia," she said.

"Kourtnee, seriously, what is going on?" I demanded.

"Apparently, ever since the first day he saw you in the garden, you are all he thinks about."

"Kourtnee, I'm sorry to disappoint everyone, but I'm not looking, nor am I ready to start a relationship with anyone right now. Besides, if I were, he would be a mature Randolph Scott type."

"Randolph Scott? Who's that?"

"He is my favorite cowboy actor."

For the next several weeks, I changed my morning routine enough not run into Chad. There was no way I was going to allow him to get to me. It was terrible, but my heart was empty; my mind – forever tainted. I could not see myself trusting anyone.

"Julie, I need to talk to you," Teresa said. "We have to move Chad to another room, and that's not the worst of it. In four days, we will have to move him again. Julie, I feel bad. Can you tell him for me? These people booked their rooms months in advance."

"I'll figure something out, Teresa. I'll talk to him for you, don't worry." I thought about the money he was spending. I gave him a discount but still…

It was the end of October but for some reason Chad still liked to sit on the side porch. Someone should have told him the scenery was much nicer out on the back terrace.

"Chad, I'm sorry to bother you. Mostly, I'm sorry because we have to ask you to move to another room."

"I don't mind."

I thought for a moment, "Chad, perhaps you might be more comfortable in my cottage."

"Your cottage?"

"Yes, I have my own private quarters. Would you like to see it? I could show it to you now if you have time." He stood up and I explained, "You would still be able to enjoy all the privileges the inn has to offer, and the cottage has ample room, especially for your maps. It's about a ten-minute walk. Shall we?" When we reached the front porch, I opened the door and told him to go in.

"This is incredible. It even has a view of a pond. I would love to rent this for the rest of my stay." Chad bent down and kissed my cheek. "You're the best."

I was frozen. No smiling. No reaction. I just stood there. I didn't know what to say.

"I should never have done that. Julie..." His face was the color of a ripened red apple.

"Does that mean you'll take it?"

"Yes."

"Good. You can see Teresa and she will give you a key. If you have anything heavy to move, I'm sure Kevin will be glad to help you."

"Julie, I've walked through every garden on this property, but I never noticed this cottage. I wonder how I missed it."

"Don't worry, we'll put it on the map for you, so you don't get lost coming back from dinner one evening." Still trying to break the uncomfortable moment, I asked him, "Chad, how long have you had your pilot's license?"

"For thirty-two years, but it seems like yesterday. I inherited the business from my father and flying came with it."

"That's interesting. How often do you fly?" I asked because he never seemed to leave.

"Whenever my clients call me." He flashed a quick smile before adding, "Right now, I'm working for the governor."

"Chad, you do realize the staff leaves next month for the Christmas holidays?"

"I'm aware. Julie, I really am sorry about what just happened." "Please, I've already forgotten about it." I was numb inside. My heart was hollow. His kiss, good looks, even his mannerism had no effect on me. I wished it did.

The day before Thanksgiving, I stopped in the kitchen to see if

Michael had my list of recipes. "Good morning."

"Morning," Christine said as she entered the pantry, carrying several bags of groceries.

"Christine insisted on stocking the kitchen for you." Michael said, while shaking his index finger at me. "Make sure you eat. One more thing, I was thinking since Chad will be here on Christmas, maybe you should ask him to join you for dinner. So you're not alone."

"Michael, I think that would be a very nice gesture, except I'm sure Chad has plans to be with his family."

"No. I know for a fact that he'll be here for Christmas."

"Really? How do you know this?"

"Chad asked me about your plans for the holiday and I told him that you will be here alone."

"Michael!"

"Julie, come on. What are you afraid of?"

"I'm not afraid of anything. What I am is just fine at being alone for the holidays." I spoke more sharply than I meant to. "Michael, I'm sorry. I didn't mean to snap."

"Julie, please." His voice grew softer, "I know you like your solitude, what do you want me to do? You're both living here, and you'll both be here on Christmas Day." He cocked his head to one side before adding, "What should I tell the guy?"

"Michael, you're right. I'm sorry."

Michael kissed me on the cheek. "We love you. That's all I'm saying." Then he carried the rest of the food into the pantry for Christine.

I could not figure out what Chad saw in me. I wondered if maybe God did have His hand in it. For so long, I had been denied affection. I didn't know if I could trust myself to know it when it did come along.

In a few days, everyone would be gone. The gardens would lie dormant, and I would have no one to turn to. I was worried about the next few weeks alone with…"

"Hey, Julie, did you say something?

"Teresa, I…no, I don't think so." I shook my head.

Friday, I said goodbye to everyone. A few days had passed and I was grateful for the company of a good novel. The only time I slipped out of my room was to get a bite to eat and make a fresh pot of tea. I never saw Chad. At one point, I thought maybe he *was* traveling.

Christmas morning, I started writing in a new journal. "Page one. Someone once said, 'Find out what you love to do, and then figure out how to get paid for doing it.' I smiled. "I have done just that. I love running the inn. I wish we were doing it together. I miss you, Dan. More than you will ever know. Hugs and kisses, Julie." I closed the leather book wondering about Dan, Lady, Lynnae...

I decided to shake it off and treat myself to a stack of whole grain pancakes covered in blueberries and clotted cream. After breakfast, I headed straight to the library with a cup of coffee and my old standby – *The Christmas Box*. When I entered the room, I could not believe my eyes. There was a small Christmas tree next to the fireplace. Someone had lit a fire and placed a vase of white roses on the table next to my favorite chair. I opened the small envelope, and a warm yet nervous feeling came over me.

The note inside read, "Merry Christmas, Santa."

I stood there not knowing what to do, or how to react. Ten minutes later, I set the book down, took my coffee and went back into the kitchen. I gathered the remaining pancakes, made two eggs over easy, collected the pot of coffee, some orange juice, and headed out the door.

I had to keep reminding myself he was just a guest. He was just someone staying at my inn.

As soon as I stepped onto the front porch, I could smell cinnamon and cloves. I took a deep breath, and then knocked on the door. "Good morning, I made enough pancakes for an army, would you like some?"

Chad smiled at me, and my damn heart started pounding.

"Good morning, beautiful. Merry Christmas." His voice was soft and tender.

"Merry Christmas. I made you a couple of eggs, along with some milk, and orange juice as well." I held up the bag. I was rambling like a fool.

"Thank you, would you like to come inside or do you intend on standing out in the cold?" "Sorry, I can't stay. I have a date with Richard Paul Evans. Please enjoy your breakfast, and Chad, I mean Santa, thank you. Thank you for lighting my fire and for the beautiful Vendella roses." "Vendella?"

"Yes. Large creamy white roses. Thank you. That was very sweet of you."

"You're welcome. A beautiful woman like you deserves to be showered with roses."

"Do I smell cinnamon and cloves?"

The scent was even stronger with the door wide open.

"Yes, I tossed a bag of your scented pinecones into the fireplace this morning."

"Merry Christmas," I replied, remembering I'd left bags of them in the firebox.

As I walked away, I could feel his eyes on me.

When I reached the front porch of the inn, I felt a breeze go through me. It stopped me cold. I paused for a moment and wondered about the roses. Of all the colors. He had to buy white. Red was for love. White meant friendship. How was he to know they used to be my favorite?

By January 2nd, everyone had returned to the inn after spending time with their families. I was so glad they all came back. I couldn't wait to hear their voices, their stories and see their smiling faces. My first stop – the kitchen. "Good morning, Michael, where's Christine…"

"Morning, Julie. Christine will be right back. She went to see Kevin and Kourtnee and ask about their ski vacation."

"I was still up when they got home last night. They had such a great time," I said.

"Good to hear. So, Julie, how was your time alone?"

"Time alone? Michael. What time alone? Chad was a few hundred feet away. In fact, I don't think he ever left the cottage. Teresa came back the day after Christmas, and Molly returned a day after her. Peaceful. Very interesting, yet peaceful. How was your visit with Christine's family?"

"Nice. Come on, did he come up and spend any time with you?" "Michael, you are worse than an old gossip. Chad is our guest. I treat everyone with the same respect." I smiled at him. "I'll have you know, I left the front door open the entire time."

"Julie, yeah, yeah, yeah, did he…come and spend time with you?"

"Yes, and for your information, I even brought him down a tray of pancakes on Christmas morning."

"Now you're talking. Come on, what else?"

"Nothing, really. I am very busy when you leave. I have upcoming events, Teresa's calendar to go over. Never mind prior to your return, I had your new menu to look at. Anyway, Chad is gone for a few days. So you'll have to wait until this weekend to hear his side of the story."

Michael stood there staring at me, shaking his head. "Julie, you know that wall you have up? It needs to come down."

"I love you, too, Michael. Most of all I love your new soup recipes. Now if you don't mind, I'm going for a long jog."

On my way back up to the inn, I went past the cottage. I could live in that cottage for the rest of my life, and it wouldn't bother me one bit if I never had a visitor. When I reached the inn, reality set in. There were a dozen empty picnic baskets on the front porch. Christine ordered the baskets for the garden tour to be held on April 29th.

Kourtnee prepared and printed a bunch of maps of the entire property. Christine planned to make a few hundred-cucumber sandwiches to go along with Teresa's homemade lemonade. Both Bea and Molly volunteered to be tour guides.

Chapter 24

W e were all in the kitchen when Kevin kissed Kourtnee on the cheek and said, "Now?" with a bit of a thrill.

I saw Kourtnee reach behind Kevin's back. She held up an infant's onesie that read: Baby Elliott due in June. Everyone was excited for them. The inn was about to hear the sound of tiny little feet.

Valentine's Day, Molly ordered from the local florist and created an enormous floral display of black magic roses and magnolia leaves in the lobby. On the tables in the dining rooms, she had small square vases filled with red ranunculus, dark red dahlias, chocolate cosmos and red hypericum. Each room was eloquent and romantic. Michael served shrimp and white bean soup, salad with brie en croûte, poached pears in port wine and seared sesame tuna with pear-mango salsa.

On St. Patrick's Day, Christine took orders for additional soda bread and Michael's green beer was a huge success. Easter Sunday, the dining room, porches, patios and the back terrace were overflowing with guests.

Before I knew it, it was the end of April. My high season was about to kick in. I made myself a salad topped with some leftover grilled chicken from the night before, sat out on the terrace and welcomed the warmth of the spring sun on my face.

"Great minds think alike," Kourtnee said, pulling up a chair and setting her own salad plate down on the table. "Did Teresa tell you, we're booked solid for Mother's Day. Good thing you moved Chad to the cottage."

I looked away for moment. "Has he said anything about how long his assignment is going to last?"

"Not to me. I know he's away this week. Want me to ask him, when he gets back?"

"No." I looked down at my salad. Moved a piece of arugula with my fork.

"You know he sets his alarm clock for five every morning just to watch you out on the pond," Kourtnee said, before she took her first bite.

"It's just coincidence, that's all," I said. Eight months he's been here. My God, I could install a new swimming pool with the money he's spent.

"Julie, you said yourself, he's a tall drink of water."

"What's a tall drink of water?" Teresa asked, as she and Molly came out to join us, holding Reuben sandwiches.

"I'm sure I'll regret telling you all this." I shook my head, giving Teresa a half smile. "A tall drink of water is something you drink fast and furious when you're hot and thirsty; or savor real slowly when you have the time, and don't want it to end."

"Oooh, I like that," Teresa said, as she glanced over at Kourtnee.

Molly whispered in my ear, "Who knew you had a wild side..."

I ignored her. "Kourtnee, have the pamphlets arrived yet? Miss beautiful drink of water herself."

"Yes, and they include a tour of the pond."

"I thought we were going to keep people away from the pond." But I knew why Kevin wanted to include the pond area.

"I know, but Kevin said the pond is his shinning gem, now that he planted all those blue hydrangeas."

"They are beautiful," I agreed. "I have to run into town. Michael asked me to buy a few things. Anyone care to..."

"I'll drive you," Teresa said, taking hold of her pickle. "Catch you guys later."

"Tell me about Sal," I said, as she started the car. "You haven't mentioned him in a few days."

"He wants me to move in with him, Julie, but I don't want to leave the inn. I'm not giving up my job. I like what I do."

"Teresa? Sal *owns* an inn. You could…"

"I know. I guess, I'm just not ready to settle down. Did you feel that way, when you first met your husband?"

"No, I knew I wanted to be with him from day one. I remember the day I met him. At a friend's wedding. He was the most handsome man I had ever laid my eyes on. He literally astounded me. Dan wasn't like the other men at the wedding. I knew from the first moment I saw him that he was different, and when I got to know him, I knew my instincts were right. He's smarter than he gives himself credit for. He's great at everything. When Dan put his mind to something, nothing and no one can stop him. He has guts. He's full of ambition and I admire that in a man."

"See, I don't feel that way about Sal. I like him, but he just doesn't shake me like that. Julie, you must have loved him to stay for as long as you did."

"I probably stayed for so long because I was able to see the good over the bad. I saw him for the person he was. I really did believe in him. I thought he was my soulmate. I actually thought Dan was a gift from God. Every morning, before my feet hit the floor, I thanked God for shining down upon me. For thirty years, I had so much love in my heart for my husband. I just knew that a love like that could only come from God. I was just a small-town girl. My dreams weren't very big. I wanted to get married, raise a family, live in a beautiful home and live happily ever after."

"Julie, you're the strongest, most successful woman I know. You're a good woman with a heart of gold. God will give you healing and victory to get through your situation. Keep holding onto your faith and you will be amazed at how God will bless your life."

"Teresa, He already has."

"How old were you when you met Dan?"

"It was four months before my nineteenth birthday. Going to school, playing field hockey and working full-time didn't leave me much time to go out on many dates. Let's face it, I lacked experience in the dating world."

"Whoever he is, he's a fool to let someone like you go." She touched my hand. "Obviously, you still love him. I can hear it in your voice. When did you know he was the one?"

"The night he called me and sang Bob Dylan's 'Lay Lady Lay' to me over the phone. He promised to make all my dreams come true. Apparently he and I dream differently because never did I ever dream about all those other women."

"Do I dare ask how many?"

"Truthfully, Teresa, I don't know. From time to time, I would get a nudge. When I suspected him of having an affair with a woman he had worked for, I developed panic attacks. Those attacks brought me to a level so low, I not only lost control of everything around me, I lost my self-esteem, my ability to trust, and my faith. When your faith is gone, all hope is gone."

Teresa wiped her nose with the back of her hand.

"I was married to a man I adored and loved with all my heart. I was devoted to him. I worshiped my husband – a man who had affairs, I am sure, even though he only ever admitted to one. My instincts were probably true."

"Julie, I can't imagine you would let any man cheat on you, even once. If you suspected him so many times, why did you stay?" "I loved him so much I actually blamed the women. Thinking how dare they tease my husband? Then one day, Dan told me the truth. I no longer looked at him the same. From that moment on, I stopped blaming the women."

"Good for you. Sorry, but, I have to pee," Teresa said stopping the car in from of George's of Galilee. "Want to come in? I'll buy you a shot of honey whiskey."

"No. I'll wait for you in the car. Let's go to Empire Tea and Coffee in Newport. I'll buy."

Teresa came out of George's. "They're so friendly in there." "They have great reviews," I said.

"Julie, can I ask you a question?" she asked as we headed to Newport. "What is this life book you keep talking about?" "It's not a book you can see or touch. It's held within your heart. Guarded by your soul. You and I have shared a wonderful chapter. I still remember the day I heard you in the drugstore. That day, I felt a flutter of a page turn. Now, I thank God you are in my life. Your name will always be in my book."

"I'm happy God wrote my name in your life book. You're very special to me." Teresa added, "I'm so glad you came here. Where in New York did you live?"

"We lived in a small town. An hour and a half north of New York City and an hour south of Albany."

"Julie, I used to babysit for a woman who cheated on her husband, constantly. They had a house on Block Island, and an apartment in Boston. It would break my heart to see him. He was so good to his wife. He gave her whatever she wanted. Told her every day that he loved her. It didn't mean a damn thing to her. The cook told me that she was sleeping with their driver. When her husband started drinking, I stopped working for them, and went to work for myself. Julie, I think people like that are sick. I'm serious. They must have a sickness. Some people are just wired wrong."

"Teresa, if a man goes to see another woman instead of coming home to his wife, and he has to lie about where he was, he doesn't have the best of intentions, does he?"

"No, Julie, he doesn't. You're trembling."

"Whenever I think about him with another woman, this is how
I get."

"Did you ever confront him?" "Every time. He would just look at me and tell me I was crazy. He swore to me. Looked me right in the eye and told me that he was not having an affair."

"Bastard!"

"It wasn't totally his fault. I should have talked to him more about my suspicions, feelings but I didn't. I closed the conversation out of fear. Oh, Teresa, every one of them was from the same pond. Except the last one. She was from the bottom of the barrel.

Seriously. When I saw her, I asked myself, 'how bad is my marriage that he has to turn to her?' She was so bad, so hard on the eyes, no one believed me. Not even my best friend. I *had* to leave. He gave me no other choice."

"You had every right to leave him for cheating on you." "I didn't leave because of his cheating. I left, because it was time to set him free. And myself from my prison of sadness and self-doubt."

"That's so sad, knowing how much you love him. Did you guys try counseling?"

"I talked to a marriage counselor once. The damn fool actually told me, 'You're an American woman, you take adultery much too seriously. When a man dies in Europe, his wife stands next to his mistress at his funeral.'"

Teresa's hand went to her mouth. "Oh, no. What did you say to...?"

"I didn't say a word. I got up and left. Listen, like the arborist who takes down trees for a living; after thirty years, you become an expert. The tree expert knows the good tree from the bad. A tree can tell you when a storm is coming. Even a tree will give you the right signs. All you have to do is recognize them. After thirty years, I became an expert. I learned to read Dan very well. I learned to read the signs." I took a deep breath. "A forest has to burn in order to stimulate new growth. Trust me, I got burned."

We enjoyed our tea, along with two sconces, fresh strawberries and clotted cream, before returning to the inn.

Chapter 25

The inn had been open for an entire year. Thankfully, I had managed to keep myself busy, and my mind occupied.

The next morning, I was up at dawn. I went down the stairs and noticed Kevin standing in the lobby.

"Good morning, Julie. Are you ready for your big day?"

"I hope I am. I heard you included the pond area as part of today's tour."

"Why not include the garden at the pond? It's unique, and it does remind me of an oasis. I think people should see what we've created." He walked closer to me. "Julie, he's a really great guy. Listen, Mike and I would never let anyone hurt you."

At that moment, Kourtnee came out of the office. "Never mind them, I would kill to protect you."

Kevin gave Kourtnee a kiss and placed his arm around her, just as she banged her hip into his. "Good morning, handsome. Julie,

Kevin's right. Chad's a nice guy, and he cares about you. We all think you should give him a chance."

"What am I going to do with the two of you? Trust me; no one is going to hurt me. So I don't need any protection. Right now, I need to get through this little garden tour. So, if the two of you don't mind, I…"

Kevin patted me on the shoulder, and took Kourtnee by the hand and went out the front door.

I followed them out to the front porch and of course, I saw Chad coming up the path from the cottage. I went over to the side porch, sat down and said a quick prayer. I asked the Lord for guidance and ended my prayer with, *I know they all mean well.* I hoped they didn't think I was a miserable crank.

Before I opened my eyes, I felt someone sit down next to me. Chad had his hand on my knee, whispering in my ear, "Good morning, beautiful." Then he got up and walked away. I do believe my ear was wet. Hot wet.

Michael and Christine had prepared an early morning feast for our visitors. We served coffee, herbal teas, homemade muffins and pastries, along with every kind of Danish you could imagine.

I pointed out to one of the groups that all along the entire porch, we had hand-selected hanging baskets, all chosen to attract hummingbirds and butterflies.

The day actually went by very fast. I don't think anyone sat down for two seconds. I even noticed Chad walking through one of the gardens with a group of five guests. Who knew?

"Julie," Teresa enthused, "people are signing up for next year's garden tour, and most of them want to stay at the inn for the weekend."

"That's great, Teresa. So what you're telling me is we are all booked for *next* April?"

"Exactly!"

"Teresa, would you go and let everyone know that I would like to schedule a meeting for next Friday? At seven-thirty in the morning, in the kitchen. I'll let Kourtnee know right now."

I didn't walk through the inn, I floated. "Kourtnee, I'm calling a meeting for next Friday. Can you and I get together for an hour prior to the meeting?"

"Sure. I have time today."

"Okay, I'll need to look over the books, and then we can meet an hour from now." I went up to my room, looked at the numbers and made my decision. Then I went back into Kourtnee's office. She was glowing more and more every day.

"Kourtnee, from now on, I want to give each person a percentage from the inn's annual profit. After the inn paid all its expenses, we were left with a profit."

"That's fantastic."

"Kourtnee, please write eight checks for the amount of three-hundred and thirty-five thousand dollars."

"Eight checks for…?"

"Yes, eight: me, Kevin, you, Michael, Christine, Bea, Molly, and Teresa. That means by next Friday you need to write the checks.

Actually wait, leave my share in the account."

"For each of us?"

"Can you transfer the funds from the money market to the checking account prior to Friday's meeting? Please."

"Julie."

"Kourtnee, you're very deserving. Don't look at me like that." "Julie, why are you being so generous? You don't have to…"

"Kourtnee, I have everything in life that I need." I smiled at her.

"My life has never been about the money. I am more about living my best life. This inn makes me happy."

"Then why do you keep your distance from us? For so long now, you have isolated yourself from all of us. I don't understand you at all." Kourtnee blew out a long breath. "I know you're hurting.

I…I want you know I love you, Boss Lady."

My eyes filled up. "I love you, too." I had to leave her office.

Friday morning, I handed everyone their envelopes. "Remember, I am hoping that you are all saving for your retirement."

"Goodness," Teresa said. "I thought I was retired and living in my dream retirement home."

Kevin laughed, adding, "Hey, Teresa, don't worry, by the time Julie is done with this place, you'll be living at a dream resort."

They were happy and *that* pleased me. Because Lord knew… they all made me happy.

Chapter 26

A huge tent had been set up in preparation for the wedding. Michael had a few of his old classmates coming to prepare all the meals, and Christine and Michael did as promised: they kept the guest list to just under one-hundred.

Molly had the activities mapped out for the entire weekend. Michael's brother and Christine's sister were hosting the evening's rehearsal dinner. I was standing on the front porch wondering about Lynnae and Barry. I still had the Samsung tablet. I could log onto the website and see my bakery, Lynnae, Brooke and Stephanie. But *that* would be too painful for me.

"Hey, you okay?"

"Kourtnee, I didn't hear you come outside."

"You're breathing into your hand a lot these days. What are you thinking about?"

"Just wondering how the plans for this evening are coming along," I said.

"Great, we're gonna have such a good time tomorrow."

"You think so?"

"Oh, yeah." Kourtnee smiled. "Molly is something else."

"What does she have planned for tonight?"

"Molly has arranged for a dance instructor to come in and teach us how to square dance."

"That's a great idea. Is that why we are having a barbeque out on the back terrace?"

"Yes, and to make sure everyone gets into the mood, she has these red bandanas and cowboy hats for everyone to wear." Kourtnee rolled her eyes.

"I like the idea of country casual on rehearsal night, and then tomorrow we bust out the crystal and sterling silver. Kourtnee, you have to agree with me, Molly always does a fantastic job when it comes to planning a party."

"I'll tell you just how smart she is. She has an artist coming tomorrow to draw everyone's picture. She thought it would be nice to have our picture drawn while we were dressed up."

"Really? What a great idea. Um, very different. I like it. As long as the bride and groom are happy, I'm happy."

Kourtnee read a text message from Kevin. "Hey, Kevin needs a check, I'll see you later."

I started to go down the driveway when I heard Chad calling my name. I stopped and waited for him to catch up. He stood in front of me, smiling.

I grinned. "What are you...?"

He was holding one hand behind his back. I inhaled deeply when he handed me a single red rose.

"Thank you, I'll put in a vase right now." I stepped away and explained, "Kourtnee needs my help with a problem in the office."

The next morning, Michael was pacing the floor when I entered the kitchen.

"Michael, are you a little nervous this morning?"

"No, not at all. I just hope I can make her happy."

"Michael, loving only her, believing in your wedding vows, and in the Seventh Commandment, trust me, Christine will be the happiest woman in the world."

Michael smiled, nodded and kissed me on the cheek.

"Hey, what's going on in here?" Kevin said, coming into the kitchen. "Michael, why are you in the kitchen, man? Come on, let's go."

"I'm coming, but first I want to send down a tray of fresh fruit, chocolate covered strawberries and croissants to the ladies."

Suddenly the guest chef, Russ, entered the kitchen, holding up a bottle of champagne, and a silver platter in his other hand. "Here you go, chef."

Michael took the tray from him. "Thanks."

Kevin laughed. "It doesn't get any mushier. Can we please play golf now?"

"Leave him alone, I think that's very romantic." I patted Michael on the back. "Nice touch." "That's because you are a girl, Julie." "Oh, stop!" I said to Kevin.

"Good morning, everyone. Good morning, beautiful." I felt Chad's hand on the small of my back.

"Good morning, Chad." I stepped aside and turned to face him. "Thank you for giving up the cottage this weekend."

"My pleasure. Hey Michael, ready?" Chad looked at me. "I'll miss you today."

I raised an eyebrow, offering a quick response, "I will be missing all of you today."

"Chad, kiss her and let's get going," Kevin hollered. "I want to play some golf..."

"Kevin!" I shouted, forgetting for a moment that we had guests in the room.

"Go and play golf," Russ said. "I'll kiss her for you, and take good care of all the ladies."

Everyone laughed. When the men left, I told Russ that I would be happy to take the tray of goodies down to the cottage.

Holding the tray in my hands, I noticed a small envelope that read, "My darling, Christine." I always knew Michael was a romantic man. I wondered if he counted the chocolate covered strawberries, because there was one missing.

The women were all getting ready for a day of pampering and relaxation. I filled the cottage with DVDs like *Maid in Manhattan* and *Pretty Woman*.

On my way back up to the inn, I noticed Kourtnee heading down the path. "Hey, how come you're not at the cottage?"

"I didn't think I needed to stay at the cottage when my bed is only ten minutes away."

"Okay, sunshine, but if you need anything, let me know."

"I will, I promise. Julie, he's in love with you, you know."

"He called me beautiful. And this morning, your foolish husband told him to kiss me."

"Go get dressed," Kourtnee said as she walked past me.

Even though my heart was focused on the wedding, my mind was on Chad. How could he be in love with me? I gazed out the window thinking about how far I had come, how strong my heart had become. I wrapped my hair up in a French twist. My black heels matched my black lace dress. At five o'clock, I was ready.

As the men escorted the guests to their seats, Michael stood patiently at the altar waiting for his bride.

Chad leaned in toward Kevin and I heard him say, "I have butterflies."

Kevin laughed. "Why?"

"It feels like prom night. Hey, I got this one." Then he quickly made his way to me. "Good evening. May I escort you to your seat?" He smiled and held out his arm.

I nodded. "Yes, you may. Thank you."

"You look even more beautiful tonight."

"You look very handsome, Chad."

When he took my hand and held it to his cheek, I thought I was going to die.

"Tell me you're going to dance with me tonight."

A warm feeling rose within me. "I make no promises."

He kissed my hand. "You'll dance with me."

I sat in my seat. Every time I looked at Chad, he was looking at me. There's something to be said about a man in a tuxedo. The ladies were to arrive by horse-drawn carriage. Everyone looked so happy. Even the weatherman was kind on wedding day.

Kinder to Michael and Christine than he had been to me on my wedding day, when it had poured the entire day. But at six o'clock, just as we were saying our vows, the rain had stopped.

I sat there remembering how handsome Dan had looked in his tan jacket, white shirt and gray tie. In our wedding photo, he looked like something out of *Casablanca*. That was the happiest day of my life. *Please, Lord, I know you can stop the rain. Can't you mend my broken heart?*

The music started, and the carriage arrived on cue. For a brief moment, even the birds remained calm.

As the women walked down the aisle, tears of joy began to flow. Christine appeared, and everyone stood. She was strikingly beautiful in her wedding gown. Molly had done a magnificent job. She had ensured every detail was to perfection. She had created a halter dress, with hand-sewn pearls on the bodice. The dress accentuated Christine's figure perfectly, making her appear even taller than she was.

Before she reached the altar, Christine stopped. She stood there, staring at Michael. All eyes were on her. You could have heard a pin drop. *Something is wrong. What is she doing? Oh, no,* I thought. Then I looked at Michael. Instantly, I knew exactly what Christine was doing. She was taking in the moment. It was breathtaking. Michael was crying.

The smile on his face was as big as the day itself. The tears rolling down his cheeks told the whole story. Michael walked past the minister. Up to his bride, took out his handkerchief, and she gently wiped his tears. There wasn't a dry eye under that tent.

They wrote their own vows. Michael promised to love and to cherish only her for the rest of his life. Christine promised to feed him Oreo cookies dipped in chocolate every night.

The music began to play and once again, I was back in 1989. We were on top of the world. For that one brief moment, I was ready – ready to get married. At 5:30 in the evening, we headed out into the rain. We both wanted a simple ceremony. By 6:00, we were married. Happily, the four of us walked outside Judge Cantele's home, looked up and noticed a bright rainbow in the sky. It was directly over the judge's house. Dan's brother, Bill said, "Now, that's a good sign." I was married to the man I loved, which meant

I had everything. The music stopped and I heard, "You may kiss the bride."

Michael's friends did a fantastic job with the food. Molly hired the band, ensuring everyone was up on their feet the entire night. They were the most eclectic band I had ever heard.

I had insisted on baking everyone individual wedding cakes. They were slightly larger than a cupcake, filled with chocolate custard and decorated with edible peonies. When Christine tasted the sample I made for her, she looked at me and said, "You're hiding something and it's not the damn recipe." I just smiled at her.

I watched as Michael swirled Christine around the dance floor. I felt a warm sensation come over me. I hoped Teresa and Molly would find that same happiness.

"May I have this dance?" Kevin said, reaching for my hand.

"Of course, you may, but where is your wife?"

"Over there, dancing with Chad."

"Your wife is very beautiful tonight, and if I may say so myself, you look fantastic in your tuxedo."

"Thank you. Julie, give him a chance."

"Kevin, please. I'm not ready."

"He's in love with you…"

"Kevin, he doesn't even know me."

"Julie, come on."

I saw a hand tap Kevin on the shoulder. "May I cut in?"

Kevin smiled. "Only if I can have my gorgeous wife back."

Chad stood in front of me. First, he extended one hand out to me, and then he reached around my waist with is other hand. "I told you, you would dance with me tonight."

"Chad, asking someone to dance and cutting in on them, well that's just not the same." I put my hand in his.

"I've been watching you all night. Julie, please don't make me beg – because I will, you know."

"You don't have to beg. I'm right here." I had to close my eyes, not to let the tears flow. I tried not to notice how close he was.

Chad twirled me around the floor as if we had been dancing together forever. My heart was aching. For the first time, a man who wasn't Dan was holding me close, and it felt good.

"You smell wonderful, Julie. What are you wearing?"

"I can't tell you, it's my secret." I stepped back, looked at him, and said, "I'm kidding. I'm wearing vanilla."

"Vanilla? It smells fantastic on you. You smell delicious."

"Someday, I'll tell you where I got the idea from."

He pulled me into him even closer. "Tell me now, or I swear I will never talk to you again." He smiled and winked at me.

"Umm, tough choice." I raised an eyebrow. "I love to watch westerns. In one, a cowboy said, 'I want to make love to a woman who smells just like vanilla.' I've been wearing it ever since." A big smile spread across his face.

I tilted my head. "What?"

"Just a thought. That's all."

"Men. You're all the same."

"Trust me, we are not. Look at me. I'm not…" He looked away. "They're getting ready to toss the bouquet. Why don't you catch it?

And I'll catch the garter."

"Nice try, except I made the toss bouquet, so I can't catch it."

"You did not."

"Yes, I did. Watch. It will separate into five smaller bouquets, each with a ribbon. Each ribbon says something different: 'You will be married next,' 'Love will come afar,' 'Someone here adores you,' 'Romance awaits you,' and 'Forget about it, you're never getting hitched.' No, I'm kidding about the last one; but it will separate.

Watch."

"Amazing," Chad said just as the bouquet separated.

"Chad, I really did have a great time. Thank you for asking me to dance."

He gave me a long look, then he kissed me on my forehead. "Julie, I'm hoping you will dance with me for a long time to come." By ten p.m. Michael and Christine had left for their honeymoon.

Michael was surprising her with a week in Hawaii.

Chapter 27

S unday evening, Teresa and I were out on the front porch, enjoying a cup of sleepy time tea.

"Hey, do I hear a car?"

I looked at her. "Do we have someone checking in?"

"No. Not that I remember. Wait, I did ask Bea to cover for me the other day. Maybe? Oh look, it's Chad."

Chad stepped out of his car. Two drop-dead gorgeous young women got out of the other side of the car. They looked like models from a *Vogue* cover.

I was frozen. I could not breathe or speak. *I can't do this again. My heart cannot take another break. I never want to feel that pain again. How could he do this to me?* I had my shield up, and my hedge of protection. Why the hell wasn't it all around me? Why did I let him stay? I didn't want to be rude, yet all I could do was stare at them.

"Teresa. Julie?" Chad put his hand to his chin. "I was at the airport, when I overheard them say they were staying here, I offered to give them a ride. This is..." Chad turned to face the two women. "I'm Christina Stellate and this is Michelle Eggink. We're only here for one night. We have a photo shoot in Narragansett tomorrow morning at six..."

"Michelle Eggink and Christina Stellate, yes I remember now," Teresa said. "Oh, I just *love* this inn," one of them gushed.

"Where do we check in?" the other one asked. "We have an early shoot at the ocean tomorrow. Sun up."

"Come, I'll show you," Teresa said. "Will you need a ride in the morning?"

"No thanks, they're sending a car for us."

"Welcome to our inn," I barely spoke the words. I knew better than to try and stand up. My legs felt like Jell-O.

"Julie, are you feeling sick?" Chad asked.

"I just have a headache." What was I supposed to say, umm, I can't breathe? Because I was a fool.

Chad walked up onto the porch and sat down where Teresa had been sitting. "I'm sorry, I didn't mean to upset you like that."

"It's fine, really."

"No. It's not, and anyone can see that you're upset. Julie, I promise I will never surprise you like that again. Ever." Chad looked at the other guests. "If you're not too upset with me, may I suggest we go for a walk?"

Guests. For a moment, my mind wandered away. Is this how a crazy, jealous, paranoid, tainted mind reacts? I'm not even in love with the man, and still, my mind was spinning out of control. I heard Chad say something. What, I don't know.

"Julie. I thought about you all day. I would like to spend more time with you. Just the two of us."

"I can't do this. I'm sorry." I could feel his eyes on me.

"Look at me. I will never hurt you. What are you afraid of?" He stood up, extended his hands out to me, and said, "Take an evening stroll with me."

He helped me to my feet. When he did, he held my trembling hands in his own. He pulled me into his arms, and whispered, "I am not going anywhere. Please give me a chance."

I wanted so much to believe him. To feel his love. But what about my promise? I promised myself that I would never let another man hurt me. Or have that kind of control over my heart. My mind was forever damaged.

We left the porch in silence. Chad led me over to the rose garden. He sat me down on the resting bench, then he sat down beside me. "It's just you and me. No one can hear us."

"Chad, I'm sorry, if I did something to make you believe…"

He held one finger in front of his lips. "Shh, it's all right. You didn't do anything." He put his arm around my shoulder. "You're shaking, Julie. See for yourself. I'm not like anyone else. Just give me a chance – the chance to prove to you that my love is real. You're trembling. Listen to me," he said, with his finger under my chin, lifting my face to see his. "There's nothing you can tell me or do that will change the way I feel about you. Nothing."

I tried not to let him see my tears, but he was so close, he had to see them fall.

After a few minutes, I exhaled. "I'm very tired. Can we please go back now?"

"Absolutely. I insist you let me take you to your room." He held me by my waist. I felt dizzy. From time to time, I had to rest my head on his shoulder. When we reached my room, he opened the door, bent down, and kissed me. "Sweet dreams. I'll see you tomorrow morning, beautiful."

"Chad…?" I inhaled, trying to catch my sighs. "Goodnight."

My entire body was begging for him to lie down next to me. As I fell asleep, I could still feel his lips pressed on my own.

The next morning, I felt lightheaded. My heart was on an emotional rollercoaster – from dreading my life to imagining a life full of excitement. I went downstairs and asked Teresa if she could drive me into town.

She drove to the very tip of Point Judith, where only sand and large rocks set by the town kept everyone from driving their cars into the ocean. Teresa parked the car in the parking lot near the pier and we watched the boats coming in and out of the harbor for a short while.

For a moment, I felt calm and peaceful. I loved the smell of the ocean. It was simply delicious. The air was warm and inviting. I could have sat there for days.

Teresa and I got out of the car and headed down toward the beach.

"Dan brought me here once, and I fell in love with the place. I couldn't think of a better place to start over."

"Sometimes, starting over is exactly what a person needs to do. A lot of people don't have that kind of courage to do something like this."

"Well, I have to admit, I'm scared, because once again, I've let a man come between me and my happiness. I would rather eat cat shit with a knitting needle than feel that way again." Teresa laughed.

I looked out at the ocean. Teresa had been one of the first people to befriend me at the inn. I glanced over her way. She never left her room barefaced; her hair was always perfectly in place. She can be a little chatty, but in a close friend kind of way. We were visibly different. She stood five-two to my five-six, weighed one-ten to my then one-thirty-five, and she spoke in a much sweeter voice than I did. Since neither of us had been born there, we both avoided the where did you attend school, and how long have you...nonsense. Thankfully, we never discussed the past. It was our unspoken agreement. Our friendship was about teatime and the inn.

Everyone had secrets. If anyone could restore my balance, Teresa was it. She was caring, loving and charming.

"Hey," she said as she shook her index finger at me. "Let's work on a new project together. Something that keeps you busy and makes you happy at the same time."

"Oh, Teresa. In the beginning, the inn did allow me to keep myself busy, and it allowed me to disappear. For the first time in my life, I had something to look forward to. I couldn't wait for the first guest to arrive. Now, there's a guest staying with us who scares me to death. Last night, I wanted him to lie down next to me. I miss my husband so much. The way he would reach for me every night. Even if we didn't make love, my husband always held me tight until I fell asleep. Last night, my body longed for someone to spoon with me." "Listen, I know what you're doing. I see it in every one of your projects. You're building your own safe haven. Julie, you better figure out what you are going to do, because I have a feeling that this one is not going away."

I didn't know what to say.

"Come on, let's take a nice walk down the beach," Teresa said, tapping me on my head.

That made me smile. We kicked off our shoes and carried them as we strolled along the water's edge, sending the gulls and the sandpipers scurrying out of our way. "Maybe, I can just toss every one of those other women into the ocean." We both laughed at the thought. "Hey, maybe, you can buy me a new heart."

"You got it. I'll take you to see the heart doctor first thing tomorrow."

Teresa and I walked in silence, kicking up sand with our toes. We must have traveled a mile along the ocean.

"This is so sad. I don't know how women like you do it. You know it's not you…"

"Teresa, when I hear someone say 'it's not you,' I have to ask why not me? Obviously, I wasn't doing something right. Or he would have been just as happy as I was. Are you hungry?"

"Starving," she replied.

We sat in the restaurant for an hour or so, and then we headed back toward the car. The sun was still warm on our faces. We both stopped and allowed our bodies to be kissed by the sun.

"Julie, were the two of you ever happy?"

"I was happy every day of my life. I looked forward to going home and spending time with him. Dan was my best friend. We did everything together. To me, it didn't matter what we were doing, as long as we were together."

"I don't understand. How can one person be so happy while the other person is so…"

"I've come to think it's a disease. A terrible sickness. I'm afraid to say that it kills a lot of what should be really good marriages."

"Do you regret marrying him?"

"Not for one single day. Teresa, I thank God every day for Dan. I'll never regret loving him." I was looking out where the ocean and the sky become one. Once again, I disappeared, lost in my own memories.

We sat down in the sand. Several minutes went by. I felt peace when Teresa starting humming *Amazing Grace*.

Dan's favorite song.

She stopped humming. "Julie, where were your friends? Didn't anyone reach out to you? Why didn't someone say something to Dan? Like, you're a damn fool. Or how could you do this to such a wonderful woman? How about someone slapping him upside his head and saying wake up."

It was hard to find malice in anything Teresa said. Every word came from her heart.

"You're the first person I've told. I was afraid they would think I was pathetic or worse, that I was crazy. I was too embarrassed."

"The damage of secrecy. Never be embarrassed to share your heart with those who love you. You need to open up to someone. They say it can be very rewarding and therapeutic to get things off your chest. Oh, Julie, your husband was a stupid, foolish man, and his punishment is…he lost you."

"Teresa, that's the nicest thing anyone has ever said to me."

"It's too bad the marriage counselor you talked to was such an ass."

"Actually, I tried to open up to a friend, but it was hard. She loved Dan as much as she loved me. Lynnae was like a daughter to both of us. When I did tell her about my suspicions, she said they were unjustified. She just couldn't see Dan – the perfect, loving and attentive husband – cheating on his wife."

"No children, right?"

"We were both tested. The doctor said Dan had a low sperm count, and I might need fertility drugs. For some reason or another, we never did anything about it. Fate, I suppose. I didn't go without. God blessed me with an abundance of nieces and nephews."

"I'm sure they miss you. Don't you think they are wondering where you are?"

I shook my head. "Right before I left the state of New York, I mailed a letter to each of them, explaining everything and that I was finally taking care of myself. They know I'm planting a garden somewhere."

"That's why we have so many gardens?"

"I have to be outdoors." I held my hands up above my head. "I am happy when I am outdoors. I could pull weeds for the rest of my life."

Teresa and I found a couple of empty lounge chairs along the beach. At first, we sat in our own silence. I knew what Teresa was trying to do. And I knew what she meant when she said talking about a trauma can be very therapeutic. I was not sure my heart understood, because it hurt.

"Julie, I've had my heart broken a few times. My last relationship was the hardest breakup. His girlfriend, the one he left me for, came into the drugstore every week. She was in the day I met you. She was the woman complaining about the wrong color of lipstick. She claimed the packaging said crimson, but the lipstick inside was a primrose. As if that never happens. I wanted to say, deal with it, bitch."

"Teresa!" I had to laugh.

"Well, she is…"

"It's fine. I've used a few choice words myself. Tell me about your…"

"No. Some other time. You're in my path. When I'm in yours, I'll tell you about my life."

"Where did you come from?"

"God," she replied and I laughed.

We inhaled the salty air at the same time. "Do you know why I insisted on baking Christine's cupcakes? Because I missed being in the kitchen, baking for others. I missed my life. I worked my ass off to build that business up. Everyone thought I was crazy for opening a bakery in the middle of nowhere. I knew how to hit the pavement. I walked into every business, school, and establishment I could. I was not afraid to ask for their orders. I was so happy back then. I loved the women I worked with. Especially Lynnae."

"You're a lot braver than I am. I'm not courageous at all."

"Brave? I don't know about that," I laughed. "I was thirty-nine when I decided to teach myself how to ride a motorcycle. I purchased a Honda Rebel."

"A motorcycle? Now that's cool."

"Not so cool. On a beautiful Sunday afternoon, about thirty of us were heading to Connecticut for the day. Two experienced riders were in front of me. Dan and his best friend Jesse were right behind me. We weren't into the ride more than ten minutes when I lost control of my breathing. I looked at the oncoming traffic and noticed a big SUV coming toward me. I blacked out. Liz, the only other woman in the group, drove past the men so she could use her foot to steer my bike away from the oncoming traffic. They said Liz stopped me from crashing my bike. She kept yelling at me to wake up. Dan said she hollered 'breathe' at least a hundred times."

"Did you get hurt?"

"No. No one got hurt, thank God. I eventually snapped out of it and followed Liz to the other side of the road. Everyone parked their bikes and we all started to breathe again. A few of the men looked as if they saw a ghost. Dan made me leave my bike. I got on the back of his motorcycle and cried as softly as I could. Several times, I felt

Dan's hand tap the side of my leg."

"I'll bet he was scared to death."

"He never said a word about it. A week later, we sold the bike to a friend. For an entire year, I had to have someone else drive me everywhere I had to go. I was afraid of everything."

"So that's why you don't drive?"

"No. Out of fear that Dan would find me, I decided not to register a vehicle in my name. My license is still good for a few more years. I suppose I was afraid that if I saw Dan, I would take him back."

"Julie, don't get mad at me, but did you ever think that maybe he did it to get your attention? Maybe he liked seeing you jealous. It still makes me sick that they didn't even care that he was married." "I know what you are saying but it doesn't make it right – blaming the women. I made that mistake. If only these awful women would leave my wonderful husband alone. Although I have to say, one of them was crazy enough to leave him a pleading message." "I'm afraid to ask. What did you do?"

"I'll tell you what I did. I went to the fish market. Bought a whole fish. Opened its mouth and stuffed her message inside. Then

I mailed it to her. Trust me, I was furious."

Teresa might have been laughing, but the thought of that wench still made me fuming mad.

Teresa was laughing so hard a group of men playing volleyball in front of us stopped and looked. "Oh, I'm sorry, but you know that envelope must have stunk."

"The whole situation stunk."

She sat up abruptly. "Julie, what if Dan does a Google search and finds out that you're an innkeeper in Rhode Island? What will you do if he shows up at the inn?"

"Teresa, calm down." I smiled at her. "I don't exist. When I sold my rental properties, I put my money into a money market. When I sold my business, my attorney formed an LLC for me. She created a trust fund. All the money went directly from the money market and into the trust. The trust fund owns the inn. Kourtnee is the trustee. She signs all the checks. Me, I am just the phantom gardener."

"You're unbelievable. You are one clever individual."

"No, I am a very cautious woman. Hey, it's getting late. We had better head back."

"Yeah, or Michael will send out a search party."

"Teresa, thank you."

"Julie, thank you. Thanks you for trusting me. Your secrets will always remain safe with me. My life is pretty boring, compared to yours. One question though, what are you going to do about Chad?"

"I don't know."

"What did you do in the past, if a man made a pass at you?"

"I showed him my wedding band."

Chapter 28

The next morning, I was sitting in the library. The window was open. Kevin and Chad were sitting on the side porch. I could hear their entire conversation. "I don't understand what's happening. I thought she felt the same way about me as I do her. I can see it in her eyes. I know why she is holding back. I would never cheat on her."

"Why would you say that? Do you think that's why she's here alone?"

When I stood up, the book fell from my lap onto the floor. It made such a loud noise; I rushed out of the room.

Teresa was in the lobby. I informed her that I would be in my room for the rest of the day.

"Julie, are you feeling okay? You're extremely pale."

"I'm feeling fine. I just need to tend to a few things. If anyone has a problem they cannot deal with, I'll be in my room."

I spent the rest of the day lying on my bed. I tried to read a few times. However, my mind kept going back to the same thing. Did my eyes really show that? I tried to shake it off by telling myself that he was just assuming things about me.

I was sitting in front of the window, looking out at the rose garden when I heard a knock on my door. I heard Michael's voice, "Dinner time."

I opened the door. "Thank you, Michael. How did you know I was getting hungry?" "Because you haven't eaten all day and it's my job to feed you. Besides, how are you going to keep that great figure of yours if you don't eat? Listen, sweetheart, you can stay up here all you want, but at some point you're going to have to face the fact that he's not going away on his own."

I took the tray of food from him and set it down on the desk, turned back around and said, "Michael, I'm scared. You have no idea how scared I am."

"What are you so afraid of? I can't tell you what to do. But I can tell you this, he loves you."

With tears in my eyes, I looked at Michael. "I'm trying. I need time. I need to think about this." I looked away. "It's a little more complicated than it looks." "Okay, sweetheart. We'll take care of everything downstairs. You take all the time you need. Would you like me to send Teresa up with some tea later?"

"I would like that. Michael, thank you." He gave me a bear hug, literally picking my feet up off the floor.

After Michael closed the door, my tears became uncontrollable. My heart was heavy. My mind was racing from thoughts of romantic evenings to long walks in the woods one minute, to a broken heart in the end. I never touched the tray of food. I did eventually go downstairs. I went into the library and noticed my book was still on the floor. I picked it up and saw Chad sitting out on the side porch.

Then I heard Michael's voice.

"Would you like a little anisette?"

"Hey, Michael. Sure, thanks. She's not coming down, is she?"

I sat quietly in the wingback chair, facing the window. The room was dark enough that no one could see me, but the lace curtain allowed me to see just enough movement on the other side. I watched as Michael sat down and poured two glasses.

"Chad, you have to give her some time. Give her space, or you will lose her before the first kiss. I'm telling you. She's a smart woman. She knows what she's doing. Most important, she cautious."

"I know. But why be that way with me?"

"We can only speculate. No one knows her story. We only know that she's not the type to make the same mistake twice."

"I would never hurt her."

"I know that. Listen, Chad, I'm guessing that woman has had her share of heartache and sadness. Enough to sing the weeping willow blues for a long time to come."

"I'm in love with her, Michael. I plan to spend the rest of my life with that woman. If she'll have me."

Michael nodded. I'd heard all I needed to hear.

The next day, I asked Kourtnee to drive me into town.

"Kourtnee, can you pick me up after dinner?"

"After dinner? Don't you want me to stay with you?"

"No, I'll be fine."

"Julie, I'm worried about you."

"Kourtnee the only thing I want you worrying about right now is Kourtnee."

Kourtnee was glowing. Everyone swore she was going to give birth to that baby right there in the office. I kept thinking, soon the inn will hear the sound of little feet. I couldn't wait.

I spent the entire day pacing up and down the beach. At one point, I actually stepped in my own footsteps.

A week had passed since I'd overheard Chad and Michael talking. Each night Chad would sit out on the side porch. I knew he was waiting for me to make my rounds. Kourtnee told me that she overheard Chad tell Kevin that he couldn't stand it any longer. That he was ready to take 'drastic measures'. We both wondered what he was planning.

I stepped out of Kourtnee's office and bumped right into him.

"Chad…"

"Julie, I need to see you down at the cottage. There's a problem…"

"What type of problem, Chad?" I asked. "Do I need to call Frank?"

"No. I just need to show you something, that's all. It will only take a few minutes. I have to work in this morning. Come by at seven tonight and I'll show you."

I knew he was up to something.

The entire day, I couldn't stop thinking about him or his little problem. First, I moved my belongings into the New Englander. I filled my old bookshelves with new books, like Baby Einstein and Huck Finn, along with every nursery rhyme CD. I wanted the baby to have his or her own room. Considering mine was across the hall, I moved downstairs.

At four o'clock, I went jogging. I was near the pond when I saw Chad doing tai chi. I had never seen anyone do it before. He was wearing a pair of jogging pants and nothing else.

Thank God for the tall grasses. I stared as he moved; watching his every muscle. He was a beautiful man. Well-defined triceps, small waist. Tight abs. I was staring at his long torso, wondering what life would be like with a man like that. I was staring at him with open-mouthed admiration, when I realized Chad had been watching me the whole time.

He laughed. I quickly turned and jogged back up to the inn.

When I peeked into the dining room, I had noticed we had a full house. "Why so many people?" I asked Christine.

She smiled. "Tonight we are serving homemade chicken potpies, baby greens with a warm vinaigrette dressing, and my delicious apple pie. That's why the full house. Hey, the couple at table number nine are the owners of the clam bar on Ballard's Beach."

"I'll be sure to say hello."

I said hello to as many guests as I could, then I headed down to the cottage. As I neared the front porch, I could hear music coming from inside. I inhaled, lifting my hand to knock on the door just as

Chad stepped onto the porch. He was holding a bouquet of flowers.

"You caught me."

With his free hand, he opened the door to the cottage. "Shall we go inside?"

When I stepped inside, I was amazed by how neat and orderly everything was. Chad set the flowers down in a waiting vase that had been situated perfectly between two lit candles. "Chad, what is this?"

"Dinner, Julie. It's just dinner."

"I'm sorry, I'm expected in the dining room. I have to finish greeting my guests. You know that."

"Not tonight. I told Michael not to expect you. In fact, Michael has Christine, Teresa, and Molly assisting Bea tonight. It's just you and me. Don't be upset. It's just dinner." "You keep saying that. But it looks like more than dinner to me. There are flowers and candles glowing everywhere I look. And in the background, Willie Nelson is singing, 'Always On My Mind. '"

"Julie, can you give me a chance?"

I can't believe no one told me. "Chad, what about a year from now? Ten years from now? How about when the new becomes old. Where…?"

"Right here with me. That's where. Julie, I'm not going anywhere. Please stay and have dinner with me. Stay with me tonight?"

Silence. I wanted to run. But I didn't, because I was a woman full of hope, dreams and desires. My body ached for a night of pleasure.

"Julie, I'm asking you to have dinner with me. I'll give you all the time you need. All the space in the world. Please, just don't push me away."

How could I resist? I was starving. I kept thinking. He's only wearing a simple pair of jeans and soft white tee shirt, yet, he looks so darn good to me. I wanted to reach up to him, but I knew better.

"By the way, you are a terrible liar. There's no problem here in the cottage."

"There is, when you're not here."

He took my hand, led me inside and closed the door.

"You made me salmon. It's my favorite."

"I made you something else, but only if you eat your dinner will

I give it to you."

I sighed. "This is such a bad idea. What am I doing?"

"You're having dinner with a man who's falling in love with you." He reached over, touched my shoulder, and whispered softly, "Open your heart. Let me in, and I will show you how much I love you." He pulled me into his arms and kissed me.

After dinner, Chad took me by the hand, led me over to the couch, and asked me to sit down for a minute while he lit a fire. Then he sat down next to me. "Julie, you take my breath away. Tell me…"

He kissed my hand, my wrist, my…

I wanted him to hold me. I wanted to feel his love and his embrace so badly. "Promise me you will never break my heart."

"I'll do more than promise you, I'll show you."

I'd spent my life waiting for someone to love me – the way I loved Dan. I believed Chad did indeed know how to really love a woman. I was scared to death that I was not that woman.

We sat together for a little while, watching the fire. Chad admitted that Bea and Molly had cleaned the cottage, and that Kevin had told him where the florist was in town. "I did all the cooking though. Well, most of it." We both laughed.

"Thank you. It was delicious, every bite. So, where's my surprise?"

He looked at me and made a funny face. "You didn't touch anything on your plate. You barely ate a thing. However, you did stay."

When he returned from the kitchen, he was holding a tray of chocolate covered strawberries. "I made these for you, but you have to let me feed them to you down here." He pointed to the blanket in front of the fireplace.

I moved to the floor, sat down and said, "You're so bad."

"Close your eyes and open your mouth."

I closed my eyes and when I did, he kissed me. "Promise me, you'll have dinner with me tomorrow night."

How could I not? I was butter in his arms. "I promise to give you a chance, if you promise to go slow."

With a cat-like smile, Chad looked at me. "Oh, I can take my time, don't you worry about that."

I inhaled. "I'll bet you can." I thanked Chad for a wonderful evening. "I'm glad I stayed."

"I'm hoping you'll spend every evening for the rest of your life with me…"

"Slow…" Before I had a chance to finish my sentence, he interrupted me by kissing me and then he held me for a moment. Afterwards, he helped me to my feet.

"Come on, I better get you home, before I get myself into trouble."

Half way to the inn, Chad reached for my hand.

"Chad, thank you. Thanks for dinner, for making me laugh, and for allowing me feel like a woman again. It was very nice."

"You made my heart beat for the first time in my life. Trust me. I should be thanking you. So, dinner with me tomorrow night?"

I wanted to say, "Yes, yes, yes, whenever you want." But things were moving too fast. "I can't. Soon. In fact, I'll cook something wonderful for you, I promise."

He stood there looking at me. I could see the disappointment on his face, but he said, "Don't you worry, I can wait. As long as it's you I'm waiting for."

"Actually, Chad, it's just dinner." I smiled.

"Kiss me, so I know I am alive. Woman. You make my head spin. That's okay, because my heart is going just as fast."

I whispered, "Trust me, you're not only alive, you're doing just fine."

Chad reached out his hands, held me by my waist, pulled me in tight and looked into my eyes. "For as long as you will have me. I will…" He wrapped his arms around me and when he did, I longed for him to make love to me. I wanted to share all of it with him – the truth – everything; but I knew I couldn't, not yet.

A few days went by, and I knew I had better keep my promise. I gave Michael a list of items I would need from the kitchen. For dinner I prepared, mushroom, squash, and barley soup. Venison stroganoff with egg noodles, sautéed kale, and individual fudgy rum chocolate cakes for us.

Then Bea and I went shopping for that perfect little dress. I invited Chad to have dinner with me in the library.

Molly made a sign for the door and Teresa kept a close eye on the guests, ensuring our privacy.

I curled my hair and put on a little more than lipstick. I tossed the dress and my new pair of XOXO strappy heels onto the bed. I stood in front of the mirror; there was something to be said about a garter belt, silk stockings, and those several inches of bare thigh. It felt seductive standing in front of the mirror and as I slipped one foot then the other into my heels, I smiled. I loved dressing like a woman; I liked feeling sexy, and I loved the moment. Seven o'clock on the nose, I heard a knock on the library door. When I opened it, Chad looked surprised, as if he were standing at the wrong door. "Well, are you coming in?" I asked him.

"Oh, yeah."

"Get in here. I made you a cocktail."

"You look amazing. No, you look, incredible. Julie, once again, you have taken my breath away."

"Thank you. You brought me flowers."

"You're killing me."

"You better behave, or you won't get your surprise."

"You better give me one kiss or kill me now." He held me, and leaned me back so far I thought my hair was touching the floor. "Woman, what am I going to do with you?"

"Come on, your dinner is getting cold." Sitting across from him,

I knew I was in trouble, not because of his behavior, because I allowed myself to be in that moment. I felt so relaxed and I was enjoying his nearness.

Still Crazy

After dinner Chad said, "Would you mind if I put some music on?"

He was killing me. "Not at all. There's some CD's over on the bookshelf."

Chad put *Cold Play* in the CD player, walked back over to me, put his hand out and I got up. He held me close in his arms and we danced. I took a deep breath, "Oh, Chad," I said. "I haven't been this..." I searched for words. "This happy in such a long time."

He whispered in my ear, "Someday, I will make love to a woman who smells just like vanilla."

He kissed me one more time and then left the room. I stood there. My body was on fire.

Chad was gone for the next three days. I didn't know who missed him more – Michael, Kevin or me. I was sitting in the kitchen, drinking my first cup of coffee. I could smell something baking in the oven. I closed my eyes, trying to guess.

"Julie, I have something to tell you."

"Hey," I opened my eyes. "Michael?"

With the biggest smile on his face, he slapped his hands together and let it out. "We're having a baby."

I immediately gave him a great big hug. "Michael, that's wonderful news."

"I wanted to tell you right away." Just then, Kourtnee entered the kitchen, followed by Kevin.

"Hey, Elliotts, we're having a baby, too." "Oh....my goodness!" Teresa hollered.

Chad, Bea and Molly came running into the kitchen. "What is all the fuss about?" Molly exclaimed.

Michael informed them of the news. Everyone was hugging.

"Good morning, sweetheart." Chad kissed my cheek. "Great news, huh?"

"Good morning, Chad, yes it is. How was your trip?"

"It was good. Julie, let's take a drive tomorrow. I want to show you something." "Okay, what time?"

"Umm, lunch time."

"Where are we going?" I asked.

"Trust me, you'll love it. We won't be gone too long. You look a little busy right now. You enjoy the moment, and I'll take my bags down to the cottage." He kissed me and walked away... again. Of course, I had to watch him go.

Then I turned to Molly, Bea and Teresa. "I think we have another party to plan. We'll invite all their families, and friends and have another shower extravaganza. How does that sound?"

"Count me in," Bea said.

"Me, too," Molly chimed in. "Hey, wait. Christine can't make her own cake."

"Julie can make it," Teresa said, and then looked at me. "Right?"

"Yeah, I can make it."

The next day I ran into Teresa in the lobby. "Hey, how's the shower plans coming along?"

"Great, we were just discussing the details. I blocked off as many rooms as I could for the entire weekend for them. Good thing it's six months from now."

"Sounds good. Thanks for helping me. Oh, gosh, I have to go. Chad is taking me for a drive."

"Have a great time. Will we see you for dinner?"

"Absolutely." I ran out the door. Chad was already waiting for me by his car.

"You're late."

"I'm sorry. I was talking to Teresa about the baby shower for Christine."

"I'm kidding. About being late that is. Are you ready?"

"Yep. Actually it will be the first time I sat down all day."

Chad reached over, took my hand into his and gently kissed it. The drive was not a long one; it was, however a beautiful one along the ocean. As we drove down the road, I couldn't help noticing how happy he seemed to be. "I love riding in a car," I said. "Especially along the ocean. What a pleasant sight."

"I want to show you the first place I stayed at when I arrived in

Rhode Island. It's called Castle Hill, over on Ocean Drive."
"Is it right on the ocean?" I asked.

"Yes, wait until you see it."

A moment later, I saw the sign. My eyes opened wide. "Chad this place is spectacular. The views are incredible."

"Wait until you see the rooms; they're not too shabby either. Julie, your inn is just like this one. In fact, your rooms are very similar."

"I don't have this view of the ocean, though."

"Julie, I could have stayed here. Their chef is out of this world." I looked at him with surprise. "Why didn't you?"

"It was missing something. It was missing you. The first day I saw you in the garden; I knew I wanted to spend the rest of my life with you. But every time I tried to get close to you, you pushed me away. Julie, please don't…"

"I hear you. I know what you're saying." I looked at him, and… "I love it when you look at me like that," he said.

"I was hoping you were going to feed me."

"You're hungry?" He laughed. "Fine, I'll take you to George's.

We'll sit topside. You'll love it."

My heart started racing. "Actually, can we just get a bite to eat at Aunt Carries? It's closer and I'm starving. Don't tell Michael, but I skipped breakfast." *I made a mental note to add lying to my resume.*

"We can go wherever you want."

After we ate, we took a long stroll along the beach.

"Let's take another drive. Rhode Island has four-hundred miles of coastline. From coves, bays and inlands."

"Let me call the inn…"

Chad handed me his cell phone.

We drove through small picturesque towns with colonial – or Victorian – era homes. Past coastal villages, historical lighthouses.

As we drove past a beautiful home, I said, "One day, I would like to visit some of the mansions."

"I'll take you this weekend." He rubbed my left shoulder and added, "Where would you like to go for dinner?"

"I'm still full from lunch."

"But I want to spend the entire day with you. Come back to the cottage with me. I want to watch the sun go down with you in my arms."

By the time we reached the inn, it started to rain. Hand in hand, we ran all the way down to the cottage. "Have a seat. I'll make us a pot of tea."

I sat there remembering the last time I ran hand-in-hand in the rain. It was pouring out – much like it was that night. It was one of the most romantic nights of my life. Dan and I were coming back from a picnic at Macedonia Park. We never made it past the front door.

Dan kissed me until we both dropped to the floor. Right there in the doorway. We couldn't get our clothes off fast enough. He made passionate love to me. The only thing I could hear were the sounds of my own pleasure. Our bodies were moving as one. There was raw heat between us.

I remembered it as if it were yesterday. The following day, Dan came into the kitchen with red marks on both of his knees. I could still see the smile on his face when I asked about them. He told me his knees were red, for the same reason I had a large red mark on the small of my back.

I reached back and felt a little sore spot. It was rug burn. I joked that he had rough sex with me. Dan replied, "It wasn't rough, it was hot sex."

Even the rain reminded me of Dan. I missed those tender moments, sharing my body with him.

I rubbed my head, trying to stop myself from thinking about him. I tried to remember where I was, and why I was there.

I felt cold. My body started to shake. When I looked over my shoulder, I noticed Chad was standing over me. He was holding a pot of tea, and several towels. "You're freezing. Would you like to go inside?"

"No, I'll be fine." I didn't know what to say. I wanted to go back to my own room. Chad handed me a towel and then he wrapped a blanket around me.

"You're all of a sudden very quiet. Care to share your thoughts with me?"

"I'm just enjoying the rain; that's all."

Chapter 29

In mid-June, Kourtnee gave birth to a beautiful baby girl. Delilah.

I was on my way down to the pond with a new book when I saw Chad standing in front of the cottage. He was looking up at the sky.

I looked up to see what he was looking at, but I didn't see anything. Then I heard him say, "Thank you…"

When Chad opened his eyes, I asked him, "Giving thanks these days?"

"For everything. Did you come down here to see me?" he asked then leaned in and kissed my cheek. "Mm, I smell vanilla."

"I was headed down to the pond to read for a while and I saw you standing here, so I thought I would stop and say hello."

"Sit down, I want to tell you about our trip."

"Our trip? Where are *we* going?" I asked, wondering how many inns he'd slept at.

"I want to take you away for two weeks."

"Chad, two weeks is a long time. I can't leave the inn for two weeks. Stop looking at me like that. I'm sorry. I can't go."

"As usual, you're not making this easy for me. Come here. I want to take you to Italy."

"Did you just say, Italy?" The word alone made my breathing stop. "Hold me, Chad," I whispered, "Hold me, so I know you are real…"

Chad reached out to me, held me in his arms. And as he began stroking my hair, I said, "Why Italy?"

"That's easy, for the same reason all men love to go to Italy – for a beautiful woman. I'm hoping to find the love of my life." He laughed aloud. "Her name is Sophia, Sophia Loren. No, I'm just joking."

"Are you kidding me? Women love her. I adore her. She is my idol. And you're right; she is a very beautiful woman."

He explained, "For a while I thought I wanted to become an architect, which is why I went to live with my mother's family in Italy. There's nothing like Italian architecture. The buildings of Italy span almost three thousand years; drawing influences from a wide variety of sources. Etruscan and Roman buildings borrowed heavily from ancient Greece, while, in later centuries, Norman, Arabic, and

Byzantine styles colored Italy's Romanesque and Gothic architecture. Classic ideas infused the country's Renaissance buildings; later giving way to the inspired innovations of the

Baroque period."

I was nodding in agreement. "Every photo I've ever seen appears as if it should be known for some great artist or another. Seriously, it seems as if all the buildings displayed the ornate and intricate decoration from one artist or another. And is it me or does it seem like every fresco is a form of visual language by the artist in order to narrate a story?"

"If you can get all that out of a photo of a painting. Wait 'til you see the Renaissance gardens."

"Did you say gardens?" I couldn't believe how fast my heart was pounding.

"The formal gardens begin at the Pitti Palace and extend to the top of the hill overlooking the City of Florence. Julie, these gardens are some of the largest and most elegant Italian style gardens you will ever see."

"Oh, I would love to see them."

"They date back to 1440. Some of the most beautiful etchings of Rome are by Giovanni Battista Piranesi, date back to 1636 and are made of marble and bronze." He leaned over and kissed me. "We'll make the gardens our first stop when we arrive in Florence, I promise. I'll be here forever. Let me fulfill your every fantasy. I want to make all your dreams come true. *Esplorare l' Italia con me, il mio amore.*"

With a big smile upon my face, I said, "You speak Italian." I ran my hand very slowly up from his knee to his heart.

He kissed my hand, and replied, "Per il prossimo tresettimane lei e' tuttoilmio, e faro' tuttisognisi realizing, cominciandostasera.

L' amo con tuttoilcuore!"

I was captivated by the mellifluous sound of his voice in Italian, even thou I knew he messed up a few of his words. Still, I said, "You make my heart smile." "Julie, you're going to love the Westin Excelsior in Rome. There are fantastic views right from our hotel room. I thought we would stay in Rome for three days, take the train to Florence. I want you to see the countryside. I have everything all mapped out."

"It sounds like a dream."

"If you wish to dream, wait until we arrive at the villa."

"The villa, Chad, where is that?"

"In Pienza. My mother's family has a small villa there. Pienza's a tiny little renaissance jewel right in the heart of Tuscany's most pastoral countryside. Before we leave Florence though, I want to take you to the Boboli Gardens. Julie, I want to take you to so many beautiful places."

"Sounds fantastic."

"Julie, I love you with all my heart. I plan on telling you that every day for the rest of my life."

I closed my eyes and listened as he spoke every loving word.

"The Opera. We have to go to *La Scala.*"

Softly, I said, "Is Milan still the fashion capital of the world?"

"It is. We can go to a fashion show if you like."

"No. No, trust me. I would much rather visit places like the Sistine Chapel."

"The earliest tickets we could get would be months away, but we'll do it someday. Where else would you like to go?"

"Right now? To the kitchen. I think I need to eat. My head is killing me."

"Oh, no. We had better get you some food. Should we test your sugar?"

That stopped me dead in my tracks. He sounded just like Dan when he said that.

"No, I'm fine. I'm just getting a slight headache that's all. I think with all this talk about Italy and traveling, I'm a little overwhelmed."

"Oh, sweetheart, I got so excited and caught up with all the details, I forgot that you need to eat every few hours. Don't tell Michael, or he'll kill me."

"Come on, silly, let's go," I said. "Chad, don't stop. Stay as excited as you are. Please."

We went up to the terrace and sat down as if we were guests staying at a beautiful inn. I tried not to think about Dan; or how he always made sure I ate on time. To the point that he packed my snacks every day.

"Chad, I still can't believe that you were never married."
"Julie, I have had many women in my life, but I have never been in love. In my family, we take marriage vows very seriously; we actually believe in the words a man and a woman exchange. I've never met anyone I wanted to spend the rest of my life with…" he reached out and touched my cheek. "Until you."

Chapter 30

I didn't understand any of it. I should have been over Dan. Why did I still have thoughts of him? Every day I would think of him. It was as if he was in my head running around. At night, I dreamt he was still by my side.

I had to keep myself busy.

I looked out my window and saw Kourtnee and Kevin talking to each other. She was pushing the stroller and he was fondling her hair, neck and shoulder. Dan used to touch me every time he went by me. I missed him so much. "What am I going to do? What am I doing with Chad?"

I picked up the phone and called Frank.

"Good evening, young lady. Don't even tell me, you want to build something?"

"Yes, I do," I said in a tired voice.

"What is it this time?"

"A small daycare with a fenced-in yard."

He chuckled, "I'll see you tomorrow morning."

"Thanks, Frank."

The entire night I tossed and turned from all the excitement. To take my mind off Italy, I thought about the daycare. I didn't want it big, I just wanted a safe room where the children could read, play and nap.

I was on the front porch when Frank pulled up.

We headed over toward the day spa. Once we were out of hearing range, I said, "I don't have a lot of cash left. But do you think we can build it for forty grand?"

"Of course we can. Bea told me we have another baby on the way."

"Yes, Christine and Michael are expecting."

Frank and I were discussing the fence for the yard when Chad approached us from behind. "Good morning, Frank. Good morning, beautiful."

Frank smiled at him. "Sorry for borrowing your gal."

Chad laughed. "So, what does she have you building now?"

I smiled and winked at Frank. Then I explained to Chad what I was building.

"Do you have any idea how long that will take?" Chad said. "Never mind, how much money it is going to cost to run the electric lines from the inn."

I looked over at Frank. "Frank, would you like to explain to Chad how you're going to do it?"

"Chad, have you ever been to a barn raising?" Chad shook his head.

"Well, whenever I have a big project, or a deadline such as this, in addition to my crew, I call about fifty of my friends, and together we can erect a building's frame in one day. We can actually have the entire building airtight by the end of a weekend. Considering Julie is going to let the women pick out the interior, I can have the entire building done before she plants the first flower."

I raised my eyebrows. "The Amish have been doing it for hundreds of years. Chad, the electric lines and the plumbing pipes are already in the ground. When Kevin dredged out the pond with the bulldozer, I told him I sold the extra topsoil to a local contractor in exchange for new electric and water lines. All I had to do was rent a backhoe with a one-foot-trenching bucket on it so Kevin could dig the lines. The contractor laid the pipe."

"You're incredible." Then he waved his finger at me. "You scare me."

"Oh, by the way, yes, I will be planting flowers all around the fence."

"I knew you would have to get your hands in on it somehow,"

Frank joked. Well, I'm off to the building department. I'll have Gina Marie call you in a few days."

"Julie, before you leave, can I ask you something? What two weeks are the best for you, for Italy?"

At that moment I wasn't sure if I was about to have another panic attack or if it was a pang of guilt from holding back my reason.

"You want a marriage proposal first? Is that it? Because if you do, then..."

"Shh." I stopped him, holding one finger on his lips. "Hey, you haven't even fed me today. You have to learn to feed me, if you're going to argue with me." I kissed him.

He mumbled something in Italian, and said, "I'll have lunch with you anywhere, anytime."

The next morning, I jogged a little longer than usual. My head and my mind were less in line those days.

During the next few weeks, I made Chad promise me that he would not speak of things that upset either one of us. I told him he needed to learn to pick his fights. Not seeing my clothes hanging in his closet was not worth the stress we were both feeling. And for now, Italy was off the table.

During our thirty years together, Dan and I never fought about the little things. The only time we did argue was during the storms that blew in and out of our marriage.

I was in the library filling the shelves with the books from my old room. When I stepped back, I fell over a box full of books. "I need another shelf or ten." I added Diane Chamberlain's latest bestseller. I still had Delinsky, Deveraux, Evans, Sparks, Steele to name just a few. I picked up the house phone and called Frank.

When he arrived, I was sitting on the floor in the library. "I have nowhere to put these."

Frank put his hand out. "Get up off the floor. I'll take care of it."

Frank helped me to my feet.

"I don't know what I would do without you."

"It looks like you know exactly what to do." Frank picked up a book from one of my piles. "Toni Morrison. Hmm, a favorite of mine. Did you enjoy *Beloved*?"

"I did."

"You read a lot…"

"Frank, with the days I've been having lately, I need my reading time. Can I ask you something?"

Frank sat in one of the chairs. I sat in the other. "Am I being overly cautious with my not letting anyone into my heart?"

"You have a very big heart, young lady. I don't blame you one bit for protecting it. I would never want to see anyone hurt you. Not sure what I would do, in fact. So you be careful who you give that heart of gold to."

"Thank you, Frank. You're very sweet and kind."

After Frank left, I went into the kitchen. "Hi, Michael, what's for dinner?"

"You're happy today."

"What do you mean? I just asked what's for dinner tonight."

"Maybe because you practically skipped into the kitchen."

"Michael, I am happy."

"Well, Miss Happiness, you should know that we are serving grilled sea bass tonight."

"I love sea bass. Really?" For a moment, I wondered who had the crystal ball.

"Yes, really. Can you guess who insisted on picking it up?" He smiled. "Julie, you should marry that guy."

"Easy, chef."

While everyone else got ready for the evenings fireworks, I had spent my entire day in the bulb garden. My knees were killing me. I longed for a cup of tea, and a few minutes alone with my feet up and a good book.

I was headed up to the inn when I heard Chad calling my name.

"Hey, you," he said.

"Hey. Can I get a glass of something, anything?"

"Sit down; I'll make you a pot of tea. What kind?" he asked.

"Mint would be great," I replied, then collapsed on a chair.

Chad came back outside with a glass of ice and the pot of tea. I didn't wait for it to seep, I poured the whole pot into the glass and drank it entirely. "Thank you," I said before Chad even had a chance to sit down next to me.

I fell asleep in Chad's arms. When I woke up, he told me that I'd slept for a half-hour. "You snored the entire time. You didn't even wake up when I kissed you."

"I had a dream. I ran away."

Chad looked at me. "I'd find you. If you ever left *me,* I would search for you."

I put my head down. Thought about Dan, wondering if he was trying to find me.

"Julie, I have to go away, and you need to go with me. I won't go without you. I'll book us separate rooms."

"Chad." I sat up. "No. Not when I…"

"Julie, it's only for five days."

"I can't leave. Not now. I…"

"Julie, he's a new client. He wants to surprise his wife by taking her to Paris for their twenty-fifth wedding anniversary. Julie, it's good money. It's Paris. I want you by my side. I'm asking for us to spend a little time together away from the inn. It's *Paris,* Julie."

"When do they want to leave?"

"In three weeks–"

I interrupted him. "Chad, you have to understand." I raised my voice. "Try to understand, I *can't* leave."

"Yes, you can. You don't have to be here twenty-four-seven."

"I don't know what to do." "Go to Paris. Julie, listen to me. I recommended another pilot. They offered to bring as many people as I want. Think of it, Julie, we can take Teresa, Bea and Molly. Michael says he has plenty of backup staff. Kourtnee doesn't want to fly, with a new baby."

"You *talked* to them?"

"This might be a once in a lifetime chance for them." How could I say no? "Hold me. Promise me..." This time I caught myself.

"You'll go? Julie, that's wonderful!"

Chapter 31

T hree weeks later, the six of us, including Dr. Ellis and his wife, boarded Chad's sleek-looking Gulfstream G100 at Greene Airport. I was so glad Teresa and Bea came with us. I fell asleep listening to the two of them laughing and chatting about their plans to go shopping.

The next thing I knew, I heard Chad's voice: "Please fasten your seatbelts everyone. Ladies and gentleman, welcome to Paris. Thank you for allowing us to fly with you."

Chad booked two adjacent suites at the *Villa des Ternes,* a charming boutique hotel on the West Bank. Each suite had a common living area and two bedrooms. Teresa and Bea shared one suite, leaving me to share mine with Chad. I knew what he was expecting, but I also knew my heart.

The first night, we all had dinner at a *petit bistro* near our hotel. Immediately after dessert, Teresa and Bea excused themselves. They said they wanted to check out the Paris nightlife.

When they got up, I felt uncomfortable. "I think I'll go across the street tomorrow morning and get breakfast over at that cute little bistro."

"Do you mind if I go with you, mademoiselle?"

"Of course not."

I was surprised when Chad escorted me to my room, kissed me on my cheek and said, "I'll see you at six tomorrow morning."

Chad left immediately after we had our breakfast. I spent the rest of my morning pacing in my room. At one o'clock, I decided to buy Chad something special for taking all of us to Paris.

I stopped at the front desk and asked for a map. The young man handed me a piece of paper, folded in four. "This is our most current guide. You won't get lost, but if you do, our number is at the top."

He winked at me. "You call me and I will come and get you myself." I thanked him and assured him that I would be just fine.

Two blocks down from the hotel, I found a jewelry store. "Good afternoon, Madame, may I assist you with something?"

"Yes, I would like to buy a gift for someone. For a man, thank you."

I bought Chad a new watch.

Then I took a stroll down the crowded streets, gazing in the windows. A person could get drunk looking at all the beautiful merchandise. It almost seemed as if no one had anywhere they needed to be. People just sat outside the restaurants for such a long time. Talking, laughing as if they had not a worry in the world.

When I arrived back at my hotel room, I noticed a large box sitting on the bed with a note that read: "Tonight, you are my pleasure, my every fantasy. Meet me at Le Cinq 31 Avenue George V, at seven o'clock." I opened the box and found a little black dress, a pair of high heels, and an amazing diamond brooch inside.

"Hmmm, that's funny, no panties?" My heart was pounding, and he wasn't even in the room. I sat on the bed thinking about how

I had allowed myself to get there. "Maybe, Chad is a gift from God."

I took a long hot bath. I curled my hair, put on the little black dress, high heels and the magnificent brooch.

Not long ago, I would have been the one praying to God for no wind, because I purposely would have not worn any panties. I used to be bold. *Now, I am cautious about everything.*

I still had an hour before I had to meet Chad. I grabbed my book, sat down, and turned to the first page. Even in Paris, I had to bring along my favorite author. I was reading *The Gift.* For a moment, it took me back. I remembered a special gift I once created. I purchased a Playboy calendar for my husband. Except in that calendar, all the faces were the same. To keep things secret, I had Lynnae take the photos. Miss February was my favorite. I stood behind a large red heart, wearing only a pair of black stockings and a pair of stilettos much like the ones I had on.

If that was not enough, the following year I videotaped myself stripping very slowly to, "Because You Loved Me" by Celine Dion. I don't know why I tried so hard; but then again, I would have walked on fire for him. Now, I walk on eggshells.

"Damn it," I shouted. I had to re-do my makeup. Outside the hotel, a car was waiting for me.

When I arrived at the restaurant, Chad was sitting in the corner at a quiet table for two; looking as handsome as ever. The garçon took me by my arm and escorted me to the table. "Madam, please." Chad stood up.

"Thank you for my gifts. I have something for you as well." I set the box down in front of him. I waited for him to say something.

"Can I open it?"

"Please." It almost felt like we were strangers seeing each other for the first time. I had nervous chills.

"Thank you. Julie, I love it."

The waiter came over to our table, opened a bottle of champagne, and asked if we would like a few moments.

Chad spoke up immediately, "No, we are ready to order." He ordered for the two of us.

When the waiter walked away, Chad reached for my hand, holding it in his own. Then he leaned over toward me and said, "I better make sure you eat your dinner before I give you your surprise."

I could only smile. "You mean my very large diamond brooch isn't my surprise?"

"Those diamonds are just the little ones. I have much bigger plans for you tonight."

Champagne, surprises, big plans.

After dinner, we walked the streets of Paris. Even the air in Paris was romantic.

The entire evening was just too perfect. When we arrived back at the hotel, Chad insisted that I have one drink with him before heading off to bed. "I ordered a nice bottle of red wine for you. I thought it would help you sleep."

I knew Chad expected me to sleep with him. And why not? His heart was sincere. My own body ached for a night of passion. *Dare I use the "I have a headache" routine? I'm sure Chad would understand, besides he hasn't asked or mentioned it once.* Except we *were* in Paris.

We walked into Chad's suite. "Um, that's odd. Perhaps they left our bottle of wine in your room."

We walked through the common area and into my bedroom.

There must have been a hundred candles glowing. There were a dozen vases, all filled with creamy white roses. I was in awe. I stood there for a minute. The roses smelled amazing. I whispered,

"Chad, you have taken my breath away." Then I slowly turned back around to kiss him.

He was down on one knee, holding up a little black box, exposing the largest diamond I had ever seen. He reached for my hand, held it gently and said, "Will you marry me?" My other hand went to my mouth.

"Marry me."

"Chad..." He stood.

I tried to explain, "I came to Rhode Island, hoping to find peace in my life. I never set out hoping to find love."

"Julie, I want to spend the rest of my life with you. As your husband."

"Chad, trust me, I know what you want. It's not that easy. I have the inn, and I have a…"

"What? Are you all right? Julie, you're scaring me. I am asking you to marry me, and you're looking at me as if... what?" he said very sharply.

"I can't do this. I never meant to hurt you. I'm sorry."

"Julie, I don't care what it is. I don't give a damn about anyone else. The hell with him."

"What did you just say?"

Chad reached out, held me in his arms. I didn't even have the strength to pull away. "I love you. I can take care of you. You're stronger now. You can do this."

With tears in my eyes, I looked up at him. I could hardly whisper, yet speak. "I'm sorry; I couldn't tell you this before. I'm..."

All of a sudden, the entire room went black.

He held me tightly in his arms. He kept telling me, "It will be all right. I love you. I love you with all my heart."

My breathing became erratic, I heard him say, "Julie, I'm going to call a doctor, I'll be right back, sweetheart. You'll be all right."

It was as if I had no air. I was fighting for my life just to breathe.

"Julie, I'm afraid to let go of you. I have to call a doctor." I shook my head, no. I knew what was happening.

"Julie, I think you're having a heart attack, please let me call someone. I'm scared, I can't lose you. I'm calling a doctor."

I shook my head once more, held up one finger and moved slowly down to the floor. Chad immediately sat down beside me, held me in his arms and rocked me until my breathing became normal again.

An eternity had gone by before I finally regained my composure.

"Sweetheart, please tell me what is going on, I want to help you."

All I could say was, "I'm sorry you had to see that."

"I'm here. I love you." His face was calm. His words were sincere.

"You deserve the truth and I know it. I am so sorry." I took a deep breath and looked at the floor. I was embarrassed that I allowed it to go this far. Yet, I knew I had to tell him.

When my eyes met his, I allowed the words to come out. "I have a husband. He lives in New York."

Chad pulled me into his arms. Kissed my face a thousand times and rocked me back and forth – as if he didn't care.

"Chad, I just told you I'm married."

He pulled back a little. "Do you know how much I love you? Do you understand that no matter what, I will always love you?

You're my life, even if there is a husband somewhere in your past.

Julie, look at me. It's time to let go of him."

His words hit me like a brick. No matter how much I tried, I couldn't stop my tears. For such a long time, I locked every emotion up inside.

I vowed I would never open my heart. Once again, my heart was hurting. For a different reason.

"Julie, let me help you." "Chad, you already have."

"You know what you need?"

"A good spanking?" We both laughed.

He kissed me. "No. A cup of tea."

"Wait…"

He threw his hands up, like a stop sign, called downstairs and ordered chamomile tea in spite of me asking him to wait. It was as if he was on a mission and no one was going to stop him.

By the time the tea came, I had stopped crying, and I had began to breathe like a normal person. "I'm sorry I wasn't strong enough to get a divorce. I know that would have been the right thing to do, but my heart couldn't go through that."

"Julie, that's because you have such a big heart. He's a fool to let someone like you go. Julie, trust me, it is time – time to move on."

Never in my wildest dreams did I ever think anyone could or would love me like that. I sighed, "I loved him with all my heart. I loved him more than I loved myself."

"I know how much you loved him, and I'm sorry it didn't turn out the way you wanted it to. I'm sorry he broke your heart. Julie, don't let him break your spirit. It's time to move on. Look at me.

Things happened for a reason."

I cried, "I wish I knew the reason."

"Julie, have you ever loved a man other than the jerk you were married to?"

"Why a jerk?"

"He lost you, didn't he? Any man who'd do that has to be a jerk."

A moment had passed and I was glad when he said we both should get some sleep.

"Good night, sweetheart. I'm going to my room." That time when he kissed me on my lips, I felt his pain.

Chapter 32

Back at The Inn in Rhode Island, where I belonged. The next morning I had the urge to call Frank. There was just one problem; I didn't have a thing for him to build. I just needed to hear his voice.

I went down to the kitchen, grabbed a cup of coffee, and went down to the pond before anyone had a chance to see me. I hadn't even paddled for ten minutes when I got out and ran back up to the inn. I had to call Frank.

Michael was waiting for me with my list of herbs. "Good morning, sunshine. Did you go down to the pond already?"

"Yes I did." I paused for a moment. "I woke up early. I must be on Paris time."

Michael handed me the list, "Is there anything I can do?"

I stood in front of him, gave him a kiss on his cheek and told him, "Michael, I'm glad I have you in my corner. Thank you for always having my back."

"Always." He pointed a finger at me. "Remember that."

After I picked the herbs and gave them to Michael, I went to my room, took a shower, and vowed never to cry again. It was time I pulled myself together. I didn't leave everything that I loved to end up a total hot mess. I was stronger than that. I called Frank, and he agreed to meet me at the end of the driveway in one hour.

I leaned against the signpost and waited for Frank, thinking about my life. The family I left behind. My two best friends. And of course, my baby, Lady. I was glad I had someone like Frank in my life; he had wisdom, a sweet soul, and years of experience.

Most of all, I trusted him enough to tell me the truth. I had carried that chapter around long enough.

Frank pulled up, opened the door and hollered, "Come on, young lady, let's go. Where are we going?"

"Let's just drive." I told Frank all about Dan. About my life back home. "I didn't like myself very much. I was a vehement soldier fighting a losing battle. Dan wasn't capable of change, so I changed my lifestyle."

"One question. Are you happier without him?"

"Frank, I was so in love with my husband, I can't be with anyone else."

"You didn't answer my question."

I was looking at Frank, pondering his question, when he said. "Think about what you're doing."

After Frank and I spoke, I was convinced I had made the right decision.

When Frank dropped me off at the inn, I heard Teresa, Molly and Bea laughing about something. "Hey, what's going on?" I asked.

"We were just gushing about Paris, that's all. We were telling Molly what a blast it was," Bea said.

"It was interesting," I said. "Umm, Teresa, can I see you for a minute?"

"Sure. Let's take a drive."

As soon as I got into the car, I got right to the point. "Teresa, I'm going to ask Chad to leave."

Teresa slammed on the brakes. "Julie... What? Why? Did something happen in Paris?"

"I have to let him go." I tried to explain. "He asked me to marry him."

"Oh, nooo. He loves you so much."

"Can you drive, please?"

Teresa took hold of the steering wheel for all its worth and slowly started down the driveway. With my heart in my mouth, I watched her drive down the two-mile stretch.

When she approached the open road, and I could breathe, I said, "I know that. But he deserves so much more than I can give him. This is hard for me. You have no idea. Do you know how long I have prayed to God for a man to love me like this?"

I had to turn my eyes away from Teresa. Unlike me, she adored adoration. The air felt heavy. Like a thousand pounds was lying on my heart. Teresa kept her eyes on the road, hands on the wheel, and her expression benign.

For ten minutes, we drove in silence. We were both in a daze. When we approached the center of town, she asked me where I wanted to go. "Do you want to walk? Or do you need to sit down?"

I looked out at the crowd of people. Across the street, a woman was setting her merchandise out on the sidewalk. Her pink hair matched the sign above her head. "We Are Women Hear Us Roar," I said reading the sign out loud.

"Let's walk," she suggested. "It will do us both some good.

Wow, I never expected that. Okay, I'll stop saying that." Teresa parked the car. Turn the engine off and asked, "Julie, what are you going to do?"

"Teresa, Chad is absolutely perfect."

"But...then, what's the problem? Why are you letting him go?

I don't understand any of this. You can't let him go. Julie, you just said he's perfect."

Suddenly, I felt a pang of anxiety. "Everything Chad does reminds me of Dan. When he makes me feel romantic, I long for my husband. I can't do that to him. I cannot lie down next to him or anyone else for that matter, and keep wishing he were Dan. I wish I could erase him from my mind." I looked over at her. "We're talking about a lifetime. A life that took thirty years to build. Together, he and I created so many wonderful memories. I don't know how to live without him. He's on my mind, and in my heart, forever. I know it's hard for you to understand, but I was happy."

"Somehow, I'll help you get through this chapter in your life. I will."

I kissed her cheek. "We truly lived a fairy tale life; two young lovers, two hearts with the same desires in life. We were two people who had it all. Believe me, I am not saying that I was happy with his bad behavior, nor am I saying that no matter what he did, I was able to look the other way. My heart is just saying it will always be in love with him."

"That is so sad. I'm sorry. He has no idea how much you love him, does he?"

"It doesn't matter anymore. As long as my heart is still in love with him, I cannot be with anyone else. Chad deserves someone to love him as much as he loves her."

"Julie, so do you."

"I won't do that to Chad, I can't. I know what it feels like to love and I mean really love someone. Dan was the love of my life.

There isn't an eraser big enough to change the way I feel. Honestly, with all his faults, Dan is still a good man. We were meant to be together. I just have to accept the fact that it was for thirty years and not forever."

"Julie, you can't be alone for the rest of your life. You deserve to be loved by someone. I beg of you, please listen to me, before you tell him goodbye."

"Can you give me a new heart? Can you...? Then I have no other choice."

"I seriously need to walk," she said.

"Me, too." We got out of the car and walked down the beach. "Julie, I'm the only person who knows about Dan, correct?"

"I just told Frank this morning. And Chad knows. After his proposal, he deserved to know the truth."

"I see, okay." She had that look on her face again. I felt bad when I did that to her.

"Teresa, I know what you are trying to do. But, I can't change the situation. I know you're looking out for me. I'll tell you what, tomorrow, I'll go and see Dr. Oz, and maybe he can give me a new heart."

"Oh, Julie, I am so sorry you're going through this."

"Don't be sorry. I'm a fighter. Most of all, I am a woman of faith. I know deep in my heart that God will get me through this." I had to turn and look away. I was staring at the ocean. A few miles out, I could see a sailboat. For a moment, I wished I were on it, sailing away.

"Teresa, every time Chad goes away, I'll wonder if he is with someone else. Every time he is on his cell phone, I'll have to fight off the feeling that he is speaking to another woman. That's not the way a normal woman should act. There's nothing normal about me now. I am, and I will always be, a paranoid, jealous woman. I will never be able to trust a man again in my life. My mind is so tainted, I'm ruined and I know it."

"God hears you. He sees your pain. He's just a breath away. Don't let go of Him. He…"

"I promise you, God is first in my life. He's the reason I survived all of this. I've made it through so many heartaches, because *He* loves me…unconditionally."

"Julie, do you think your husband realizes what he has done? Maybe he misses you more than you miss him."

"He really is a good man, in a lot of ways. He has a wonderful heart. I remember when his mother was first diagnosed with Alzheimer's. Her television was broken. That year for Christmas, Dan went out and bought her a big flat screen. Dan was always good to his family and to our friends. For years, he took good care of his mother. Whenever we made something good for dinner and we had a little leftover, he would take it to her.

"It didn't stop with family. When his friend Jesse needed money to buy a truck, Dan handed over the cash – all of it. One day, an acquaintance came to the house. Said he was behind on his mortgage. Dan handed him fifteen-hundred dollars. I told him, 'God will bless you for that.' I've seen the good in him. There was so much about him to love. I know in my heart that he was worth loving. I just wish I'd captured his heart the way he did mine."

"Julie…"

"It's okay. I know what I have to do. I'm comfortable with my decision. Most of all, I am not afraid to be alone."

Chapter 33

I was sitting under the arbor, remembering when Kevin had ordered it. He had said, "Once the roses fill in, no one will know you're under here." I thought about my old weeping willow tree and the hours I'd spent reading one novel after another.

Suddenly, I felt a breeze. The kind of breeze that felt both warm and calming. I closed my eyes and tried to imagine I was sitting down by the ocean. I wanted to capture the smell and feel the mist of the sailboat sailing into the sunset. But all I could feel was my heart beating in my chest. It felt as deep as the ocean. Powerful, strong, and yet painful. I knew the day would not be easy for me but still it had to be done.

I remembered the day I left my home; the feeling was the same. All I ever wanted was for Dan to be happy. I hoped he was happy. I prayed that he had found what he had been searching for. I wondered if he moved on with his life. I was sure his heart didn't ache like mine.

I opened my eyes for a moment, but then I closed them because I could see Dan's face. I could still hear his voice. I longed to taste his lips.

I bowed my head. "Take my heart. Just take it." My head fell into my hands. I was trying to stop myself from thinking – from remembering.

Kourtnee said we had four weddings coming up. Maybe they would allow me to bake something, or do their flower arrangements.

The scent of roses was all around me. When I opened my eyes to look at them, I saw Chad standing in front of me. There it was, my heart, racing again.

"I wanted to spend a moment with you before I head out," he had said.

I started trembling. "How long have you been standing there?"

Chad cocked his head to the side. "I just told Teresa the cottage is empty. I packed all my belongings last night."

My heart was pounding. I felt as though I was going to pass out.

"All right, you're doing it again. Julie, I don't know what else to do with you. What do you want from me? You're as white as a ghost."

He sat down next to me. I could hear him crying. A few minutes went by, when I heard him say. "I love you so much. It hurts me to see you like this. Julie, you have to be strong. I can't stay here with you."

I was shaking so hard my entire body felt like I had the chills.

Suddenly, Chad began screaming. He was screaming so loud I jumped. He kept yelling, "Why? Why? Why?"

I didn't know what to do. I was in a catatonic state. I couldn't even cry. All I could do was hate myself.

"Julie, when you asked me to leave, I lost my heart. You tore a hole in me." Chad lifted my chin, raising my eyes up to meet his. He spoke softly, "After spending time with you, I wanted to be your cowboy. I wanted to make love to you." He stopped speaking for a moment, but I knew what he was saying. "I wanted to be the one who made all your dreams come true. I wanted you so much. I was willing to wait for you. For our wedding night to be our first night together." Tears were running down his face.

"I'm sorry," I said.

"Julie. You have nothing to be sorry about. Look at me. I didn't know my heart could feel this way. Because of you, I know what love is supposed to feel like. You taught me the meaning of love. Sorry? I'm sorry I'm not him." He gently rubbed my back, gave me a kiss and then said, "Oh, sweetheart, it wasn't supposed to happen like this. I wasn't supposed to fall in love with you. I was sent here to find you…"

I stared at him. "What do you mean? *Sent?* I barely got the words out. "Who sent you?"

"I was supposed to tell you that you did nothing wrong. That it was okay to love with all your heart. Not everyone loves the same. Some people have a hard time showing others how much they care and love them. I wasn't supposed to fall in love with you. I knew you were married."

My head was spinning.

"But when I spoke to Dan, and heard all the wonderful things about you, I fell in love with you even more. I didn't think Dan deserved you."

"What do you mean, you spoke to Dan? When did you speak to Dan…? Chad, answer me…"

"Dan hired me two days after you left." He got up and started to leave. "He was supposed to start clearing my property in Patterson but instead of him working for me, I agreed to help him find you. He was devastated and I…"

I listened to what he was saying but I couldn't believe what I was hearing. I closed my eyes, rubbing them trying to regain my composure. When I opened my eyes, he was gone.

I waited a few minutes before I headed back to the inn. When I reached for the gate to close it, two small birds landed on the trellis overflowing with yellow garden roses, tweeting, "Julie, Julie, Julie." I latched the gate closed and entered the inn through the kitchen. No one was around.

A minute later, I stood in the library looking out the window. Teresa was standing on the front porch, watching. Kourtnee and Bea sat on the bottom step and cried openly. Molly and Christine held each other and allowed their tears to fall in silence. Chad hugged Michael, then Kevin, before getting into his car; he looked back at the inn.

When he drove away, both Kevin and Michael had tears in their eyes. Everyone waved goodbye, knowing that things would not be the same.

In a stern voice, Teresa shouted, "We have an inn to run."

Christine went to Michael, hugged him warmly. Michael told her that Chad made him promise to keep me safe, secure and to make sure I ate.

Molly walked over to the front desk and asked Teresa, "Why? Why did she send him away?"

Kevin interrupted her, "Where is she?" Both women shrugged their shoulders.

"I saw her heading toward the rose garden, but that was an hour ago," Kourtnee said.

The curtain moved and so did I. I cleared my throat, "I'm right here." I sat down on the leather chair.

Kevin turned around. "I was looking for you," he said. "Are you okay?"

"I will be."

Kevin nodded. "I hope so."

He could be very serious at times. I wasn't sure if he was genuinely concerned, or if he was looking at me like I was crazy.

The mood for the rest of the day was as somber as a funeral, and everyone looked distraught.

I had planned to write in a new garden journal, but instead, I decided to write a letter. Even though I had no one to give it to.

Like Cinderella, all I ever wanted was a man with a good heart, a soft touch and a tender voice. Unlike Cinderella and Snow White, I am living in the real world. Unfortunately, I have had to deal with some hard challenges. Difficulties no lover should have to face.

No matter how much two people love each other. No matter how strong they think they are, a sickness, any sickness, whether it is adultery, drug abuse, or alcohol, has the power either to make a relationship grow stronger or to be torn apart.

My life was not about a simple love story. It was about faith, loyalty, and the sacrifices I had to make after discovering that my life did not turn out the way I had planned. The past thirty years have not been easy. I am human; and yes, I have made a few mistakes of my own. I am sure my husband wishes I were more like him when it came to saving money. But, I cannot.

I am glad that I saved and held onto this old rugged cross. I owe a huge thank you to my favorite minister, Pastor Bacino. Pastor was a great teacher. He taught me not to preach to others, but to live my life according to God's plan: to be a good person, someone others could look up to; and for a little while he allowed me to be a part of the Dover First Baptist Church family.

I'm glad I know how to pray and ask for His blessings. One of my favorite scriptures is, Timothy 6:10

I set the letter in the back of my journal. I had not been out of my room for two days. I thought it was time; I got back to the living.

I made my bed, took a shower and ordered a few new books from the local bookstore. Then I looked at the upcoming calendar, and smiled when I read Molly's note about ordering 24 tepees for an upcoming wedding.

Before I could pull the dress over my head, I heard a knock on my door.

I opened the door and saw Teresa's pretty smile. "Good morning. Can I come in? I brought you your breakfast."

"Good morning, sunshine. Of course, you may."

"I thought I would let you know that everything is back to normal. Michael is shopping for this weekend. Big wedding on Saturday, in case you're interested. Christine is baking her ass off, and Kevin is mowing the grass for the tenth time this week." Teresa made a clicking sound in her mouth. "So, what the hell are you still doing in your room?" On the tray next to the pot of coffee, I noticed my Do Not Disturb sign.

"Well, you're a spunky little rabbit this morning. I'll have you know, I was reading my Bible, and remembering when I used to teach little girls; nice polite, young ladies, at my church." I smiled.

"Teresa, thank you. Thanks for giving me some time. I've been writing and reading." I picked up the sign and tossed it on the chair. "I was getting ready to come downstairs. Believe it or not, I'm actually hungry."

"Good, you eat while, I tell *you* a few things," she said rather curtly.

My eyes opened wide. "Okay, I won't say a word."

"First, it doesn't say in the Bible that you should stay with a man who has no respect for you, or with a man who commits adultery." Teresa reached over the table and touched my wrist.

"Julie, it's okay to love someone with all your heart. You're not alone. Adultery is everywhere. Adultery isn't selective. From backcountry roads to the steps of the White House. It's a sickness. It just sucks that you had to experience it."

"Did you just say sucks?" I laughed; actually, I almost choked on my coffee.

Teresa threw both her hands up. "I'm serious. Julie, you can't be Miss Independent forever. I can't sit still and watch you drown yourself in sorrow."

"I'm not drowning in sorrow."

"Then prove it." She dropped into the chair. Closed her eyes, opened them and said, "Tell me a funny story?"

"I don't have any funny stories. Just tell me what you..."

"Yes, you do. You're full of damn stories. Come on; tell me something that will make me laugh. Please make me frigging laugh"

Something was going on with her. "Do I have to?" The little witch sprang from her seat and hollered, "Yes. I insist!"

"Awe, you're killing me. Teresa, I don't know what you want from me. What do you want me to tell you?" She wasn't budging. Her stare was serious, and I knew she was up to something.

"Fine. I'll tell you a funny story. One day, Dan said I needed to get my pistol permit. You know how much I love westerns; so of course, I said I wanted a Dirty Harry." I raised my eyebrows at her. "I bought a Smith and Wesson all right. A fifty-caliber model fivehundred. The one that has a bullet the size of a pen."

Teresa shook her head. "That was supposed to make me laugh?"

"I'm not done. We went to the gun shop to pick up my pistol, and right before it was my time to make my purchase, a little boy got off the school bus, and came into the shop. Walked behind the counter, greeted his father and said, 'Dad, is that the man who bought the largest handgun in the world?' The shop owner said, 'No son. She's the person buying the gun. 'The boy said, 'Dad, what does that say about her personality?'"

Teresa laughed. "Ha ha, obviously Dan thinks you're a saint. Either that or he's the stupidest man in the world. Cheating on his wife and allowing her to buy a handgun. Hello! Okay, that's not funny. Julie, I have to ask you something. What would you do if your suspicion were right? And you found out that Dan was in love with this woman?"

I thought for a minute. "I can honestly say all I ever wanted was for him to be happy. I took my husband for better, for worse, in sickness and in health. I loved him with all my heart. When he made love to me, it was the first time, every time. When I think of him, I remember the most amazing man I have ever known. Dan was the only man that made my heart beat."

Silence fell upon the room. Teresa was the only person with tears in her eyes.

"Julie, every person should know love that deeply. My goodness."

"I agree with you. There are many women in my shoes. Trust me, adultery is a sickness."

"Julie, it doesn't matter how strong a woman is, if she is married to an adulterer, she's living a hard life. I feel so bad for you."

"Don't feel bad. I'm a fighter. Teresa, as much as I hated dealing with one suspicion after another. Every day, I asked my parents, when you look down upon me, do I make you proud? That's all I ever wanted. Teresa, I took my husband's adultery as a gift." "A gift? Explain that…"

"Everything in life happens for a reason. Right?" "I suppose." Teresa rubbed her forehead.

"No matter what life threw at me. I refused to let it break me. Teresa, when I moved to Rhode Island, in the end it wasn't just for Dan. I've learned so much about myself. The first thing I learned was, I had to stop saying, 'I'm fine' when I wasn't. Marriage takes two people committed. I should have communicated more. Instead of standing up for myself, I was willing to bend. I take full responsibility for not calling Dan out on his bad behavior. I should have said, 'this is *not* acceptable behavior for a married man. And

I'm not tolerating it.'"

She sat down again and I thought she was going to give me a lecture but instead she opened up to me. "You know, there are behavioral issues with Sal that I need to address."

"Teresa, you should stand up for yourself. Speak your mind. That's what I'm trying to tell women. My blog has thirty-eight hundred followers."

I took a sip of my coffee. "Wisdom comes from experience. I made peace with the past. I left Dan because I loved him. That was my gift to him. Truth be known – it ended up being a gift to me."

"Julie, it's what you believe about yourself that determines how others see you. Well, one thing is for sure; I will always look up to you."

I smiled warmly at her. "I love you with all my heart Teresa. Love every sip we share."

"And when did *you* start a blog?" she teased.

"When I first arrived in Rhode Island. I'm a working bee, not a social butterfly. I had to spend my time doing something. If I'm not reading, gardening or kayaking, I'm writing."

"That's what you do down here all day…"

"One more story and then we better get going." "Wait, what's the name of your blog?" "Be Strong Enough," I replied.

Teresa grinned. "Tell me your story."

"One morning, Dan and I were headed out the door to sand a customer's driveway. I went to get into the truck, but instead I slipped on the ice. I hit my head on a cement step and blacked out. When I opened my eyes, Dan was standing over me. First, he kept asking me if I was okay, then he said, 'You need to be more careful.' I fell and hit my head the same day Natasha Richards fell on the ski slope. I cried so hard that day. I was mad. Furious at God, for taking her home and not me. She had two children to raise and *she* had a husband who loved her.

"I didn't understand why God would take her and not me. I had been begging Him for a year to take my life. That's how bad the pain in my heart was. I loved my husband more than I loved myself.

"I don't know why God calls some people home when He does. But I do know this, when you start begging God to take you home, it's time to do something different with your life. I spent the next few months reflecting back on my prayer, the promise I made to myself one day. I prayed for my husband. Asked God to watch over him. To bless him with a woman that could make him happy. I packed my bags and woke up in Rhode Island. Teresa, I know God loves me. And I know He hears my prayers – even the unanswered ones."

Chapter 34

At noon, Teresa and I headed up to the inn, ate a delicious spinach salad with feta cheese, cranberries, red onion, and toasted pecans. Afterwards, we enjoyed a cup of tea in the rose garden.

"I promise you, with what I know about myself now, I'll be fine." I held my hands out in front of me. "How could I not be?"

Teresa looked at all the beautiful roses. "I love the yellow ones," she said.

"They're David Austin. Cabbage roses or garden roses. Depending on if you live in America or England." I patted her on the knee. "Back to work."

Teresa went back to the front desk, and I went into Kourtnee's office for a pad of paper and some recipe cards. The baby was in her bassinet and sound asleep.

"Hey, boss," Kourtnee said softly as I stepped inside. "Are you ready for this weekend?"

"This weekend?" I paused, trying to focus on what she was telling me.

"Big wedding…Saturday." She stretched her arms out to her side.

"Oh. Yes. The wedding. You're all set, right?" Kourtnee pushed her chair away from the desk. "Yes."

"Okay, good. Me, too." I replied as I left her office.

Friday morning. Day one of the wedding weekend extravaganza. As usual, I woke up at dawn, kayaked around the entire pond, wrote in my journal, ate breakfast, showered and got dressed. When I approached the cottage door to go up to the inn, I let go of the doorknob and turned around. For a moment, I thought someone was in the cottage with me. I looked in every room. I was alone, and yet an eerie feeling came over me.

I loved my cottage. Loved having Hayden Lambson prints all around me. He had a way of capturing animals. Especially the deer. I looked at the fireplace, my bookcase and my meticulous home. "Home," I said, feeling good about myself, and my future. Before I reached for the doorknob again, I ran my hand along the oak frame hanging next to the door. It was a gift from Frank. He had a quote by Robert Muller framed. I liked it so much; I hung it where I could see it every time I walked out.

"To forgive is the highest, most beautiful form of love.

In return, you will receive untold peace and happiness." Brushed my hand along the frame's bottom. "I hope so," I said and then headed out the door.

The inn was already buzzing with early arrivals for the wedding.

When I stepped inside, I heard the usual bustle. Teresa greeting our guests. Molly asking Christine and Bea if they needed help with the afternoon tea and pastries. Kourtnee instructing Kevin to check on the baby. And Michael asking one of the guests if she needed help carrying her luggage.

"My journal." I had left my journal on one of the Adirondack chairs down by the pond. I immediately turned around and headed back. When I picked it up, I found a copy of the lyrics to Alan Jackson's song, "Remember When." I looked around, wondering how on earth and who could have put the note next to my journal in such a short period of time.

I read the words to that damn song twice. As I turned to go back to the cottage, the paper fell into the hydrangeas.

When I stood up, I saw a man with his back toward me, he was looking in the front windows. I held my journal close to my chest. He had a dog with him. My hand immediately went to my mouth when I saw her.

"Lady?" I said under my breath. Then I looked closer at the man. *Is that Dan?* It couldn't be, I had to be imagining things.

He stepped off the porch and started walking up the path toward the inn, still with his back to me. Then he turned around. His memory was hard enough, vivid and strong. Seeing him was harder than I ever imagined. I watched him take a deep breath, smelling the things I had planted. All were calming, alluring and mine. Watching him, knowing it truly was him, brought memories – simultaneously beautiful and horrific. I returned to the present with pain in my chest.

I didn't know what to do, but seeing him that close, I felt a moment's panic.

Lady was sitting on the porch. "Lady, let's go."

I started to cry when I heard his voice. Dan sounded choked up.

Lady didn't move.

My heart was racing. I wanted to run into his arms. But I was frozen. Confused.

Dan rubbed his face with his hands. "Come on, girl, I know how you feel but she's not in there." He slapped the side of his leg. "I'm leaving."

Lady stepped off the porch, and slowly made her way to her father. My heart melted when Dan bent down and hugged her. "I'm sorry," he said aloud.

Dan kissed Lady on her head, stood up and she followed him. "Dan..." I whispered. But no one heard me.

My head was saying let him go, but my heart was screaming, "I am *still crazy* in love with you."

My heart came back to life, and I hollered, "Dan!"

Lady streaked down the path and jumped up, almost knocking me over, covering my face with wet kisses.

"Oh, Lady," I cried, kneeling beside her, holding her in my arms. I hugged her.

"Julie," I heard him say from across the lawn and goosebumps rose on my skin. Dan's raspy voice would always be that familiar to me. And there it was, a jolt hearing his voice again, a rush in my veins.

Dan was barely able to walk down to where we were. He knelt down and wrapped his arms around Lady and me. He was sobbing.

"I'm sorry. I am so sorry. I love you. I love you so much. I'm sorry.

Please..."

Swallowing, I took a slow, palliative breath. Seeing Dan's paleblue eyes, his striking gray hair, I just wanted to look at him. To feel his embrace. I hugged him tight. "Shh..."

"No, Julie. Please let me say this. I will never..." He looked at me. Held my face in his hands. "I will never hurt you like that again.

Ever! I can't live without you."

This was no dream. I was wide-awake and with each passing second, more aware that the eyes that held mine belong to the love of my life. He was still as enchanting as ever, and it went beyond his eyes. Someone I wanted, longed for in the middle of the night. Despite the hell that had torn us apart, the attraction, the love in my heart, remained.

I wanted to throw a temper tantrum, to scream, "Why did you come here? To punish me? To torture me?" but instead, I said, "I won't live with a man I can't trust." I pulled my hand back when he reached for it. "You broke my heart, my trust." I inhaled and suddenly my voice was shaking. "You broke *us.*"

"Let me fix it," he cried.

I shook my head. My whole existence was shaking. My voice cracked, I gulped for air.

Dan appeared shaken. He had never been cruel. Thoughtless maybe. I looked away from him. Careless. Most definitely.

"Julie, look at me. Please," he pleaded.

"You need to leave," I cried but hated myself for having said it.

He started to say something but stopped. And there it was, that look in his eyes that melted my heart every time. He stared at me for a painful moment.

"Go home," I told him.

"I can't."

My chest felt heavy. I felt a sharp stab of fear. Finally, I blurted out, "It took me nine-hundred and ten days to learn how to live without you."

Dan was bracing himself on the ground with his free arm. "I love you."

I held his gaze. "I've always loved you."

Dan looked wary. He wasn't moving. So I did. I started to get up, but his voice stopped me. "I understand why you're so upset. I didn't expect what happened to happen, but it did." He wasn't done. In a low deep voice, he added, "When you left, my life stopped.

Days? I counted seconds."

My eyes went wide. We stood up, staring at each other for a long, awkward moment, but I wasn't letting him off the hook. He was serious. He was someone I had never seen before. His lips moved and then I heard him say, "Can you ever forgive me?"

Forgiveness was easy for me. Forgetting how I felt hearing him say the last person I fucked was...

"I'm begging you." I felt his hands heavy on my shoulders.

"Please, Julie. Don't send me away–"

I cut in, whirling to face him. "This is about *you?*"

"It's about us," he said, those bluer than blue eyes defiant as ever. "I can't move on. Not without you." I didn't budge.

He lowered his voice. "Fine," he conceded, moving his hands away.

My shoulders sank. Somewhere during the outburst, his eyes had filled with tears. Dan was no actor. I was touched – of *course* that he found me. Found out what it was like to live without me.

"Come with me."

We walked in the warm air up to the cottage, with Lady glued to my legs. Inside, I handed Dan the box of tissues, then I collapsed onto the floor and held my baby girl in my arms.

Dan sat down on the sofa. "You look amazing. You're skinny as…"

I looked up at him. "So are the two of you," I said. Then I got up and poured us each a glass of water. I set a bowl of water on the floor for Lady and told her to drink.

"Julie, so much has changed. I've sold most of the equipment, I…"

"You *sold…*"

He nodded. "Yep, one of the backhoes, bulldozers and one of the excavators."

"But… you always said you had to have two of everything?"

Dan shook his head. "Not anymore. A month after you left, I took the motorcycle and the Cobra off the road. I haven't worked since then." Dan hitched his chin toward Lady. "We sat by the phone. I didn't want to miss your call. Then a client of mine said he could find you, but he never found you. I spent hours on the phone with him telling him all about you. I told him how you always made the house smell like cinnamon during the holidays. I laughed when I told him I didn't eat fish until I met you. That we've always been the couple others looked up to and admired. I told him that you're my best friend and that I was planning to take you to Italy for your fiftieth. I believed him when he said he knew how to find you. I was so upset when he never got back to me. Even Jesse tried to call him, but he never returned any of our calls."

I sat down next to Dan. "I can't believe you were trying to find me."

"I read your letter." Dan patted Lady on her head. "Lady showed me where you kept your journal. Julie, I cried when I read your journal. Your words made me understand how much I hurt you.

The pain I've put you through. I blame myself. I'm the only person who needs to be held accountable. Perhaps you can't forgive me, and to be honest with you, it wouldn't shock me one bit if you don't. And maybe you'll never be able to trust me again, but isn't what we have worth fighting for? My therapist thinks what we have is worth a second chance."

"Your *therapist?* You went to a therapist?"

"I go to a therapist. That is helping me so much. Julie, no matter how damaged our marriage was, it was one of the greatest love stories. We were two high school dropouts who didn't let anything or anyone stop us. You and I built our home, the businesses and a wonderful life together. Julie, together we can survive the storms that test a marriage. I *know* we can. I'll continue to see Barbara..."

"Barbara?"

"My therapist. Barbara's my therapist." He put his head down and then looked over at me. "My self-image is much better, thanks to her. Barbara has taught me so much. I got her name from

Lynnae."

When I heard him say her name, I stopped breathing.

Dan took my hands in his. "One day, Lynnae asked me why I cheated on you. I had no answer. Not one reason. That's when Lynnae said, 'You need to answer that question before you find

Julie.' Then she handed me Barbara's phone number." I looked away from him, hiding tears.

"Julie, you're right. I don't deserve to be forgiven and I know it. I want you to know, I love you and I'm sorry. I'm sorry I slept with other women..."

I sucked in a breath. My hand went to my mouth. I closed my eyes. Thank you, Lord. For allowing Dan to be strong enough to admit the truth, after all these years.

"Julie, Barbara said, 'Julie will never be able to heal or forgive if...'"

Opened my eyes and reached for the tissues.

Dan leaned forward and touched my wrist. "Julie, please. You need to hear this."

"I'm listening." I held the tissue in my hand.

"I can't go back in time." Dan reached for a tissue. "I'll continue going to therapy. Julie, I can tell you this. You were the best thing that ever happened to me. I screwed my life up and I know it. It didn't matter where they were from or what they said, I wanted to be with them all for the same selfish reason. For my own satisfaction and low self-esteem." "And now...?"

"I'd rather cut my arm off than live without you. I can honestly say I will *never* make that mistake again." *Mistake?*

He looked at me for what seemed like forever. "I love you so much."

He went to get up.

I put my hand on his leg. "I've learned so much about myself these past two and a half years. It's not all your fault. I should have communicated more with you. I should have told you what I was feeling. Dan, I have to tell you something. I met somebody new, someone who would never break my heart in two. A good man with nothing but good intentions."

Dan's bottom lip began to quiver. He nodded his head. Blew his nose. He reached out and touched my hand.

I pulled back my hand. "Dan, I didn't *stay* with you all those years because I needed you. I stayed because I wanted you in my life."

"And now you don't...?"

"Dan." I laced my fingers together. "Your friend found me. Chad is the man I'm referring to."

"Chad? He *found* you? Did he came onto you? That bastard." I took both of his hands in mine. "He's gone. My heart *still* belongs to you. But I will not live that life. I won't. I would rather live alone in a cardboard box..."

"Julie, when you left, I was beyond devastated. At night, I would close my eyes, hoping for one more chance. Every time I thought of you, I could smell vanilla. I know what I did wrong. I'm telling you, my therapist opened my eyes. I know my affairs devastated you."

"Devastated?" I looked at him. "I had panic attacks. Dan, I couldn't breathe."

Lady whined to go out. I opened the door for her and stood there glued to the floor, looking at my baby, the pond and my beautiful hydrangeas while rage built up inside me. Blew out a breath loud enough for the world to hear. "I'm glad your therapist opened your eyes. Lord knows I couldn't." Frank's sign was staring me in the face, tugging at my heart. "I was a good wife. You didn't deserve me." I moved to face him, but his head was hanging. I turned back around and watched Lady lie on the ground next to my Adirondack chair.

"You're right, Julie, I didn't deserve you and yes I cheated on you. I'm sorry. Julie, if you knew I was having an affair, why didn't you say something?"

"I did, and you called me crazy. Remember?"

"Then why didn't you...?"

I spun around. "Stop you?"

"Yes...! Julie, you don't *talk* to me. You don't... You're tighter than a clam's butt. I swear I didn't mean to hurt you." "But you did," I said under my breath.

"I didn't hear you. What did you say?" he asked me and I could hear him breathing heavier, louder, closer to me. "Julie, please. Sit down, talk to me. I promise you..."

"I don't want to hear your promises, Dan." This time I spoke a little louder. "You can't just show up and think the past is forgotten." I closed my eyes for a second, remembering the pain. "For thirty years I lived with suspicion. Loving you was not easy." I folded my arms and tried to calm myself. "Dan, I want you to know that I forgive you..."

"Julie, please give me another chance. I'm here, Julie, talk to me, sweetheart. I'm begging you to give *us* a chance. I would have traveled the world to tell you this. You did nothing wrong. I was a fool for letting those women get to me. I was weak, with no selfcontrol."

Tears rolled down my face. Watching Lady as she peacefully soaked up the sun, I remembered every damn night, how I would cry. I prayed to God, begged Him to change Dan, fix him. Make him love me the way I loved him. "Dan, you were the only man I ever loved. You were my every dream, desire and prayer. And yet, I couldn't trust you. I would rather live alone than to live that way again." My heart became numb, my breathing had settled and I was calm. "I need…"

"I understand," I heard him say, then I felt his hands on my shoulders. My own eyes blurred, tears gathering as he reached out and touched the small of my back. *How that part of me missed him.* "I love you so much," he whispered in my ear and then he kissed my right temple before stepping outside. His kisses always lingered. How was I supposed to fight that? He stole my breath.

Lady ran to him. I stood in the doorway – frozen. "I love you more," I whispered as I watched him move closer to the pond.

Chapter 35

M y head started pounding so I went into the bathroom and
swallowed three aspirins. A moment later, I heard a voice
out in the other room.

"Hello," Teresa hollered from the living room. "Where are
you?"

I stood in the doorway. "I'm right here."

"Are you okay?" she asked and closed the door. "Umm, I
have to ask. Was that *Dan?"* I nodded.

"Wow, he's gorgeous."

"Did you see Lady?"

"Yeah, I saw them. Long enough to notice he was crying
pretty hard."

I leaned against the door jam. "What am I going to do?"

"Hmmm, I don't know. What did you say to him?"

"Oh, Teresa. I...I need to get out of here. Can we go
somewhere? Anywhere..."

"Let's go." Teresa opened the door and I followed her to her
car. I didn't see Dan's truck but he could have parked in the guest
parking lot. We rode in silence. I didn't mean to cry but I did.

When she parked the car in front of George's of Galilee, I told
her I needed a strong drink.

"It's not even noon yet," she laughed. "Oh, hell. Come on."
We went upstairs and sat at the bar. I ordered two dirty Martinis.

Then I said, "Forget this, I need to walk."

Teresa paid for our drinks. "How the hell did he find you?"

"I don't know."

"What are you going to do?" I shook my head.

"Julie, what exactly did Dan say to you?"

"He said he was sorry and that he loves me."

"Do you believe him?"

I turned to face her. "It's not Dan's love that I question. It's his loyalty and devotion."

"Maybe he's learned his lesson…"

"I love him so much. You have no idea." I glanced out at the ocean. "I suppose that's why I stayed with him for so long."

Teresa bent down and picked up a seashell. "Julie, there's more to a relationship than love." She tossed the shell out into the water. "Listen to your heart."

"Teresa, I don't want to live without him but yet I can't live like that again. I've never told anyone this." I stopped walking and sat down on the beach. Teresa flashed a grin before joining me. "Instead of talking to my husband – the man I truly love with all my heart, I wrote in a stupid journal. I literally wrote every suspicion, heartache and pain down and no one can take those words away. I'm telling you. My insides are trembling thinking about it. As much as I love him, I can't go back to that life. I just can't."

We sat on the sand. Teresa stretched out her legs and arms. Then she rested her head on her knees. Glanced over at me and cried,

"That had to be horrible. I wish I'd been there to help you. If only…"

She sat up straight. "I'll support whatever decision you make."

"My heart aches for him."

"Julie, based on everything that you've told me about Dan, I'm sure he still loves you. Tell him if he wants you back, he has to see a therapist. Make him go to couples' therapy. Put your foot down."

"He's been seeing a therapist…"

She interrupted me. "See, he's trying. Maybe he has changed."

My cell phone rang. "Hello." I looked at Teresa. "It's Frank." Teresa smiled.

"Of course. Yes," I told him. "I'm with Teresa. I'll ask her to drop me off."

Teresa held out her hands, pulling me up. "Where am I dropping you off?"

"At Frank's. That's a switch; usually it's the other way around.

I'm worried about him, he sounded upset."

Teresa stopped walking. "Did he say what the problem was?" "No, he just sounded different. I hope he's not sick."

"Sick?" Teresa asked and then started running to the car. "He sounded serious, that's all," I called, running after her.

Teresa started the car before I got in. A few miles down the highway. I pointed. "Turn right. Frank's the last driveway at the end of the road."

Teresa put the car in park, reached over and patted my leg.

"Give Frank my love. I'll say a prayer for him. In fact, I'll say one for all of you. Call me if you want me to come back and get you."

I leaned over and gave her a hug. "Thank you." I got out and met Frank at the front door.

Frank waved goodbye to Teresa, looked at me, took my hand and led me upstairs. "I haven't been in this room for some time now." He opened the door and I looked inside. It was a library very similar to the one Frank had built for me. I moved closer to the bookcase.

"Have a seat."

I sat in a chair and when I did it rocked. I was definitely sitting in a woman's room. The wallpaper had beautiful delicate pink roses. Above each bookcase, there was a vine of ivy and numerous photos of Frank and a woman. "Is that your wife? She's beautiful, Frank."

Frank reached up and took down a photo of the two of them when they were in their twenties or early thirties. He kissed her face. Set it down and picked up another photo of the two of them sitting in a flat-bottomed boat. "We laughed so hard that day." He handed the photo to me and I thought she was even more beautiful with gray hair.

Frank had an enormous smile on his face. "We never would have shared the best years of our life if I hadn't forgiven my wife."

I was shocked at his words. I looked at her. "I'm sorry," I said. Frank took the photo from me. "Young lady, I would never let anyone cause you pain. I would not have called him if I thought

otherwise. That man loves you. I can see it in his eyes."

"And I love him…"

"Then go to him."

I stood up. "I don't know where he is. He came to the inn but now he's gone."

I heard Frank make a familiar noise, "Mmmm."

I followed him down the stairs. When he reached the bottom, Frank pointed toward the living room. He kissed my cheek and I heard him say, "It's time."

I moved toward the archway. Inside, waiting for me, was my world. I stepped in and Lady ran to me. Dan was standing in front of the big bay window, looking out. When he turned toward me, my heart started beating faster. For a moment, we just stood there looking at each other.

Dan moved closer to where I was. "Can we talk?"

I looked into his eyes and thought about all the things I wanted to do with him. We sat down on the sofa together with Lady at our feet. Dan started to cry. "I'll do whatever makes you happy."

I looked into his eyes. I loved but didn't. I wanted him to hold me, but not by any account did I want him to be that close or ever far away again. "I got used to not seeing you, not caring about you." "I understand."

I shook my head and held out my hand. The instant he took it, I felt new.

I reached up and wiped away his tears. "Can you make love… to… me?"

Dan looked shocked. His face lit up and my heart skipped.

"For the rest of my life." Dan hugged and kissed me before adding, "Julie, you'll see. I won't let you down. I'll prove my love and my devotion to you every day."

I kissed him and that time, my insides surged. Dan couldn't stop kissing me, telling me how much he loved me. I leaned back to look at him. "I've missed you so much."

Dan reached into his pocket and handed me an envelope. I recognized her handwriting. I held the envelope to my heart. "How is she?"

"Lynnae's good. She misses you terribly. We all do."

"Dan, I love you with all my heart, but I'm not the same girl I was when we got married. I'm definitely not the same woman I was when I left New York."

"And I'm not the same man I was. I no longer have low selfesteem. I don't need a new woman to make me feel like a rock star." Dan's face turned gray. "The day you left was the hardest lesson of my life. Julie, I love you more than you can imagine. Tell me about your inn. Are you happy?"

"I am."

Dan nodded. "Lady and I took a look around before we went down to the cottage. Impressive. Remember all the times we talked about retiring and opening an inn together…"

"I remember."

"Julie, Lady and I want you in our lives. We need you. Did you ever think about coming home to us?"

A smile rose up inside me. "Home? Dan, Rhode Island is home now." I looked at my baby and she looked up at me. "And you know what The Inn in Rhode Island needs? A chocolate lab. Right, Lady?" Lady sat up and kissed a salty tear from her father's cheek.

"Julie… are you… serious?"

"Oh, yeah." Then I kissed him long and hard.

Frank came into the living room holding three bottles of Corona. I laughed when he pointed his finger at Dan and said, "You were right about the pickle. It is rewarding."

"Excuse me, how long have the two of you been…"

Frank kissed me on the cheek, tapped his bottle to Dan's and then mine. "To the best years of your life!"

Frank said he had a celebration to attend. We followed him outside, down the driveway and for most of Ocean Road. Dan reached over Lady and stroked my hair. "Where's the envelope?" Both hands hit the steering wheel.

I held it up. "Right here." I was still holding it.

"She would have killed me if I lost it." Dan ran his hand through his hair. "I want to see your face when you read it."

I opened the envelope and of course, I felt a lump in my throat.

"Oh, my…"

Dan looked at me. "She asked me to walk her down the aisle."

"Oh, my goodness."

Dan pulled over to the side of the road, dialed a number and handled me his cell phone.

"Hey, Dan."

"Lynnae. It's me."

"Julie…?"

"Lynnae, I've missed you so much. I can't believe this. You're getting married…"

"Barry, Brooke, Stephanie, come here. Hurry. It's Julie!" I heard her scream. "I'm on the phone with her right now. Yes. Julie, I'm not getting married without you. Come over to the bakery right now. We're all here."

"Lynnae, I'm not in New York, I'm in Rhode Island." "She has the best little inn in Rhode Island," Dan yelled.

"Rhode Island? I'm coming to see you. Right now. Barry and I are on our way."

"Seriously?"

"Yes! Put Dan on the phone. And don't you move."

"I know, right," Dan said. "The Inn in Rhode Island. Mallard Way. About twenty minutes north of Point Judith. Yes. I know. Sounds good. Three or four hours, depending on traffic." Dan put the phone down. "There's no stopping her. She'll be here Sunday." Dan picked his phone back up. "Hang on. I wanna send Barry a text."

When Dan started driving again, he vowed to make me happy every day of my life. A moment later, we were on Mallard Way.

Dan reached over and kissed the back of my hand. "Wake up, Lady, we're home."

Molly approached us the minute we stepped up onto the front porch. "Wait right here," she said and then went inside. We heard her yell, "They're here!"

A moment later, I introduced Dan to Molly, Kevin and Kourtnee. He said hello to Bea. Then he shook Michael's hand before saying, "Congratulations," to Christine.

"That's my girl." I heard Frank say.

"Frank!" I ran into his arms.

Dan hugged Frank. "Thank you. I don't know what I would have done if you didn't call me."

Frank stepped back and pointed his finger at Dan. "I'm glad I called you and I'm glad you stopped to see me today." Then he winked at me. "They're all so young," Dan said to Frank.

Frank grinned. "They have to be, to keep up with her." He patted Dan on the back. "You take care of her; she's very special to me."

"You can count on it." Dan reached for my hand. "It's like one big family here…"

I saw Teresa standing back, eyes narrowed a little, sizing Dan up. I knew she would be the person to hold his feet to the fire. "Dan, this is Teresa. Teresa… this is Dan."

I looked past her, down the driveway, just in time to see a box truck with a big pink elephant on the side pulling up. The teepees had arrived. Teresa was waving me away. "Go. We've got this." She blew me a kiss.

Dan and I went back to the cottage.

When we stepped onto the front porch, I pulled Dan's hand back. "I've missed you so much. My body is aching for you." I whispered in his ear, "Make love to me."

Dan picked me up and carried me inside. We made love in front of the fireplace. Hours passed. It was dark outside when Dan let Lady out. When he let her back in, we made dinner for the three of us. After we ate, I made love to Dan. I couldn't help myself. I was sitting on his lap, facing him and I wanted more.

"Italy. I'm taking you to Italy," Dan said as he began rubbing my shoulders.

I looked at him. He *was* a changed man.

"Julie, Monday morning I'll call Barbara and ask her to recommend a good therapist for me in Rhode Island."

"That means a lot to me." I ran my hand up from his chest to face. "I wanted so much for us. I had plans for you and me."

"I know," Dan smiled impishly. "Hey, Frank said you want to put in a swimming pool. I told him Jessie and I will do all the digging. Julie, we'll sell whatever equipment we don't need and the rest we'll trailer to Rhode Island."

"Jesse... how's he been?"

"He's good. He was a pain in my ass at first. Calling me every day. Stopping by the house. You must have put the fear of God in him, because he told me if I called the police and reported you missing, you would never forgive him or me." "He was right about that," I laughed.

"Truthfully, Julie, I don't know what I would have done if it weren't for Jesse and Lynnae."

Dan picked me up. Carried me over to the warm fireplace, went down on one knee, then the other. Until, we were both on the floor.

"Turn over," he whispered in my ear. Knees in mine, breathing in the knap of my neck. "Lie with me – just a while."

I don't know how long we lay there. I breathed in the scent of comfort, understanding, love, caring, and remorsefulness. Dan fell asleep. He was a part of my Point Judith life. In a split second my life had changed. Taking in the moment, I faced him and focused on the possibilities. Sheer pleasure rose within me.

"Are you happy?" came his voice in a low hush followed by, "That's all that matters." His eyes held mine for a moment before shifting off. His chin came up. "Are you hungry?" he said with a smile.

His thoughts must have gone there, too, because he seemed suddenly awake. "Your eyes hold doubt," he said as sat up, reached out and touched my face. My heart faltered for an instant. "Are you…?" he asked with the slightest emphasis on the – *you.*

Teasingly, I scrambled the air with frantic hands. Quietly, I replied, "Yes…I am now."

"I'm glad," he said solemnly. The look on his face was familiar. He sputtered a dry laugh. I might have laughed, too, if I'd known what was so funny. "I'm happy for you, Julie. I am. Do you like running the inn?"

"Yes." We were back to the present.

"What's the best part?"

"My staff," I said. "I love working with them.

"Like Frank?"

"Frank is the best, he's good to me."

"He cares about you, y' know?" I nodded.

"Are you as close to the women as you are to Lynnae?"

"I started out as an innkeeper, but now this is my home and they're all my family." I looked into Dan's eyes, and I remembered how hard it was for me in the beginning. Thinking about Dan and wondering whether he would come or call. On those days, I kayaked a little longer, hiked deeper into the woods, anything to take me away from my thoughts.

"Uh huh," he said as he touched my back just lightly. "I'm glad you had them here with you." He kissed me and said, "You're hungry? I'll cook." Then he jumped to his feet.

Chapter 36

S unday morning, August 7th. Eight a.m.

Dan and I were making breakfast when we heard hollering. "It's the boys!" I ran to open the door.

Sam and Max were hugging my legs. When I embraced Lynnae, I could not let go of her. Several minutes passed before I stepped back to look at her. Lynnae had tears in her eyes.

I started bawling my eyes out. "Hi, Barry," I said as I wiped my nose with the back of my hand and started laughing. "Oh, boy. It's so nice to see everyone."

Dan made breakfast for us all. Then he and Barry went up to the inn. When they returned, Dan said, "One o'clock." He pointed to

Lynnae. "I said I'd make it happen." Lynnae looked at Barry. "Seriously…?" "Julie's staff said they love weddings." "What about a dress…?" I said.

"I don't give a damn about a dress. I'll wear your underwear, if it means you'll be there."

Barry was shaking his head. "I've got everything. Dan texted me and told me what to bring…"

From behind, Jesse picked me up and held me in his arms. I saw Dan grinning from ear to ear. Once again, I cried. This time, happy tears. Dan and I both love Jesse like a brother. "I'm never letting you out of my sight," he cried.

A while later, I chased the men and the boys back up to the inn.

I needed time alone with Lynnae.

I wrapped her hair up in a French twist; put a silver clip in her hair.

Lynnae looked at me in the mirror, standing behind her and asked, "Am I dreaming?"

"Nope, now go get dressed."

A moment later, we heard a knock on the door. "Is the bride ready?" Dan asked.

I opened the door, and Dan kissed me. "Everything's set."

"Then I'll see the two of you momentarily," I replied.

Everyone was there. Frank, Gina Marie, Sabrina, Jessica, Bea, Cathy, Amanda, Michael and Christine. Teresa and Sal, Kevin, holding Delilah, and Kourtnee, and Jesse.

Molly filled the yard with lavender hydrangea, purple lisianthus and ivory roses. I sat up front, in the first row of chairs. I wanted to see her come down the aisle.

I heard the music start *The Wedding March* and everyone stood up.

First Sam, Max and Lady, then Brooke and Stephanie made their way down the aisle. I looked back and saw Lynnae; she was a vision of beauty. She was wearing a short lace, ivory halter dress, and matching shoes. Dan smiled and winked at me, and then he kissed Lynnae on the cheek.

Lynnae wrapped her arm through Dan's and together they slowly made their way toward Barry. Her eyes were on him the entire time. Barry was beaming. Dan kissed Lynnae one more time, and then extended her hand to Barry, before taking a seat next to me.

Dan took my hand in his.

Their vows to each other were perfect.

The minister looked up and said, "Who has the rings?" Sam raised his hand and replied, "Hey, down here. I do," as he handed the rings to the minister, and everybody laughed.

Soon, Barry was saying, "I do."

"I do. Forever and forever after," said Lynnae.

When Lynnae and Barry kissed, the violinist started playing "A

Thousand Years."

Dan wiped my tears away. Then he kissed me tenderly and whispered in my ear, "I love you with all my heart. By any chance

does the inn have October 2nd available?" I looked at him.

"I'd like to start over. Let's renew our vows. Marry *me...* Julie."

Coming 2022

THE INN in RHODE ISLAND

Acknowledgments

In all likelihood, the idea for this book would be compared to jumping off a high bridge into shallow water, if not for all the love and support from my family, friends, and book club members. My love and profound appreciation to each and every one of you for your loyalty and for being my book friend forever. Because of you, my dream came true. Thank you, thank you, thank you all!

To the wonderful editors who took the time to read Black Hawk Literary Agency's submission of *Still Crazy*, I thank you for your time, consideration, encouragement, and kind words.

To my literary agents, Jan Kardys and Barbara Ellis-Uchino. Jan, I offer my deepest thanks for reading my first draft, for your wisdom, years in the business and for introducing me to Barbara. Barbara – the incredible agent/book doctor, coach, cheerleader, and friend – how can I possibly thank you enough? Your dedication, long hours into the middle of the night, 3 a.m. messages, brainstorming, trimming and tweaking every line in this book, I could not have done this without you.

To my friends, Ellen Levine and the late Dr. Richard U. Levine, thank you for believing in me.

My fellow author, Carol Caton, you are my inspiration.

To my family, thank you all for allowing me to use your names, personalities, and your voices.

David – my love. I am still crazy in love with you. I could not have done this without you, your love and support. Thanks for my laptop, printer, and for building me a writing studio.

Finally, above all, I'm grateful to my Lord and Savior. Thank You for walking with me, and for Psalms 45:1

JUDY PRESCOTT MARSHALL
Earned her certificate - Write Your First Novel from
Michigan State University

She lives in Dutchess County, New York

judyprescottmarshall.com

Letter From the Author

As a child, what delighted me the most was reading under a street lamp, under a shade tree, or in my room with a flashlight. To say I love books is an understatement. I still love to hold them in my hands. I love meeting new friends, discussing books, characters and settings; and that makes me a huge fan of book clubs. Today, I host fifty-two book clubs – one in every state – and in ten countries around the world. I'm grateful to my street team across America. Honored when my book is chosen by an entire group.

As a way of saying thank you, I offer weekly giveaways on Facebook, and each spring, I surprise one group with an evening of dining out and drinks. In the summer, I host a picnic on my one-hundred acres along the majestic Ten Mile River. All book clubs are invited. To enter, all you have to do is email me at judyprescottmarshall@aol.com. No book club is too small or too far away. If you don't have a book club, start one. Or join one of mine. I would love to have you. Go to Facebook and type the state you live in and the words, Be Strong Enough Book Club. Example: Alaska Be Strong Enough Book Club.

March 3, 2020, I landed in Nashville, Tennessee. I was so excited to kickoff the Be Strong Enough Book Tour. A tornado, however, had other plans for me that day. Still, I met so many wonderful people. We cried, prayed and promised to meet again. When I got home, I read every one of their emails. Each full of hope, and inspiration for the future of Tennessee. Yes, I do read all of my emails. I love connecting with my readers. So drop me a line from time to time and let me know how you're all doing. I promise, as soon as we are through with covid-19, I will be back on the road again. Until then, if you would like a signed bookplate, bookmark and tea from me. Email me at judyprescottmarshall@aol.com

The Inn in Rhode Island

Chapter 1

With the morning sun beaming on my face, I tried to focus on the day. Our six p.m. ceremony down by the pond.

Then a celebration dinner outside on the back terrace. Dan and I wrote our own vows. No minister needed this time. Only our dearest and close friends. We both wanted something simple yet elegant.

I rolled over onto my back, opened my eyes and stared at the ceiling. Dan was sound asleep. He's the man of my dreams, and I am still crazy in love with him. I'm so happy he's comfortable in the cottage.

I closed my eyes for a second, but then quickly opened them. A chill ran up my spine. Last night, I dreamt I was sitting in my rocking chair, outside on the front porch. All of a sudden, I heard Dan hollering my name. I ran down to the pond. Dan reached for my hand. He told me he loved me. He promised me he would never break my heart again. Dan kissed the back of my hand, before adding, "I only have eyes for you. Julie, you're my one and only love. I love you Julie Holliday." Then his hand slipped out of mine and he was gone.

"Good morning, beautiful."

"Ahh, you're awake. Good morning, my love." I kissed him on the cheek and started to get out of the bed. I needed to shake that dream. "Coffee?"

Dan reached for my arm and asked, "Are you marrying me today?" Then he raised an eyebrow and gave me a seductive smile. "Oh, yeah!" I replied, glad for the reality check.

"I love you, Julie. I want today to be... Julie, I wanna move forward with our lives. It's the first day of our *new* life together. I'm going to make you feel my love every day. You'll see."

"Dan." I inhaled. "I believe you and I'm so happy you found me."

"I started looking for you the day you..." Dan looked over at the clock. "Holy crap, I have to meet Rose at nine o'clock."

Dan was in the shower before I could throw back the covers.

Out in the kitchen, I sipped my coffee, scrambled some eggs and buttered the toast, thinking, *it's a good thing she's his therapist!*

Dan inhaled his breakfast, before kissing me goodbye. "I love you..."

"And I love you, Dan Holliday."

After I took my shower, Lady and I headed up to the inn. She's such a good dog, we never ever needed a leash for her. I wanted to make sure Lynnae's room was ready. In each of the guests' rooms, I put a welcome basket. Lynnae's room had a few extra goodie baskets for the boys. She promised me they would be here by ten. I hated the fact that my dearest friend lived in New York. I wanted her here with me in Rhode Island.

As soon as I saw Jesse's truck pull in, I stopped walking, to wait for him. The big lug made it. We knew he would, after all, he's Dan's best friend and best man. He may have the physique of a lumberjack and the tattoos of a biker, but to me he's a big old teddy bear. In New York, he never missed a Friday night out. He'd get dressed like he was posing for the cover of GQ. Women never knew how to take him, or how to hold onto him. I told him he needed to wear a sign on his back that reads: "I'm not here for a long time, I'm just here for a good time."

After he parked his truck, I waved so he would see me, then I told Lady it was okay to go see him. My beautiful chocolate Lab bolted for his truck. She loved Jesse and he loved her. But he ignored her and went to the passenger side and helped a woman and a young boy get out of the truck. That was odd. He hadn't said anything about bringing... "Oohhh. Oh, my!"

Jesse hitched his chin my way. The woman's clothes were torn.

"Is that *blood?*" I ran to assist Jesse. When I approached them, it was worse than I imagined. She appeared weak and bruised.

"Julie, this is Erin and this is her son, Kyle." Jesse sounded choked up and I thought I saw tears in his eyes.

I reached for the little boy, who was clutching a brown stuffed animal by one of its feet.

Jesse took Erin into his arms. When she rested her head on his shoulder, he placed his sweatshirt between then the carried her to the inn.

"Come with me, Kyle." When I picked him up, his teddy must have fallen to the ground. A moment later, Lady scampered ahead of me. I stopped and bent over. Kyle reached down and patted Lady on her head before taking back his teddy bear. Lady barked joyfully, certain she had done a good job. Kyle held his teddy close to me as we went inside.

"Oh, my Godddd!" Teresa screamed in a spine-chilling voice.

"What happened?"

"Teresa, grab the first aid kit!" Jesse yelled to her. Then he went into the library and sat Erin down on the sofa.

I stopped in the doorway and told Lady to stay in the lobby. With my right foot, I closed the door, sat Kyle down next to his mother and began to breathe again. On the other side of the door, I could hear Lady whining. Kyle looked past me; his eyes were searching for her. When I let her in, Kyle immediately sat on the floor and hugged her.

"I'm sorry. I... I had no idea where I was going." Her voice was broken. We could barely hear her when she said, "I just knew I had to get away from him... before he..."

"Who?" Jesse asked, making a grumbling sound.

"My husband," she said brokenly as she glanced over at her son.

"C' mere." Jesse knelt down and embraced her in a bear hug.

"No one is going to hurt you. Not while I'm around."

"You're so sweet." Erin's voice was barely above a whisper.

Her pain was so keen we both felt it. When she started crying, I bit down on my bottom lip. The urge to cry was so strong I had to look away for a second.

"It's okay," I said sadly. "You and your son are safe. We'll take care of you." Behind me, I heard the door close. Erin jumped in her seat.

"Here." Teresa handed me the first aid kit. Then she took off her sweater and wrapped it around Erin. Her right breast was exposed. Jesse's sweatshirt had fallen onto her lap when she jump. Teresa had to help her put her arm in the sleeve.

I pulled myself together, opened the kit and said, "Erin, this is Teresa, she's the receptionist here at the inn." Then I introduced Teresa to Kyle.

My heart was bleeding for this woman. By the color of her pale, pale skin, I could only assume she hadn't been out in the sun in a long time. I bent down and gently wiped the dried blood from her cheeks, neck and right hand.

"Julie." I felt Teresa's hand on my shoulder. "Jesse took the little boy to the kitchen for something to eat. I heard him tell Jesse he was hungry. Would you like me to get something for her and bring it in here?"

I looked at Erin. "Erin, are you hungry?"

She shook her head and wiped her tears with the back of her hand. "No, thank you."

"You have to eat something." I swallowed hard, fighting back more tears. My blood was boiling. Who could do such a thing? I hugged her. I didn't mean to cry. But the moment I looked at Teresa, I, too, started bawling my eyes out.

CPSIA information can be obtained
at www.ICGtesting.com
Printed in the USA
BVHW041612200121
598103BV00009B/22/J

9 780991 027330